ORIENTAL COOKERY

ORIENTAL COOKERY

**CHARTWELL
BOOKS, INC.**

A *Quill* BOOK

This book was designed and produced by
Quill Publishing Limited
32 Kingly Court
London W1

Art director Nigel Osborne
Editorial director Christopher Fagg
Senior editor Liz Wilhide
Project editor Sabina Goodchild
Designer Steve Wilson
Design assistants Philip Chidlow Timothy Rowe Andrew Haslam
Illustrators Yvonne Shaw-Bins Richard Phipps Carol McCleeve
Paste-up Hugh Schermuly

Filmset by Leaper & Gard Ltd, Bristol
Origination by Hong Kong Graphic Arts Service Centre Limited, Hong Kong
Printed by Leefung Asco Printers Limited, Hong Kong

AUTHOR'S ACKNOWLEDGMENTS
Accompanying my husband on a posting to
Malaysia for three years was to open the door
to the joys of cooking oriental. One of the main
influences on this was Ah Moi Thong, our
amah, who gave me a great insight into the
cuisine. Anita Wong was a good friend who was
a great inspiration. She shared many of her
family recipes with me.
    This book has also fostered many
friendships and I would especially like to thank
the following: Mrs Konzah, who was most
generous in her help and in cooking on the
Japanese chapter. Pohk and Posim Moeng, who
now live in England, gave me the recipes from
Cambodia. Winston Sharma and Susie
Thompson gave me a lot of first hand
information on Burma. Moira Smith and Sheila
Marks both knew the Philippines intimately and
spent a lot of time assisting me on my research
Elizabeth Ashton Edwards and Patty Watson

had up to the minute impressions on China
which were fascinating and had to be included.
The Embassies of Thailand, Philippines,
Indonesia, Korea and Vietnam were also very
helpful.
    To my husband, Johnnie, and my children,
Alexandra and James, I owe my love and thanks
for their constant support while this book (and
the piles of washing up) grew and grew. To
Beryl Castles who, in her spare time, typed
every word, my warmest thanks. To Anne de
Gier Wintermans, who helped me test all the
recipes, I want to express my sincere
appreciation. We both love food so the
memories of our oriental cooking days are truly
happy ones. And, finally, to all the colleagues,
friends and others who gave of their time to
taste and pass comment on the fascinating
cuisine of the orient, thank you for sharing this
with me.

*Quill would also like to extend thanks to the
following:*
ML Taw Kritakara
Ban Suan Restaurant, Chiang Mai
Benkay Restaurant, Royal Orchid Hotel,
    Bangkok
Gaeo Everingham
Kaiwan Restaurant, Chiang Mai
Korea National Tourism Corporation
Oi Wallingford
Rainbow Vietnamese Restaurant, Hong Kong
Seoul Jib Restaurant, Bangkok
Siriporn Buranaphan
Spice Market Restaurants at the Bangkok
    Peninsular Hotel, Hong Kong Hotel and
    Marco Polo Hotel, Singapore
Wila Laap Ped Restaurant, Chiang Mai

CONTENTS

INTRODUCTION

In the countries of the east can be found a fascinating diversity of peoples, religions, cultures, traditions, and, of course, cuisines. On this culinary tour of the orient I hope to show that, despite centuries of exchange between these different countries and their customs, and various influences from the west, each cuisine continues to retain its own special character and charm.

This book deals with the distinctive cuisines of ten regions: Malaysia, Singapore, Indonesia, the Philippines, Thailand, China — north, south, east and west — Korea, Burma, Japan and Indochina — Cambodia, Vietnam and Laos. Perhaps the main reason for the continued vigor of these regional cuisines is the way that they use to the full all the local food resources available to them. Rice is the staple ingredient throughout the Far East, but these lands also produce an abundance of delicious fruits and vegetables, which can be seen displayed in teeming markets from Burma to Indonesia. The sea and richly stocked rivers provide an endless source of fresh and unusual fish and shellfish. In fact, from wild herbs and spices to chicken feet and shark fins, everything edible is ingeniously transformed into exotic and mouth-watering delicacies.

With years of experience in the culinery field, cooking utensils throughout each of the countries have been kept to a minimum: the wok, for example, is common to all oriental cuisines. However, presentation and table etiquette are unique to each specific area, and make their own special contribution to the experience of a truly local cuisine. In the following pages, I hope to have captured some of this flavor and, also, to have provided recipes that will prove to be a real taste of the orient.

Far right *Map of the countries and regions included in this oriental tour, showing principle cities, capitals, rivers, seas and islands mentioned. Inland waterways and open seas both characterize the area and provide fish and seafood for the cuisine* (above). *Fertile plains and uplands* (right) *also ensure good growing conditions for a wide variety of produce.*

SZECHWA

Ava
Mandalay

BURMA
Irrawady River   Pagan

Chiang Mai

Mekong River

Rangoon River

THAILAND
Chao Phraya River

Bangkok

Battambang

Tonle S

ANDAMAN
SEA

CAMBO

George
Town   Kuala Kangsar

Cameron Highlands

Penang Island   Trengganu
Balik Palau   Kuala
Lumpur   M A

Kuantan

Malacca

SINGAP

SUMATRA

STR. OF MALACCA

INDIAN OCEAN

Traditions of oriental cookery

In the freshness of the food available all over South East Asia, in the skill of its cooks, lies a success story. Although life is changing in urban areas, the markets there are still thriving social centers, in many places marketing for fresh food is still a daily ritual. I was frequently struck by the shabby surroundings of these markets, but the array of food, so artistically arranged, is something one could never forget. One market that was extremely picturesque was by the banks of the river in Kuching, opposite the palace of the Rajah Brooks — the White Rajahs. It was a feast to behold: fresh vegetables and herbs, bottles and plastic tubes of fish sauces, sambals and palm sugar, turtles' eggs, which look just like ping-pong balls, dry spices and those mounds of wet spices in rich colors.

When it comes to preparing meals in a traditional way you should expect to spend quite some time at work. However, short-cuts have slowly crept in with the marketing of wet spices, although some people still prefer to pound by hand rather than use a machine. Slicing and chopping of food for a Chinese stir fry is also a lengthy business. Long ago it was realized that food cut to the same size would cook at the same rate and be ready at the same time. Meat cut across the grain would be more tender and vegetables cut thinly and diagonally tended to cook more evenly with a greater surface area exposed. Food prepared in this way looks prettier, too.

Quick cooking undoubtedly evolved from a scarcity of fuel. Charcoal and coal would be used in the brazier if available, but if not, straw, wood or even manure might be used and rapid cooking caught on, being an economical use of these scarce forms of fuel. This in turn led to one pot cooking — not just putting in everything that was available, but a combination of textures and flavors to complement each other. Resourcefulness is, thus, a key word in oriental cooking.

Below *The markets of the east are renowned for the freshness and variety of their produce. Fruits, vegetables and meat, always displayed in immaculate rows.*

Right *The wok, pestle and mortar and wooden slab are traditional tools of the orient. Spices are another classic feature of the cuisine, throughout the region.*

Basic equipment

The traditional oriental kitchen is extremely simple. It contains nothing that is superfluous, and often one tool is required to do many jobs. The cleaver, for example, does not only chop, it shreds and grinds, and the wok is used not only for stir frying, but also for steaming. With just a few of these basic utensils the people of the east are able to produce their varied and exotic dishes, and with a knowledge of these tools and how they work, we, too, may attempt to cook 'oriental'.

The wok
The wok, to my mind, is an essential piece of equipment if you are to cook oriental food successfully. It is a wide, circular pan with a curving base, which was originally called a *wo*, and then wrongly translated into English. it is also known in Malaysia as a *kuali*, *wajan* in Indonesia, but universally as the wok. It has many advantages over a frying pan, which soon become apparent when you use one.

In the first place, very small quantities of oil are required for stir frying, and, also, for deep frying it does not require as much oil as a conventional pot. The actual shape of the wok is carefully designed so that the heat is spread over a large area, allowing a greater quantity of food to be cooked simultaneously. Many oriental dishes also require a certain amount of evaporation, which is easily achieved with this large surface area. The curved sides then reduce any spluttering of oil and ingredients tend to fall back into the pan.

When buying a wok choose a good size one — I have two 12in (30.5cm) and one 14in (35.5cm), with lids. They are cast iron and *very heavy* with a handle on either side. The weight is very important. Avoid those lightweight models that burn the food as the pan is too thin for the high temperatures required in stir frying. There are a number of Teflon-coated woks with flat bases suitable for electric stoves. I have little experience of cooking with electricity, but if you do have this type of stove it might be worth investing in these coated woks or borrowing a friend's before you buy. I have a gas stove and was able to buy a metal stand on which to rest the wok when cooking, which I highly recommend. Stable as you may think the wok looks when placed directly on the stove it is not a good idea to do this.

If a new wok sticks, melt some pure oil or lard in it, leaving it over a gentle heat for a while, then cool it a little before rubbing vigorously with a pad of newspaper. This may have to be repeated several times until a surface is formed. Immediately after using the wok wash it quickly in soapy water with a washing-

Right **Steaming** *This cooking technique can be used for all types of food from fish and meat to vegetables, but is perhaps most well-known for* dim sum. *The bamboo baskets, which come in a variety of sizes, are generally used for this, one stacked on top of another. However, for steaming anything larger such as a fish, a metal trivet in a wok with a lid to cover is extremely practical.*

up brush — no abrasives — rinse and dry. Brush over the inside surface with oil. I have employed this system with unqualified success. One tip that I was taught was to heat up the pan over a gentle heat first, before adding the oil. This will prevent ingredients sticking to the sides.

Steamer
This is a popular method of cooking and the attractive, stacking, bamboo steamers can be used for both cooking and serving. Line the criss-cross bamboo cases of each steamer tray with a rinsed and squeezed muslin. Arrange the food in steamers, stack up one on top of the other and set a lid on top. Place the steamers over boiling water in the base of a wok, enough to touch the bottom rim, but *not* the food. Cook as long as the recipe suggests, replenishing the water as necessary. I also have a round metal trivet which can be set over hot water and used for steaming a whole fish. The fish can then be cooked on a large dish covered with foil to retain all the cooking juices. The wok is covered with its lid.

The slicer
This wide-mouthed spatula is used in conjunction with the wok, as its shape is much more suitable than a fish slice.

Chopping board
This block can be found in most oriental kitchens. It is like a round slice of tree trunk and is very heavy.

The cleaver
This is a fiersome looking implement. It is heavy and used for slicing, chopping, cutting up poultry and shellfish and for grinding meat if a good processor is not at hand (do not use a grinder — it takes moisture out of the meat). Anyone familiar with the tool can use it to bruise ginger and lemon grass by placing these on the board, then pressing down hard on the blade of the cleaver.

Pestle and mortar, food processors, blenders and liquidizers
Pounding herbs and spices in large quantities can be tedious, but it never seemed to worry any cook I met in Malaysia. They found it therapeutic, rather as we regard breadmaking. A granite pestle and mortar is ideal for grinding up wet spices as it is very heavy and coarse-surfaced; it has a good grip: ginger, garlic and chilies don't fly all over the kitchen. I would recommend the use of a pestle and mortar for grinding dry spices, especially small quantities, although if you are making your own curry powder or *garam masala* then a blender, liquidizer or the small coffee grinder would do equally well.

When using the food processor or blender for pounding the wet ingredients, it often helps to add some of the oil from the recipe if the blades are not moving freely. Do not forget to reduce the oil by the same quantity when subsequently frying the spices. It is also wise to chop or slice up the ingredients before putting them in the food processor, dealing with ingredients first, such as *laos*, lemon grass and ginger. This will ensure a fine paste and that the ingredients are evenly chopped. I would recommend a small food processor if you are to do a lot of oriental cookery.

Above left **Chopping** *The large-bladed cleaver is the universal chopper in the east, but smaller knives are required for peeling and slicing.*

Left **Blending** *A food processor with slicing and grating attachments is recommended. A pestle and mortar are also handy for pounding.*

13

Techniques

Stir fry

All the ingredients must be ready before you start to cook. The pan is heated first and then oil is added. First fry garlic and ginger, without browning, to flavor the oil. Add meat slices, if using, which will splutter in the hot fat; keep turning all the time and remove. Vegetables are added after the meat as the juices left in the pan would toughen the meat pieces. If cooking vegetables select the firmest to cook first, onion, celery, carrot, cauliflower, then adding the others with leafy green vegetables last of all. Remember to keep turning all the time so that they are all coated with oil — sometimes a little broth is added —

the wok is covered and the vegetables steamed for a minute or two. Shrimp are sometimes tossed into the pan at the last minute or some previously fried meat, or a drizzle of sesame oil. If the sauce has to be thickened, a thin paste of cornstarch and water is added at the last minute. Taste for seasoning and serve.

The beauty of this stir fry technique is that the vegetables are cooked, yet remain crisp and crunchy as well as holding their natural color and, more importantly, their flavor.

Deep frying

This is another common style of cooking. The wok is ideally suited to the technique as its shape requires a relatively small amount of oil, as it tends to collect in the bowl-shaped or round base.

Above **Deep frying** *This is a useful method for cooking vegetables and meat, particularly in the conveniently shaped wok.*
Right **Stir frying** *The wok is also ideally shaped for stir frying any variety of foods.*
Far right **Steaming** *The Chinese* dim sum *is the classic example of steamed food. The selection seen here vary from vegetable parcels to sweet dumplings.*

Poaching

This is a popular Chinese technique, which is used for many types of food. A typical recipe is DRUNKEN CHICKEN, where the water is first brought to a boil. The chicken is cooked for only 5 minutes and then the pan is taken off the heat. The chicken cooks in the residual heat; this takes longer but is very economical on fuel. A chicken cooked in this way does tend to look very pale so when it is removed from the liquid it helps to dry it and rub the breast with sesame oil and soy sauce. The flesh is very moist and the bones will still look very pink, but this is perfectly acceptable to the Chinese, so do not be put off by the rather under-cooked look; it is certainly edible, and, in fact, very succulent.

Steaming

Dim sum and breads are popularly cooked by this method. Many can be cooked at the same time in the steamers, one stacked on top of the other, which appeals to the thrifty nature of the Chinese.

Roasting

Few homes have ovens and traditionally roast meats would be brought from the market.

Barbecuing and broiling

Charcoal is the most popular fuel and is used throughout Malaysia and Indonesia for cooking *satay*. In the Philippines and Korea, barbecuing of meats is a common way of preparing food.

15

Special oriental ingredients

A note on quantities

Where teaspoons and tablespoons are mentioned, the following measurements are implied:

Teaspoons	ml	g
¼	1.25	1.25
½	2.5	2.5
1	5	5
Tablespoons		
1	15	15
1½	22.5	22.5
2	30	30
3	45	45
4	60	60
5	75	75

Where specified servings are given for a dish they are intended as an approximate guide to the cook who is catering for the western-style meal. If several dishes are prepared and laid out in the oriental way then quantities should be adjusted accordingly.

Above right
Making tamarind juice
You can either use dried tamarind (right) *or tamarind pulp* (left). *Measure out the correct amount of warm water to soak either one. Strain before using, and discard the spent tamarind.*

Annatto seeds
Also known as achuete seeds, they look like reddish brown grape pits and are used to give color to shellfish in Philippino cooking. Buy in small quantities and if they are unobtainable, substitute quarter of a teaspoon paprika and one-eighth of a teaspoon turmeric.

Asam jawa (tamarind pulp)
This is used to give a tartness to Malay, Nonya and Indian dishes. It is sold in 1lb/450g packets and can be kept for several months in a jar in the base of the refrigerator or a very cool place. The pulp comes from the fruit of the tamarind tree and is also sold loose from an enormous mound in Malay markets.

Place one good tablespoon into ⅝ cup/150ml of warm water and leave for 5 minutes or so. Using your fingers, squeeze the pulp and fibrous material from the stones and then strain the liquid through a nylon sieve and use the juice only.

Asam keping (tamarind)
Dried tamarind fruit resembles dried apple slices. They are used to give a sourness to some dishes and are especially useful if added to a soup, as the liquid is clear rather than the muddy liquid obtained with the tamarind pulp. Soak the slices in warm water for 30 minutes before straining, and use only the liquid in your cooking.

Bagoong
A Philippino fish paste usually of anchovies or shrimps, this rather lurid, pink-colored sauce is made by putting the fish and salt in a ceramic pot and letting the mixture ferment for days or weeks; unlike blachan the pieces of fish are still recognizable. A pot of *bagoong* will always be found on the table so that diners can add more piquancy to a cooked dish or, in poorer homes, their boiled rice.

Bamboo shoot
If fresh ones are available, they should be peeled to the heart and then boiled. Canned bamboo shoot (choose the winter variety) are creamy and spear shaped. Cover with fresh water daily in a closed container in the refrigerator. Use within 10 days.

Bamboo skewers
I still have the skewers that were made for me from the spine of the leaves of the coconut palm. Wooden skewers are available very cheaply from oriental stores. Soak in water for at least an hour before using to prevent burning.

Banana leaves
These are used as plates in some restaurants, but also as a wrapping for some Malay and Indonesian food, giving it a special flavor. Soften the leaves by plunging into boiling water or over a flame, then grease before using.

Bangkwang (Chinese turnip, yambean)
Turnip-shaped, with a crisp, crunchy texture this is an important part of the filling for a Chinese spring roll. The taste is rather like a cross between an apple and a tart, hard pear — I have used a coarsely grated celeriac or moolie to replace it when unobtainable.

Bean curd
This is an essential source of protein, highly prized by the Japanese and Chinese. It has a smooth, baked, custard-like texture with little flavor and for convenience is sold fresh in 3in/7.5cm squares. The fresh white curd is made from setting a liquid of ground soybeans with gypsum.

DRIED — sold packaged in sheets. Wipe with a clean, damp cloth to soften, before cutting it to the required shape. Use as a wrapper.

FRESH WHITE — can be stored in a container in the refrigerator for 2-3 days; change the water daily. A long-life version is also available, but it should be used on opening.

FRIED — small cubes of the white bean curd, which have been deep fried. In Malaysia they were threaded onto strings and sold for adding to soups; here they are sold in packets. As they are rather greasy we used to pour boiling water over them, lift them out and squeeze to get rid of any excess fattiness. They can be stored in the freezer.

YELLOW — firmer textured than the white as it has had more water removed from it. Use white where yellow is not available.

Bean paste
HOT — a reddish brown, thick paste, made from pounded chilies and soybeans. Use with discretion as it is hot and salty.

SALTED — a paste known as yellow bean paste, made from soybeans. It is sold in cans or jars and can be transferred into a suitable container and stored in the refrigerator for several months. Cans of partially crushed, yellow, salted beans are also available where more texture is required. *Miso*, used in Japanese cooking, is the same.

SWEET — hoisein sauce is used as a dip for spring rolls and so on, or in barbecued pork dishes. It is made from soybeans, garlic and spices, and the dark red purée is sold in jars and cans. It will keep for several months in the refrigerator or a cool place.

The Japanese use several different types of bean paste (see *Miso*).

Bean sprouts (bean shoots)
These are usually the young sprout of the green mung bean, although in Asia, sometimes the coarser soya bean is used. They are available and cheap in many supermarkets and vegetable shops these days and make an attractive addition to salads and stir fry vegetables. Put them in spring rolls for their bulk and crispness. They will keep if covered with plastic wrap for 2-3 days. Alternatively, cover with cold water and change the water daily. Some people insist that the straggly brown roots and the skins should be removed, but this is a time-consuming business and although the finished pile of bean sprouts does look wonderful, it is not necessary.

If you grow your own beans, try not to grow too many at a time. Mung beans can be bought in packets or loose from oriental shops. They should not be grown in the open ground, but should be raised indoors in a warm, even temperature. Use a tray or flat bowl and cover the bottom with a layer of well-damped rag, cloth or cotton wool. Wash the beans and soak them overnight in cold water. Next morning wash the beans again in cold water and spread them evenly over the moist base. Keep them damp, but not too wet or they may go moldy. Place the tray or bowl into a plastic bag or cover with plastic. It is essential to exclude light, so cover them again with brown paper or newspaper. The beans will soon sprout and will be ready to eat in 6 to 9 days. They should be plump and 1-1½in/ 25mm-38mm long. Overgrowing spoils the flavor, so try to avoid this at all costs. It is always useful to have sprouts to hand, so do try growing your own.

Blachan (*balachan, terasi* or *trasi, kapi, ngapi*)
A smell you will never forget, as my son says when I cook it: 'it smells like Malaysia'. You might imagine that the smell would predominate in any dish in which it is cooked, but in fact it adds a depth and pungency, which is essential to the hot, spicy food of South East Asia. I was always told that the Penang blachan was superior and we saw it being made while we were on holiday there. Tiny, tiny shrimp are caught near the shore, which are then fermented in enormous barrels with salt. When they have rotted and formed a paste a number of lean, aged gentlemen, wearing ragged shorts and wide brimmed hats, scooped this unpalatable looking mass out onto long, trestle-table-like trays using wooden shovels. Each scoop was then broken into a portion and, I would guess that with years of practice, each must have weighed the statutory 8oz/ 225g. These piles were left to dry further in the hot sun before packaging.

The blachan varies in colour from dull pink to a darker brown. It must always be cooked before eating. This can be done by wrapping the suggested quantity in a small foil parcel and frying over a gentle heat in a dry frying pan for 5 minutes, or shaping it into a neat cube around the edge of a skewer and holding it over the gas flame to cook the outside. It can also be broiled to achieve the same result. If it is to be fried with other finely pounded spices the preliminary cooking may be eliminated. It is available in 8oz/225g blocks from oriental stores and, if well covered, will keep indefinitely in a screwtop jar in the refrigerator or a very cool place.

Above **Preparing blachan** *Either dry fry blachan in silver foil; or* *fix it onto a skewer and turn over a gas flame. Do not burn.*

Black beans, fermented
These whole beans are sold in cans or jars and complement garlic- or beef-flavored dishes. Drain, rinse thoroughly and crush with a cleaver or the end of a rolling pin to release the flavor before adding them to the other foods.

Buah keras (macadamia nut, candlenut, *kemiri*)
This chunky, hard-shelled nut is about the size of a small chestnut. They are so-named because when threaded onto the mid-rib of a palm leaf, they are used as a type of candle. Buy them ready shelled from oriental shops — crushed, they are frequently used in Malay and Indonesian cooking as a thickening for sauces. Substitute with Brazil or almonds, but be sure to double up on almonds.

Cayenne pepper
This is made from a particular type of capsicum, originally found in Cayenne in French Guinea. It is much hotter and less brightly colored than paprika, but does not have the depth of true chilli, which is also coarser in texture.

Cardamom
These are green or white (bleached pods) or black. They may be seen growing in spice gardens in Sri Lanka. The plant is a member of the ginger family and the pods form around the base of the main stem in clusters. To open the triangular-shaped pods give a sharp blow with a mortar and prise open with thumbnails. Tiny, blackish brown seeds will be revealed, which give a warm, pungent, lemony flavor to food, especially chicken. Sometimes the pod is bruised and put into the cooking pot whole, in which case remove them before serving. I like to put them into rice while cooking as they give a lovely flavor. The black variety have a much more fibrous appearance and stronger flavor — use the seeds in hot and spicy curries.

Chayote
These are becoming much more popular in Europe now, yet a few years ago they were almost unknown. They are like a pale green pear and are a member of the squash family, known as *fat sau gwa* in Chinese, or *choko* or *xuxu* in South America. Young-looking fruit may even be cooked without peeling. Cut into quarters through the central seed, or even into slices lengthwise. Steam for best results. Sprinkle with lemon juice and toss in a few shrimp before serving for best results.

Chick-peas or garbanzos (*'channa dal*)

These are usually available whole and sometimes split or ground (gram flour). They are used ground in Burmese cooking as a thickening agent, for example PANTHE KAUKSWE, and soaked and used whole in some dishes from the Philippines, such as PUCHERO.

Chilies

The two main types are either the long, finger-like chili, which is about 4in/10cm long, red or green, or the birds eye chili. Treat both with respect in preparation, open them up under running water to prevent the oils getting near lips or eyes. Use rubber gloves or wash hands thoroughly in soap and water after preparing chilies. Discard the seeds, unless you like food fiercely hot, and pound the flesh in a pestle and mortar or food processor. The tiny, birds eye chilies are even hotter than the finger-like kind and are much used in Thai cooking. Dried chilies can be deseeded then broken into pieces before grinding: 10 chilies make up one tablespoon; soak them in warm water for 15 minutes, drain and then pound, although this does take time to reduce to a paste. If you are using a lot of chili in cooking it might be worth your while to prepare a good quantity of fresh chilies and make them into a purée with some salt (two chilies make one teaspoon of ground chili paste). Store in a screwtop jar with plastic wrap between the jar and lid, and use as required. You can of course use dried chili powder, available in oriental shops. Make sure you get a good quality powder and buy in small quantities, often.

Chinese mushrooms

Top quality can be very expensive, but you need very few of these mushrooms to add their distinctive flavor to dishes. Soak in warm water for 30 minutes and remove stems before using whole or sliced.

Above *The people of the orient love their food hot and spicy. These chilies and peppers are just a few of the many that are available and much used. Red, yellow and green peppers are popular, and green or dried peppercorns. Take care when adding these ingredients.*

Cleaning a chili

1 Whether you are using a red or green chili, slice of the stalk end of it. Place it under running water and, using a knife, slit up one side of the chili, from top to bottom.
2 Make sure that you keep it under running water to prevent the oils affecting the eyes and throat, and, with the help of the knife, remove all the seeds from the inside. It is then ready to use.

Chinese rice wine

A colorless liquid that is available in some oriental stores — substitute dry sherry if it is unobtainable.

Chinese sausages

Lap cheong are dried, rather gnarled-looking, spicy sausages, which have a chunkier filling than western sausages. Steam them for 10 minutes until the skin looks plump again. Cool a little and slice before adding to dishes such as fried rice.

Chorizo

This Spanish pepper sausage is used in Philippino cooking. It is available in delicatessens.

Cinnamon

Sri Lanka and the Seychelles both produce this spice. Thin shavings of bark are rolled into quills (cigar shapes) and the not-so-perfect pieces are sold loose or powdered to be used in baking and confectionery. Cinnamon gives a spicy fragrance to curries — dry fry or roast lightly before pounding to a powder for best flavour. Cassia, which does not have such a fine flavour, is more commonly used in Malay cooking.

Citrus leaves (lime leaves)

The leaves of the kaffir lime, *papeda* or *magrut* as it is also known, give a very distinctive flavour to many Thai and some Malaysian fish dishes. The leaf shape is unusual, two glossy green leaves joined together on one stem. They are torn before adding to food. From the knobbly, lime-like fruit the juice (not much of it) and the peel are used. A tart grapefruit or lemon can be substituted.

Above *Herbs and spices are another essential part of the oriental cuisine.*

Mint, pandanus, sweet basil, coriander and magrut are just a sample.

Cloud ears (wood ears and trees ears)

This is a crinkly black fungus, which gives its special flavor to many Chinese dishes. Choose the smaller variety and store in a screwtop jar. They should be soaked before using and you will find that they expand considerably.

Cloves

These have a rich, spicy aroma and are perhaps one of the best known spices. We saw them growing on Penang Island and in Sri Lanka, although the main source of supply is now Zanzibar. The tree is one of the myrtle family and the cloves are the buds that turn from pink to brown when picked and dried in the sun. They act as a preservative and oil of cloves is a well-known cure for toothache. Select oily, plump cloves, but do not buy in large quantities.

Coconut milk and cream

Coconut milk is a very important ingredient in the traditional recipes of South East Asia. The coconut was originally called the nut of India until the Portuguese arrived and renamed it *coco*, meaning clown or monkey. If you look at the top of a nut, you will see two eyes and a mouth and realize how the name came about. The trees can go on producing coconuts for 75 to 100 years. So the old saying stands true: 'He who plants a coconut tree plants food and drink, vessels and clothing, a habitation for himself and a heritage for his children.'

Nearly every piece of the tree and fruit has its use. *Satay* (barbecue) skewers are made from the spine of each leaf. These must be stored in the freezer and soaked well in water before using, so that they do not catch fire over charcoal or under the broiler. Coconut oil, extracted from the dried flesh or *copra*, gives an essential flavor to the local cooking, and is also used in the manufacture of such things as margarine, soap, cosmetics, candles and detergents. After pressing, the remaining *copra* is processed and sold as feed for cattle and poultry. The coir, the outer fibrous material, is used to make string mats (coco matting), brooms, filling for mattresses and pouffes. Coconut cream and milk are made from the grated flesh of the fruit, known as freshly 'desiccated' coconut. The coconut flesh can be fed to hens as a very nourishing food! The brown coconut shell which houses the flesh and juice is also put to good use. Liquid rubber is collected into the shells and they make delightful spoons and ladles. Money boxes, bangles, buttons and musical instruments are also made from the shell.

Making coconut milk

1 *Measure out the correct amount of boiling water into a measuring cup and add it to the prescribed quantity of desiccated coconut in a food processor.*

2 *Blend for several seconds in the processor until the two are well mixed.*

3 *Pour out this coconut mixture into a bowl and allow it to cool — otherwise you will scald your hands at the next stage.*

4 *Lift out handfuls of the coconut and squeeze over a sieve into a measuring cup. Place the spent, desiccated coconut into another bowl as this may be used again, although it will not make such rich milk on the second occasion. Squeeze until you have the required quantity of coconut milk. This is usually ¼pt/150ml less than the amount of hot water.*

An average size coconut is perhaps 1½lb/675g. It should be shaken well before buying to make sure the nut is full of liquid. This liquid is not coconut milk, it is coconut juice, which is chilled and served as a refreshing drink. There is a special technique for opening the fresh coconut: hold the nut in the palm of the left hand, the eyes just above the thumb; the fault line runs between the eyes — not the other two lines that run between the eye and mouth to each side; strike the line sharply with the back of a cleaver, holding the coconut over a bowl if you wish to catch the liquid. The coconut will fall apart easily if the fault line is hit.

CANS OF COCONUT MILK — these are more expensive, but less time consuming than making coconut milk yourself.

COCONUT CREAM — available in 7oz/200g slabs. Add small cubes at the end of cooking as you would thick coconut cream. However, I would use the home-made or canned milk in most of the recipes unless otherwise specified.

DESICCATED COCONUT — I find this very successful. Empty an 8oz/225g packet into the food processor. Add 1⅞ cup/450ml of very hot (almost boiling) water. Switch on and process for 20 seconds. Turn into a bowl and allow it to cool to hand-heat. Have two bowls ready — one with a sieve over it. Take a quantity of coconut in both hands and squeeze over a sieve to extract the maximum amount of coconut milk, then drop the squeezed coconut into the second bowl. Repeat and, if necessary, add a little more very hot water to the shredded coconut and squeeze again.

DRY FRY COCONUT — Place the measured desiccated coconut into a wok over gentle heat. Turn continuously until the coconut is golden, crisp and quite dry. This will take 5-10 minutes and it must not be left or else the coconut will burn. Pound to a paste in a food processor until the mixture becomes glossy and the oil begins to 'show'. This mixture is added at the end of the cooking to enrich the food and thicken the sauce.

21

Coriander or cilantro, fresh (Chinese parsley)
This is sold in large bunches in many good green-grocers and oriental shops with the roots still intact. If fresh it will keep well set in a deep jug or container of fresh water, with a plastic bag loosely covering the leaves. Place an elastic band around the bottom of the bag. Replace the water daily and the coriander will keep for more than a week in the refrigerator. The leaves are used extensively as a garnish all over the east, but in Thailand the stems and roots as well as leaves are pounded and used, adding a special dimension to their food. In the summer you can grow your own in a window box or garden. Follow the packet instructions.

Coriander seeds *(ketumbar)*
These tiny, round seeds are always best dry fried before crushing to a powder. They give off a wonderful burnt orange fragrance and greatly enhance dishes in which they are included.

Cumin
An essential ingredient in a *garam masala* and curries, this seed looks similar to fennel, but is smaller and finer — rather like a hay seed.

Curry leaves
These are a multitude of small, shiny leaves on a stem, which are very popular in Malay fish curries. Try to find the dried curry leaves, but do not substitute bay leaves, as is sometimes suggested.

Dashi kombu
This dried kelp or seaweed is essential in the making of *dashi* — a basic stock in Japan.

Above *Apart from chilies, garlic coriander and fennel feature heavily on the oriental menu. This wooden chopping board is also typical of the east.*

Daikon
A long white radish that is known as moolie in Europe, it is usually about 10in/25cm long. Peeled and grated finely, it features in many Japanese recipes.

Dry fry spices
This process makes all the difference to the subtle taste of spices. Dry fry in a frying pan or wok, turning all the time over a gentle heat, until they give off their special aroma. Grind and use at once.

Daun kesom
This herb gives its strong, pungent flavor to soups, such as LAKSA PENANG. Do not try to find a substitute, but if you visit Malaysia, Singapore or Thailand look out for it, even if only to smell it.

Deep frying spices
1 *As with dry frying coconut, place the spices in a wok or pan without oil. Use a slice for turning. Cook until they begin to give off a distinctive aroma, do not brown.*
2 *Transfer to a pestle and mortar and pound until fine. Then use immediately to capture all the flavor.*

Daun pandan (screw pine)
This is a long, pointed leaf, which is tied into a knot and put into many Malay and Indonesian sweet recipes, such as the syrup for GULA MELAKA. It is also used in cooking rice and curries. They are generally obtainable, and there is no suitable substitute.

Fennel
A plump version of the cumin seed. When crushed it has an aniseed-type smell. It has 'digestive' properties and is much used in Malaysian dishes.

Fenugreek
These are small, brown, gritty seeds, which must be used with discretion in curries. Dry fry and add whole or grind to a powder. The seeds can be sprouted in a similar way to bean sprouts, but follow packet directions. They are an unusual addition to salads and are said to aid digestion — rich in iron and vitamin A.

Fish sauce *(patis, nam pla, nuoc mam)*
Many different shades of fish sauce from pale golden to dark brown are available and each national claims a superior type from a particular locality in his country. The sauce has a distinctive, strong, fishy smell and is used to accentuate other flavors in food. It is made by packing fish into barrels with salt, and the resulting liquid is drained off after a few months. It may be further matured before bottling. It is well worthwhile acquiring the real thing, rather than resorting to suggested substitutes such as soy sauce and blachan or anchovy essence.

Five spice powder
In Chinese supermarkets this aroma seems to pervade. It is made up from ground star anise, cloves, cinnamon, fennel and Szechwan pepper. Buy in small quantities as it soon loses its pungency.

Garam masala
A blend of ground spices that varies from region to region. It is used in cooking or sprinkled over food just before serving. Commercially prepared varieties are available, but always buy in small quantities.

Garlic
The whole garlic is a bulb or a corm and each section a clove. People who are addicted to it claim that it cleanses the blood and aids digestion. (When planted under a rose-tree it is said to eliminate greenfly.) No home should be without garlic — it adds a new dimension to food of all kinds. A garlic press is an essential piece of equipment; to make it easier to clean, just trim off the root of the clove of garlic — do not peel — squeeze it in the garlic press and lift out the skin.

Below *Garlic is not just a French ingredient, but is much used by the orientals.*

Preparing ginger
1 *Scrape or peel the outside of the ginger root. You do not need to be too meticulous.*

2 *Thinly slice the root with a sharp knife so that you are left with slender rings, which will be used for pounding.*

3 *The ginger is then ready for pounding in a pestle and mortar. It should be used immediately.*

Ginger
Young ginger is creamy colored like a new potato, with pink root areas and green stems. It is much less pungent than the older ginger usually available, which has a silvery brown outer skin and is easy to recognize by its odd tuber shape; it is actually called 'a hand'. Scrape or peel it, then slice and chop finely or cut into shreds before cooking. Some recipes, like a fish stock, call for a piece of bruised ginger — scrape and knock it with a rolling pin to release the juices. If ginger juice is required either push a piece through a garlic press or grate it on the finest part of the grater; young ginger is easier for this. Store in a paper bag or newspaper in the bottom of the refrigerator for several weeks. Check on it from time to time.

Ginger flower
We used to have these growing in our garden. The flower was picked when it was in tight bud and looked like a candle flame. Finely shredded as a garnish over a bowl of LAKSA PENANG, it looked and tasted wonderful.

Gobomizuni
A long root, about the thickness of asparagus but more like salsify, it is used in Japanese cooking. Soak well before cooking as it discolors the water. It can be bought in cans.

Ikan bilis
Just off the island of Pangkor in west Malaysia we would often see two huge boats, fishing in tandem for these little whitebait-type fish. As the nets were hauled up these tiny fish *en masse* glinted like silver in the sun. On board they were cooked in enormous vats and then taken ashore where they were laid out on straw mats to be dried in the sun.

Ikan bilis are an indispensible part of Malay cuisine. They are deep fried and sprinkled over food, served as an accompaniment, or added to vegetable dishes. Buy the cleaned variety.

Jaggery
These are compressed, wheel-shaped cakes of sugar from the Nippah palm. Use very dark brown sugar if they are not available.

Katsoubushi
Dried bonito flakes, used in the making of the Japanese stock *dashi*. Store in a sealed bag or container; it does keep well.

Kecap manis
This is the Indonesian soy sauce and is a sweet, thick variety.

Konnyaku
A yam-based product that comes in two types, either grey or white; those in the know favor the grey. Blanch in boiling water before using then drain and cut into shapes. It has no particular flavour and is used more for texture.

Krupuk (shrimp crackers)
These can be bought in 8oz/225g packets from most oriental stores. In Malaysia we used to put them out in the sun before frying, but elsewhere it may be necessary to put them into a low oven for a few minutes to dry out before frying in deep fat. They will puff up, but they should not be allowed to color. Store left-overs in an airtight container.

Kway teow — see Noodles

Laos (*lengkuas*, 'greater galangal')
Laos is a member of the ginger faily and has an earthy, rather a pine-like smell and flavor; it is a little more woody in texture than ginger. Fresh roots (which are ringed and look slightly aged) are sometimes available, otherwise there is a powdered *laos*, which should be stored in the freezer to prevent loss of flavor.

Lemon grass (*serai, sereh*)
Clumps of this grass grow profusely in eastern gardens. The bulbous stem, which is about the size of a scallion or miniature leek, is generally sold in bundles. If you buy extra, wrap it in newspaper and store in the bottom of the refrigerator for 2-3 weeks. Preparation for the freezer should be done as follows: trim off the root and cut off the lower 2in/5cm — the bulbous part, which has a wonderful aroma; reserve and wrap the upper section or stalk. Slice, then pound the bulbous part to a paste and put it into a plastic box to freeze. When it is almost frozen cut it into portions and wrap in clingfilm. Label and return to the freezer with the wrapped stalks, which can be added to the recipe too. Remove these stalks before serving.

Dried lemon grass, *sereh*, powder is also available — buy it in small quantities and store it in the freezer. Use one teaspoon for each stem in the recipe.

Preparing laos
1 *Trim off any knobbly bits from the root of the laos so that you are left with the central core.*

2 *Take a knife and peel off the skin carefully, as, unlike the ginger, it is tough and unpleasant if left on.*

3 *After slicing it, place in a pestle and mortar and pound well, then use immediately to retain maximum flavor.*

Preparing lemon grass
1 *Taking a piece of lemon grass, trim off the root end, the bottom 2in/5cm. Reserve the top section for adding to casserole dishes.*

2 *Take this bottom section, which is to be used for pounding, and slice it into rings, as you would do for the laos and giner. It is now ready for pounding.*

3 *Transfer these rings to a pestle and mortar and pound them finely. Use immediately, otherwise the root will lose some of its flavor.*

Lily buds, dried
Also known as golden needles, they need to be soaked for 30 minutes in warm water before using. They give a delicate musky taste. Some cooks insist that they should be tied before adding to food, but it is not essential.

Lotus root
These tubular roots with several waists used to be sold fresh in the market. Peel and slice finely then wash in several lots of water. Put the slices in a bowl of water and add white vinegar to prevent discoloration. The slices are very attractive served as a salad with a sesame oil dressing, or cooked until just tender before adding to a vegetable dish. Canned lotus root is also available. The dried variety must be soaked well before use.

Mange tout (snow peas)
These are available in many good greengrocers and supermarkets and are a wonderful addition to stir fry vegetables.

Mirin
This Japanese sweet rice wine is only used in cooking. Use sherry as a substitute.

Miso
This fermented soybean paste is available in two colors; the dark red is saltier than the pale brown variety. A white paste is made, which chefs can then blend with one of the other varieties for their own particular recipes. Add about a tablespoon to each 7-10fl.oz (200-300ml) of the Japanese stock, *dashi*, for soups.

Above *Fermented soy bean paste is much used by the Japanese in their stock, dashi.*

Mustard seed
Tiny, black-brown seeds used in curries. If they are to be used in a *sambal*, dry fry until they start popping, then scatter them over the food.

Noodles
EGG NOODLES (mee) — fresh, thick egg noodles, if available, must be stored in the refrigerator and used within a day or two Pour boiling water over them, then drain and dry before using. If they are to be deep fried allow at least 30 minutes to drain first and fry a few at a time. If you use dried egg noodles, it is helpful to soak them for 10 minutes in water first, then cook in boiling water. Allow 2-3 minutes for thin noodles and 3-4 minutes for thicker ones.

KWAY TEOW — flat, wide strips of rice noodles, which can be cut to the required width. They are available fresh and sometimes contain tiny pieces of scallion or dried shrimp. Scald them with boiling water after cutting and drain before frying.

LAKSA NOODLES (lai fan) — thick, white rice noodles, spaghetti size. The thin ones are referred to as *beehoon*, rice vermicelli or rice sticks. Soak the thicker noodles for 30 minutes then cook in boiling water for 10-15 minutes until tender; drain. Rinse well before serving or using in soups. The thinner variety should be soaked for 2 minutes in boiling water before using in soups.

If a crisp garnish is required, deep fry the dry noodles and they will puff up. Do not allow them to color. (See *MEE KROB* in Thailand section.) If one type is not available use the other.

WHEAT NOODLES — it is helpful to soak these 10 minutes in water first then cook in boiling water. Allow 2-3 minutes for thin noodles and 3-4 minutes for thicker ones. When using whole-wheat spaghetti as a substitute, follow the packet directions.

Nori
This is dried laver, a kind of seaweed. Hold the sheet over a gas flame before using it to seal in the flavor.

Nutmeg and mace
When the fruit of the nutmeg is ripe it splits open like a chestnut to reveal bright red arils surrounding the nut. These turn orange as soon as they are exposed to the air and are, of course, the blades of mace, which have a similar but more delicate flavor than the nutmeg. The shell of this inner nut must be cracked to obtain the nutmeg. In Malaysia the outer, fleshy casing is crystallized or pickled and sold as a snack — further proof of a thrifty people.

Oyster sauce

This thick, brown sauce of varying quality is made basically from an extract of oysters, salt and also starches. It accentuates flavors and accompanies meat and vegetable dishes very successfully.

Peppercorn

The black peppercorn is the whole berry or fruit of the peppercorn vine, picked then simply dried in the sun. We saw this being done in Sarawak. The peppercorn spikes are spread out on mats and are raked over from time to time with a wooden rake until they have dried completely. This process takes about a week depending on the time of year and sunshine hours. The spike stems are removed in the raking.

The white peppercorn is the inner core of the ripened fruit. The green peppercorn is thoroughly washed in water then left to soak in slow running water for about a week to rot the outer skin. The fruit is then trampled to remove the spikes and bruise the soft skins. The final removal of the skins is done by washing and rubbing the peppercorns by hand in a sieve. The resulting white peppercorns are dried in the sun for 3-4 days. When the fruits are satisfactorily dried they are put in sacks, weighing a picul or about 10 pecks. From the pepper garden the sacks are then taken to the Kuching merchant who sends them to Singapore, from where they are exported worldwide.

Szechwan peppercorns are different from black peppercorns and, for best results, they must be dry fried before coarsely grinding and using in recipes. They are sometimes known as Chinese brown peppercorns and there is no substitute.

Left *The fruit of the nutmeg hangs on the tree like a Christmas bauble. As a spice, it is popular in Malaysia.*

Above *Thailand is famous for its* klongs *and the many boats, laden with fresh fruit, that sail up them daily.*

Pickled ginger

This does not look remotely like ginger. It is a bright red colour in fine threads and is used mostly for garnish in Japanese cooking.

Prawn or shrimp

DRIED — used for soups and vegetable dishes. They have quite a strong flavour and must be soaked and drained before adding to vegetables while they are cooking, or pounded for soups.

POWDERED — these are sold in 2oz/50g packets and are frequently used in Burmese cuisine.

Rice

Long grain *THAI RICE* has a lovely fragrance and should not be cooked with salt.

BASMATHI RICE has a delicious nutty flavor and is for some the best on the market.

GLUTINOUS RICE PULOT (white), beloved of most people in South East Asia, is used mostly in preparation of sweet porridge, cakes and savory food black variety makes a delicious, rice pudding.

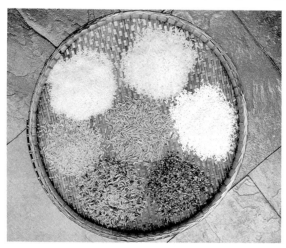

Above *Considering that the Far East is the largest producer of rice in the world, it is hardly surprising that they grow so many varieties!*

Rice wine vinegar

Try to use this for Japanese cooking to give that special flavor.

Sake

Rice wine, used extensively in Japanese cooking — if all else fails use dry sherry or vermouth. It is best warmed before drinking; immerse the bottle in a large bowl of hot water for several minutes.

Sambal rojak (*harko, petis*)

This thick, treacle-like paste is made up from soy-paste and fermented shrimp. It is served as a side dish for LAKSA PENANG. Each person puts a spoonful onto his helping of soup and stirs it in before eating.

Sambal ulek

A ready made paste of chilies and salt, this is a convenient substitute for all that pounding and grinding — two chilies make up one teaspoon. It is also sold commercially in jars.

Satoemo

These are small, sweet potatoes (about the size of a plum) from Japan that can be bought fresh, otherwise frozen or canned.

Sesame oil

A rich, dark brown oil made from crushed, roasted sesame seeds. It is not used for deep frying as it burns at a low temperature. It is best added at the last minute in small quantities to meat and vegetable dishes. Used a great deal in Korean and Japanese cooking.

Sesame paste

This is used in Korean recipes. To make it, roast and grind two or three tablespoons of sesame seeds, and add three teaspoons of sesame oil, mixing to a paste.

Despite the widespread use of rice, potatoes and sweet potatoes are used in the east (left). *Shallots are often used as an alternative to onions* (above). *Orange and tangerine — in fact any citrus fruit — rind is popular* (below).

Sesame seeds

The seeds are sweet and nutty after dry frying. To roast, place in a clean frying pan and turn over a gentle heat until golden. Do not allow to brown too much. They are extensively used in Korean and Japanese dishes.

Shallots or scallions *(Bombay onions)*

These small, strong-flavored onions grow in clusters. Each section of the cluster varies in size so it would be safe to say that each piece equals one shallot. Dark red onions are the best substitute. If using white, it may be necessary to increase the quantity to get the correct flavor.

Shiritaki

This Japanese vermicelli, made from yam and water, is sold in a pack, surrounded by water to protect the shape, or in a can.

Soy sauce

The thin soy sauce is commonly known as white sauce and is the most frequently used; the thick soy sauce is called black sauce. The latter is stronger in flavour and should be used judiciously. Both are made from salted soybeans.

JAPANESE SOY SAUCE — must always be used in Japanese cooking. Sold as *shoyu.*

Spring roll and wonton wrappers

Spring roll wrappers are available from most oriental shops in varying sizes, either round or square. They are paper thin and naturally very fragile. Open the packet and allow them to thaw, then carefully peel them away one by one and make them into another pile, covered with a slightly damp cloth so that they will not dry out before filling (see page 100); once they dry they are impossible to roll up. The same applies to wonton wrapper (see page 57).

Star anise

Used ground in five spice powder, this is a very attractive, round, star shape with eight sections, which can all be used separately.

Straw mushrooms

These are available in cans. Button mushrooms can be used as a substitute, if the straw ones are unobtainable.

Tangerine peel

This adds another dimension to chicken or duck dishes. Soak the small pieces for 30 minutes before cooking. You can make your own by drying out tangerine peel in a slow oven until dry. Store in an airtight container.

Turmeric

This is another member of the ginger family and it comes ready ground. The root is very hard and gives a rich yellow color and warm, distinctive smell and taste to food.

Water chestnuts

A wonderful crisp addition to stir fry vegetables or to fruit salads. Available fresh sometimes, but you will always find them in cans.

29

Malaysia

Malaysia is a rich land of well-ordered rubber and palm plantations, tin mines, paddy-fields, jungle and delightful little kampongs *(villages), where the gentle Malays take life in a relaxed style. Peninsular Malaysia was known as Malaya until 1963 when the original 11 states were joined by Sarawak, Sabah (part of Borneo) and Singapore. This was a short-lived union and in 1965 Singapore broke away leaving the present 13 states. Each of these states has its sultan who is very powerful within his territory, even today. All are immensely wealthy and live in considerable style. Every five years the sultans elect a new king from one of their number. Rich yellow embroidered finery and jewelled umbrellas are featured in the magnificent coronation ceremony. Malaysia itself resembles a long finger, bordering Thailand and Burma in the north and with clusters of Indonesian islands in the south, the largest being Borneo, land of the White Rajahs. A mountain range runs from top to bottom of Malaysia like a spine, almost all of it covered in dense jungle although there are dwarf forests in some of the Highland regions such as the Gentings, which are freaks of nature, but charming nevertheless. Crossing from one side of the country to the other has been made easier recently with the construction of an excellent road built by the Koreans, which goes from Kuala Lumpur, the capital, to the east coast on the South China Sea.*

The food of Malaysia richly reflects the meeting of three separate cuisines: the Malay, Chinese and Indian. Each retains their own traditional recipes, but is still able to acknowledge and use ideas from the other's cuisine. The Malays are a fine-featured, elegant and graceful people and are devout Muslims. Bumiputra *'sons of the soil' is a word frequently used in reference to the people of the rural areas where fishing and farming are the main occupations. The 'sia' in Malaysia covers the remaining population of Chinese, Indian and other settlers. Intermarriage between the races is rare unless the intended is also Muslim.*

The Chinese are very industrious people, as I learnt from our amah, Ah Moi, which means 'little sister'. They are now Malaysia's largest immigrant group. This is mainly a result of demand for labor in the mining industry almost 100 years ago, but in fact Chinese merchants had established settlements all along the coast of Malaysia, especially in Malacca, as long ago as 1500. The Indians are another important part of the Malaysian society. Large numbers came late in the last century to work on the coffee and rubber estates. There are as many different sects as there are on the mainlands of India and Sri Lanka. Each continue to cook their own regional, traditional dishes, but the greatest Indian influence is that of the Tamils from the south of India.

In Malaysia there are more national holidays than anywhere else in the world, because the three communities each take the opportunity to enjoy the other's celebrations. Malays have strong traditions, nurtured by their devotion to Islam. Hari Raya Puasa *marks the end of the fasting month for all Muslims. The day is ushered in with prayers at the mosques and then the celebrations continue with invitations to an open house for all friends and colleagues, where the best of Malaysian home-made food and delicacies are served. The Chinese New Year is usually celebrated in early February when the Chinese entertain all their friends. There are special attractions, particularly the* ang pow — *adults receive an extra month's salary in these red envelopes, and children are given money, which must always be an even amount: 2, 4, 6 or 8 dollars, as odd numbers are considered unlucky.* Deepvali *, in October, is a much celebrated occasion for people of the Hindu faith. It means 'festival of light' and signifies the triumph of good over evil. These are just three of the festivals — there are many more!*

Rice is grown abundantly in Asia, but there is still barely enough to go round. Rice growing is truly a labor of love and it is understandable why the younger generation are leaving the traditional family paddy-fields for more congenial occupations. Although mechanization is creeping in, it is amazing how much of the work is still done by hand. We are inveterate travellers and on trips to Pangkor, Trengganu and Malacca, we often stopped as we rounded a corner to see the lovingly tended acres of paddy-fields. In our experience we found most of the planters were women. They were always swathed in clothes and wore the essential, large-brimmed hats as a protection against the fierce heat of the sun. They stood more than ankle deep in mud all day, taking bundles of seedlings from the nursery and planting them out in neat rows. Depending on the variety of rice planted, the Malay farmers expect a double crop annually. Each crop takes about 20 weeks from planting to harvest. Slowly the water level is reduced in the paddy-fields as the crops ripen so that by harvest time the fields are almost dry. The land is then ploughed, often using buffalo or oxen, left for 3-4 weeks, ploughed again and harrowed. Then the field is flooded and the whole process starts all over again.

As well as being the staple diet, rice in Malaysia, and all over the east, also plays a very important part in the customs and religious traditions; our custom of throwing rice over the bride and groom to signify fertility is most probably borrowed from them. On our trip to Sarawak we were invited to the home of an Iban policeman. The female members of his family were preparing for a wedding the following day, but they still made us welcome. We drank arrak *(rice brandy), but not before a glassful had been poured out of the window as a gesture to the gods. Some of the family ate lunch in the next room, not a spoon in sight. They skilfully ate with their right hands, scooping up the rice with sauce and vegetables, never dropping a grain. Similarly, there are Indian restaurants in Kuala Lumpur where the rice and curry is served on a banana leaf and spoons and forks come only on request.*

The climate is very hot and intensely humid, with frequent tropical storms to cool the air and temperament. It is natural therefore to expect a richly spiced cuisine. After all, chilies are known to make you perspire, but the Malays also believe that they stimulate the appetite and, afterwards, create a sense of peace and benignity. Looking at them you sense the truth in this. Anything grows in this country and there is an abundance of exotic fruit available throughout the year. There are no seasons as we know them in Europe — it just gets hotter and wetter.

The food of Malaysia bears a close affinity to its neighbor Indonesia — the same cooking equipment and methods are used, as well as basic spices, coconut milk and oil, and fish, but having said that, the Chinese and Indian influence is very strong too, making it one of the most fascinating countries to visit. In Malacca, and later in Penang where the Chinese took Malay wives, another style of cooking known as Straits Chinese or Nonya developed. These recipes are included in the Singapore chapter, where the Nonya style of cooking is so popular.

Eating out is an accepted way of life. It can be impromptu and is always informal. In the morning most business people will only have a cup of tea at home, then, at 10.30am or earlier, off they go to the coffee shops or street stalls for dim sum, paus (steamed buns), siew mai (meat dumplings), NASI LEMAK (coconut rice) or FAH SONG CHOK (Chinese rice porridge), to name but a few of the foods on offer. The evening meal is usually eaten early 5.30-8pm, although there is always somewhere to eat at any hour of the day. Eating is very important; the Malaysians never seem to stop yet they retain their trim and elegant figures — men and women alike. The other appealing aspect is that food is inexpensive and there is an infinite variety in any of the cities and towns (or villages for that matter). Each stallholder pushes his stall (gerais) into the deserted car parks at about 5pm — produces benches and tables, either Formica-topped or covered with plastic cloths. In no time the benches are full of eager patrons, indulging in a vast variety of foods cooked by Chinese, Malay or Indians. In the larger cities, areas will be known for their SATAY, KWAY TEOW, LAKSA, MURTABAK.

Surely one of the best places to find out about the cuisine of the country is to visit a market. That is the place where the people who care about food (and they all do) go to select the best ingredients, and discerning they are too; every fish, vegetable or fruit is scrutinized before buying. Central Market in Kuala Lumpur — a huge building near the River Klang where there was a permanent traffic jam between 8am and noon — was a fascinating place to my mind. At the main entrance sat a bevy of people selling small quantities of fresh coriander, **eggplant, fried bean curd,** kway teow, *noodles and flowers. These were the small stallholders, most of them squatting on the floor, surrounded by their wares. On the right were all the exotic fruits such as star fruit, papaya, mango, mangosteen, rambutan, ouriam, bananas, pineapple, all beautifully displayed. To the left, a few yards away, were butchers selling lamb, goat and beef. This was a relatively small section followed by a vast area where every imaginable vegetable could be purchased. Huge baskets of glossy red and green chilies, large, medium and small, ginger, young and old,* lengkuas, *loofah, melons, yard beans, cabbage and onions in infinite variety. To the right were the mainly Indian merchants, selling spices galore — wet spices were a feature here. There were mounds of pounded, fresh chili, fresh lemon grass, coriander, garlic, ginger, and so on. Dollops of these in varying amounts were put on a banana leaf and taken home to form the basis of a curry, a fish curry mixture might have less chili than a* CHICKEN RENDANG, *for example.*

Fish came next — all very fresh, caught the previous night. People in Malaysia have great culinary skills with fish, which is evident when you look at any Malay spread or cookbook. The whole country is surrounded by sea and, being a long, narrow country, fish is available almost everywhere. Ikan *is the Malay word for fish,* ikan mereh, ikan kembong, ikan bilis, sotong *(squid). (Wherever these are mentioned in the recipes I have given equivalent and/or a suggested substitute.)*

Near the end of our market tour there are people selling freshly grated coconut in plastic bags, bean curd, both fresh and fried, and fish dumplings. On the left you would see hens' eggs galore and the famous Chinese Dragon pots — full of preserved ducks' eggs, which are definitely an acquired taste. Quails' eggs were always available and very cheaply too, so often they would feature hard-cooked, on sticks at a cocktail party or as part of a 'steamboat' recipe. Chickens and ducks squalled as they were offered for sale 'on the hoof' — not my favorite spot! Finally, the last section of this market featured pork, an area run by the Chinese in a completely separate section, so that the devout Malay Muslim need never acknowledge its existence (it is an absolute taboo as far as Malays are concerned, and yet a vital ingredient in Chinese cooking). This market really encapsulated Malaysia and its cuisine. Everything you would ever need to buy for cooking the local dishes could be found inside those four walls.

If you are invited to the home of a Malay you must remember to remove your shoes unless your host continues to wear his. When a dish

Above *The land of Malaysia is lush and green as a result of the monsoon climate found in the majority of South East Asia. The landscape is often broken up by the appearance of these long-trunked trees and mountain ranges — a spectacular sight.*

is handed to you, accept with the right hand or both hands — never the left. Similarly, food when eaten with the fingers must be eaten with the right hand only. In a very traditional Malay house all the food is put together on mats in the center of the room. The members of a family sit around, feet tucked in at the sides — it is an insult to show the soles of the feet — and help themselves. A spoon and fork might be used these days and, in less traditional surroundings, people might sit at a table.

The Chinese eat at a table with food served on platters. Each person has a bowl of rice, eats with chopsticks or takes the traditional, simple soup from a porcelain soup spoon. If you are an honored guest you will be seated opposite the door of the room. Husbands and wives frequently sit next to each other and when you wish to drink, you must toast someone else who will drink with you. In Indian households most adopt the western style of eating, but avoid beef and pork. It is wise to have two or three vegetable dishes as many Indians are vegetarians.

Laksa Penang
(Soup with tamarind)

Penang Island is a fascinating place, full of history, and we always loved going there. One of our favorite jaunts was a trip to Balik Pulau (which translated means 'back of the Island'). *En route* we passed the remnants of once-thriving nutmeg and durian plantations up in the hills. With any luck we would arrive in this small place in time for lunch, bought from a hawker's stall, whose speciality was Laksa Penang. It is a fish soup with a hint of tamarind and a myriad other flavors each complementing the other, *duan kesom*, a rather pungent green herb like basil, mint and a ginger flower, still a tight pink bud. Noodles, the soup, cucumber, chilies and lettuce, were placed in the bowl, then the ginger flower was sprinkled over the top as a final garnish. All was served piping hot in a Chinese bowl with chopsticks and a china soup spoon. We never failed to go for this lunchtime treat and without fail the same cheery man was there dispensing his Laksa.

6 small or 2
   medium-sized
   mackerel (ikan
   kembong), gutted,
   rinsed and dried.

Fish stock
fish
1 fish head
7½ cups water
1 peeled and sliced
   onion
1 piece celery
1 piece ginger
1 stem and bud of the
   ginger plant flower
   (see page 24)
4 stems daun kesom or
   basil
seasoning to taste

Soup
6 pieces asam keping,
   soaked in 2½ cups
   warm water
10 red chilies, pounded,
   or 1-2 tablespoons
   chili powder, mixed
   to a paste with oil
½in/1cm square piece
   blachan (see page 18)

20 peeled and chopped
   shallots (approx
   4oz/100g)
4 tablespoons coconut oil
1 tablespoon sugar

Noodles
1⅓ cups fresh laksa
   noodles or rice
   vermicelli (beehoon)

Accompaniments

   and shredded
3 fresh red chillies,
   seeded and sliced into
   rings
4 shallots, peeled and cut
   into slices
½ cucumber, diced
2 limes, each cut into 6
   wedges
6 sprigs fresh mint
1 stem and bud ginger
   plant flower, sliced
   finely (see page 24)
shrimp crackers
sambal rojak if available
   (see page 28)

SERVES 6-8

Wash the fish head. Remove the flesh from three of the smaller fish or one of the medium-sized fish. Shred finely and leave in the refrigerator. Place the fish bones and head and the remaining whole fish into a pan with onion, celery, bruised ginger root, chopped ginger flower, daun kesom and salt to taste. Bring to the boil and cook for at least 1 hour until the fish have disintegrated. Strain and reserve the stock.

Soak the asam in the water for at least 30 minutes, then squeeze and reserve the juice. Prepare the chilies, toast the piece of blachan on a skewer over a gas flame until it dries on the outside and gives off a strong smell. Pound with half the shallots. Fry the remaining shallots in the oil until they are just turning color. Add the chili, blachan and onion mixture. Reduce the heat and cook for several minutes to bring out the flavor. Add asam juice and sugar and leave to cook for about 10 minutes. Add 5-6½ cups/1.25-1.5 liters fish stock and adjust the seasoning. Just before serving add one ladleful of stock to the shredded fish flesh to make it into a creamy consistency, before stirring it all into the pan. Cook, stirring, for 3-4 minutes.

Prepare the accompaniments and arrange them in separate small bowls or in piles on a large platter. Serve the shrimp paste in a bowl and shrimp crackers in a dish. Prepare the noodles. Bring the stock or salted water to the boil, soak the noodles for 1-2 minutes then stir, but do not cover. Strain through a colander with boiling water.

Each person takes a helping of noodles and places them in the bowl. Add a selection of accompaniments. Top with soup and a spoonful of sambal rojak. Eat with shrimp crackers.

Laksa Lemak
(Soup with coconut milk)

4 × 8oz/225g packets
   unsweetened,
   desiccated coconut to
   make 3 cups coconut
   milk and ½ cup
   coconut cream (see
   page 21)
1 cup peeled shallots
4 cloves garlic

2 buah keras or shelled,
   blanched almonds
6 tablespoons coconut oil
3 stems lemon grass
½in/1cm square blachan
   (see page 18)
1½ tablespoon mild curry
   powder
a few curry leaves

salt to taste
2½ cups ikan bilis
   stock (see below)

Accompaniments
2oz/50g ikan bilis (see
   page 24) and
   3¾ cups water to
   make stock
3 eggplant
1¼lb/675g shelled
   shrimps, sprinkled
   with 2 teaspoons
   sugar
1 shredded cos-type
   lettuce
1½ cups bean sprouts

2 scallions, finely
   chopped
¼ cup crispy fried
   onions
2 bunches fried bean
   curd or 1 packet

Selection of noodles
laksa noodles
mee
beehoon (approx
   4oz/100g each person)
½ × 8oz/225g packet
   shrimp crackers, dry
   in very low oven first,
   then deep fry in oil
1¼lb/675g clams
   (optional)

SERVES 6

Prepare the coconut milk and cream. Pound half of the shallots with the garlic, nuts and one sliced and bruised stem of lemon grass. Fry the remaining half of the shallots, sliced, in coconut oil until they give off a good smell, then add the pounded mixture and stir well. Add the bruised lemon grass stems, blachan and curry powder — mixed to a paste with the coconut milk — fry to bring out the full flavor. Stir all the time, as you add half of the coconut cream and all the coconut milk, to prevent the soup curdling. Add the curry leaves. Simmer for 10 minutes without covering. Taste for seasoning of salt. Finally, add the ikan bilis stock and stir in the remaining coconut cream as it comes to

the boil. Add the halved, fried bean curd as described below.

To prepare the accompaniments first cook the ikan bilis in water for 30 minutes to make a stock. Strain and discard the fish. Add the eggplant to the stock and cook for 5 minutes until tender and the skins can be peeled off easily. Cut into quarters and pieces about 3in/7.5cm long. Arrange on a serving platter. Next, cook the shrimp in the stock for 4 minutes until just tender. Arrange on a platter with the shredded lettuce, bean sprouts, scallions and crispy fried onions. Rinse the fried bean curd in boiling water and squeeze to remove excess oil. Add to the Laksa soup. Finally, prepare the noodles, drain and arrange them on a platter. Serve the soup in a large tureen. The guests should spoon noodles and a selection of the other accompaniments into their bowls and top up with the soup. Eat with chopsticks and soup spoons; also hand a bowl of shrimp crackers around.

If serving the clams, clean the shells thoroughly by washing in several lots of cold water, adding salt to the last rinse. Pour boiling water over, leave for 3-4 minutes, drain and open the shells to remove the clams. Serve along with the other accompaniments.

Below **Laksa lemak** Laksa denotes a noodle dish cooked in coconut milk. The number and variety of accompaniments almost make this soup a meal on its own. It is a filling and healthy dish.

Chili Crab

I think that it was the Pacific Restaurant in the Old Klang Road where the best chili crabs were served. The only landmark was a garish mural, badly lit. It was an unpretentious place — Formica-topped tables, half in an open patch of waste ground to the side of the building — but the food was memorable: steamed shrimp, clams, pomfret. The crabs were always served with chunks of cucumber (to cool the assaulted taste buds) and slices of toast to mop up the sauce. We always used our fingers; warm face-cloths were brought around afterwards.

2 cooked crabs (1½lb/675g each)	1 tablespoon brown sugar
1in/2.5cm piece fresh ginger, scraped	⅝ cup hot water
2 fresh red chilies or 2 teaspoons chili sauce	1 beaten egg (optional) salt
2 cloves garlic, crushed	fresh coriander to garnish
4-6 tablespoons vegetable oil	chunks of cucumber and pieces of toast to serve
1 cup tomato ketchup	

SERVES 4

Remove the large claws and turn each crab onto its back, with the head facing away from you. Use your thumbs to push the body up from the main shell. Discard the stomach sac and dead men's fingers (the lungs and any green matter); leave the creamy brown meat in the shell and cut in half. Cut the body section in half with a strong knife and crack the claws with a sharp tap from a hammer or cleaver. Do crack, not splinter them.

Pound the ginger, prepared chilies and garlic together. Fry in hot oil for 1-2 minutes without browning. Add tomato ketchup, chili sauce, sugar and water, and mix well. When almost boiling add all the crab over a high heat. Just before serving stir in the beaten egg, which will scramble in the sauce if desired; taste for seasoning and serve at once garnished with fresh coriander leaves, together with the cucumber and toast.

Below **Chili crab** Note how the whole crab, including the shell, is covered in the rich-colored sauce mixture.

Right **Steaming pomfret**
1 Place the fish in the steamer on a dish.
2 Add the vegetables and herbs. Cover and cook, then drain off the juices.

Making scallion curls
1 *Trim off the white part of the scallion, which may be used in the actual dish.*

2 *Take the green part and, with a knife, make slits all around both ends, but leaving the centre section intact.*

3 *Place the cut stem into ice cold water and it will open out into a spidery-like flower, which can be used as a garnish.*

Steamed Pomfret

The white and silver pomfret are highly prized and regarded as a great delicacy — thus becoming more and more expensive too. Buy frozen pomfret or try this recipe with whole halibut, bream or sole.

2 pomfret, halibut, bream or sole, gutted but head, fins and tail left on
salt and pepper
2 dried mushrooms, soaked in warm water
1in/2.5cm piece ginger, scraped and cut into shreds
2 scallions
1 tablespoon oil

Sauce
stock from cooked fish
1 tablespoon sesame oil
1 tablespoon oyster sauce
sugar and salt to taste

To garnish
shredded chilli
fresh coriander leaves
scallion curls (see page 39)

SERVES 2-4 (DEPENDING ON SIZE OF FISH)

Clean the fish and lay each one on a piece of oiled foil. Slash twice, season and set aside. Drain and cut the mushrooms into fine slivers and shred the ginger. Trim the green from the scallions and reserve for the garnish. Slice the white part finely and sprinkle it over the fish with the ginger and mushroom. Drizzle over the oil and set in the steamer with the foil turned up at the edges to retain the cooking juices or in a shallow casserole. Steam for about 15 minutes. Lift out and set on a warm serving dish. Strain the sauce into a measuring jug and make up to ¼pt/150ml of stock by adding hot water. Heat the sesame oil and add the stock, oyster sauce, sugar and salt to taste. Pour over the cooked fish and serve with garnishes.

Sambal Goreng Sotong
(Squid sambal)

The first time we had this dish was in Kuanton on the shores of the South China Sea. As the dish with neat little squid was placed before me I thought that I had been sent noodles — someone else's order — what a delight when I discovered this special way of cutting up the squid, which curls on cooking.

8-10 squid (approx 1¹/₂lb/675g)	2 stems lemon grass
8 nuts, choose macadamia, almond or cashew	1¹/₄ cups tamarind water from 2 teaspoons tamarind pulp (see page 16)
8 tablespoons oil	1 tablespoon brown sugar
2 teaspoons chili powder	salt to taste
2 medium red onions	
¹/₂in/1cm blachan	

SERVES 4-6

Remove the tentacles from each squid, clean well, trim and remove the eyes. Reserve. Wash and peel off the reddish purple skin on the outside of each one. Remove the transparent bone from the pocket of the squid, then turn each one inside out and clean well. Score the flesh into a criss-cross pattern on the inside, then cut into long strips from tip to base. These should curl on cooking.

Grind the nuts and add chili powder, with one tablespoon of the oil. Peel, chop and pound the onions finely, then pound further with blachan. Slice the lemon grass stems into two or three and bruise with a cleaver to release the flavor. Prepare the tamarind water. Heat the wok and fry the squid without oil, stirring all the time until the liquid has evaporated. Lift out and reserve. Heat the oil, fry the chili and nut paste, then the onion and blachan and lemon grass. Cook, stirring all the time to bring out the flavor of the spices. Add tamarind water and sugar. Reduce the heat and cook for a further few minutes. Increase the heat, add the squid and salt to

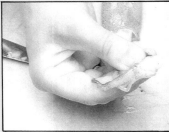

Preparing a squid
1 *Use a sharp knife to cut away the tentacles, making your incision just above the eyes.*

2 *With your fingers press up on the tentacle to squeeze out the little central bone, which should come out fairly easily.*

3 *Again with your fingers, remove the quill and innards from the body cavity of the squid. These may then be discarded.*

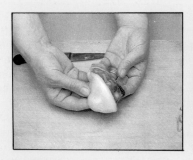

4 *Pull away the thin outer skin from the flesh, which should come off easily and in one piece, leaving the flesh in tact.*

5 *Take the knife and slit through the side of the skinned piece so that you are able to open it out flat.*

6 *Wash it well, then open it out, inside uppermost, and score the surface. Then, cut it into even-sized ribbons.*

taste. Reduce the heat and cook uncovered for about 5 minutes when the sauce should be dark red and oily and the squid just tender.

This rich dish is perfectly accompanied by plain rice and may be garnished with coriander leaves, if preferred. It is an excellent way of preparing squid.

Ikan Moolie
(Fish curry)

1½lb/675g tengirri or ikan merah, monkfish or halibut	*¼ cup fresh ginger*
2 × 8oz/225g packets unsweetened, desiccated coconut	*2 stems lemon grass*
	3 teaspoons turmeric powder
⅓ cup small red onions	*3 tablespoons coconut oil or vegetable oil*
3 cloves garlic	*3 chilies, seeded and finely shredded*
5 shelled bush keras (macadamia nuts) or almonds	*salt to taste*

SERVES 4

Remove the skin and any bones from the fish and reserve. Cut the fish into chunks and sprinkle them with salt. Dry fry ⅓ cup of the coconut in a wok, stirring all the time until it browns. Pound, using a pestle and mortar or blender, until the oil in the dry coconut begins to show. Make 2fl.oz/50ml coconut cream and 2½ cups coconut milk with the remaining coconut. Peel and slice the onions. Set one-third aside with the finely chopped garlic. Dry fry the remaining onions with chopped nuts, fresh ginger slices and sliced lemon grass to bring out the flavors fully. Pound until fine then add the turmeric powder.

Heat the oil, fry the reserved onion slices and garlic until they are just turning golden. Add the pounded paste and fry well without browning. Stir in the coconut milk and just bring to the boil. Now add the fish cubes, shredded chili, pounded dry coconut and the fish trimmings in a muslin bag if preferred. These are used to give additional flavor, but are removed before serving, of course. Cook for only 5 minutes; do not overcook as the fish will break up. Taste for seasoning and stir in the coconut cream just before serving. Sprinkle with shredded chili in a serving dish. Serve with plain boiled Malay rice.

Ah Moi's Chicken Rendang

Ah Moi, our amah, came to us saying that she couldn't cook and hoped I would teach her some European dishes. What a delight to find out that this was false modesty — she was immensely talented and I owe her a debt of gratitude for all she taught me. This was one of her favorite recipes.

1 × 3lb/1.4kg fresh chicken, jointed into 8 pieces	*1in/2.5cm piece fresh ginger*
1 tablespoon sugar	*2in/5cm piece fresh lengkuas*
2¼ cups unsweetened, desiccated coconut and just over 2½ cups boiling water to make coconut milk and cream (see page 21)	*2 stems lemon grass*
	5 tablespoons coconut or vegetable oil
	2 tablespoons dry chilli powder or to taste
4 small red onions	*salt to taste*
2 cloves garlic	

SERVES 4

Rinse the pieces of chicken and dry them on kitchen paper. Place in a bowl, sprinkle with sugar and toss in the bowl to release their juices. Dry fry ½ cup/75g of coconut in a large frying pan or wok turning all the time until it becomes dry, crisp and golden. Pound with a pestle and mortar until the oil begins to 'show'. Turn the remaining coconut into a deep bowl. Prepare the coconut milk and cream. Leave to stand for 15 minutes and spoon off four tablespoons of the thickest coconut cream. You should have approximately 1⅞ cups/450ml coconut milk. Peel the onions and garlic and scrape the ginger and lengkuas. Roughly chop up these ingredients and pound with the lemon grass until fine. Heat the oil in the wok. Fry the pounded ingredients for several minutes to bring out the flavor. Lower the heat, add the chili powder and cook for 3-4 minutes, stirring all the time. Add the thick coconut cream and salt. Stir as the mixture comes to the boil to prevent curdling. Add the chicken pieces turning frequently so that the rendang mixture coats each piece. Reduce the heat and stir in the remaining coconut milk. Cook over a gentle heat for 45-50 minutes or until the chicken is tender. Just before serving spoon some of the sauce into the pounded coconut. Mix well, then return this to the pan. Stir without breaking up the chicken and cook for a further 5 minutes.

Chicken Satay

Satay is perhaps the most widely known Malay dish. It is perfect for a barbecue, although a gas or electric broiler will suffice. The spiced meat can be prepared in advance and stored in the freezer. Allow at least 8 hours to thaw before threading on skewers and cooking. The peanut sauce can also be made ahead and stored in the refrigerator or freezer. Thaw overnight in the refrigerator and heat up just before serving. If the sauce has thickened on freezing, thin it with a weak tamarind juice or a little water.

4 boned chicken breasts, approx 6oz/175g each
approx 12 bamboo or coconut skewers — soak in water before using to prevent burning

Spice marinade
¹/₂ teaspoon each cumin, fennel and coriander seeds
6 small red shallots, peeled and chopped
1 clove garlic, peeled and crushed
1 stem lemon grass
3 macadamia, almond or cashew nuts
¹/₂ teaspoon turmeric powder
1 teaspoon brown sugar
salt to taste

Peanut sauce
¹/₄ cup peanuts
4 shallots, peeled and chopped
2 cloves garlic, peeled
¹/₂ teaspoon blachan
6 macadamia, almond or cashew nuts
2 stems lemon grass
3 tablespoons coconut or peanut oil
2-3 teaspoons chilli powder
1¹/₄ cups thick coconut milk
4 tablespoons tamarind water made from 1 tablespoon tamarind pulp or dried tamarind
1 tablespoon brown sugar
salt to taste

MAKES 12 SKEWERS

Leave the skin on the chicken breasts then cut them into ¹/₂in/1cm cubes. Fry the spices with quarter of a teaspoon of oil over a medium heat to bring out the flavor, then grind or pound. Add the shallots, garlic, lemon grass, which has been bruised and sliced, and roughly chopped nuts. Grind or pound until fine. A little oil can be added if necessary when grinding by machine. Stir in turmeric. Sprinkle the chicken pieces with sugar then mix thoroughly with the pounded ingredients until they are well coated. Leave at least 4 hours to marinate. Thread about five cubes onto each skewer and sprinkle with salt.

PEANUT SAUCE Roast the peanuts in a hot oven, approximately 400°F/200°C, for about 20 minutes. Rub off the skins in a tea-towel and grind for just a few seconds in the liquidizer. Do not reduce the nuts to a powder — this would spoil the consistency of the sauce. Grind or pound the onions and garlic with the blachan. Grind or pound the macadamia nuts and lemon grass. Fry the onion mixture in hot oil, then add the nut and lemon grass paste. Reduce the heat, add chilli powder and cook for 2 minutes. Stir all the time while adding the coconut milk. Allow to come to the boil, then reduce the heat and add tamarind water, sugar, salt to taste and peanuts. Cook for 2-3 minutes and stir frequently until the sauce thickens.

TO COOK SATAY Place skewers of chicken satay on the barbecue or under the broiler and brush with a little coconut or peanut oil. Turn as necessary until cooked. Serve on a large platter with chunks of cucumber and onion, and the hot peanut sauce in a separate bowl. For lunch serve with a bowl of rice.

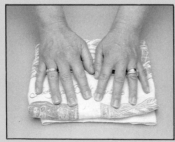

Skinning peanuts
1 *After roasting the peanuts, turn them out onto a tea-towel, folding the sides to center.*

2 *Turn the parcel over and rub vigorously with your hands, rolling backwards and forwards for several seconds.*

3 *Open out the package and pick out any odd skins that are still attached. The peanuts are now ready for pounding.*

Ayam Kapitan
(Chicken curry from Penang)

On the way up to the Kek Lok Si Monastery 'the Million Buddhas Precious Pagoda' in Georgetown, Penang, we were taken to a verandah type restaurant where Ayam Kapitan was a speciality. I must confess it didn't look special under its mound of fried onions, but the smell really was special and the taste was out of this world.

1 × 3lb/1.4kg fresh chicken, divided into 8 pieces
1½ cups unsweetened, desiccated coconut and just over 1⅞ cups boiling water to make coconut milk (see page 21)
⅝ cup tamarind juice from pulp or dried tamarind (see page 16)
½in/1cm square blachan, dry fried (see page 18)
2-4 fresh chilies or 1-2 teaspoons chilli powder

2 macadamia nuts or almonds
2 stems lemon grass
1in/2.5cm piece fresh ginger
2 cloves garlic
1-2 teaspoons ground turmeric
4 tablespoons coconut or cooking oil
salt
piece cinnamon
6 green or white cardamom pods, bruised but left whole
2 large onions, finely sliced and deep fried (see page 69), or chopped coriander to garnish

SERVES 4

Wipe the chicken and set aside. Prepare the coconut milk and tamarind juice. Dry fry the blachan. Pound the prepared and chopped chilies, nuts, lemon grass, ginger and garlic into a paste with the blachan; if using dried chili, add it to the paste. Stir in the turmeric.

Heat the oil and fry the spice mixture for a few minutes without browning. Stir in the chicken pieces until they are all coated with the spices. Add salt. Pour in the coconut milk and tamarind juice. Add the cinnamon and cardamom pods. Cook uncovered over a gentle heat for 35-45 minutes until almost all the sauce has cooked away. Taste for salt. Test the chicken pieces with a skewer. When tender serve in a hot bowl. Traditionally it is served with a topping of crispy fried onions.

Left **Ayam kapitan** *This chicken curry is served with a garnish of coriander.*

Sizzling Steak

The Coliseum Restaurant in the Batu Road (the main shopping area) serves this delicious steak. The steaks, done to a turn, were brought to the table on a hot metal platter, set on a thick wooden board. Prior to the meal you were garbed in a special, pristine white, short apron or gown. This made sense when the sauce was poured onto the steak on the fiercely hot platter – it not only sizzled but spluttered. I suggest you follow this practice at home too.

1lb/450g rump or sirloin steak	**Sizzling sauce** *strained marinade from above* *⅛ cup beef stock*
Marinade *1 tablespoon brandy* *1 tablespoon HP sauce* *2 tablespoons peanut or cooking oil* *a few drops sesame oil* *2 cloves garlic, peeled and cut into halves or crushed*	*2 tablespoons tomato ketchup* *1 tablespoon oyster sauce* *1 tablespoon Worcestershire or HP sauce* *salt and sugar to taste* *shredded scallion to garnish*

SERVES 2

Divide the steak into two portions. Mix the marinade ingredients together and pour them over the steak. Leave for 1 hour. Lift the meat from the marinade and drain before frying, grilling or broiling for 3-5 minutes on each side depending on how well done you like to eat your steak.

Pour or spoon the marinade into the pan in which the steaks were cooked, discard the garlic if it is in whole pieces. Add the beef stock, ketchup, oyster sauce, Worcestershire or HP sauce, salt and sugar to taste. Allow to come to the boil then boil rapidly to reduce by half. Taste again for seasoning.

Serve the cooked steak on either a sizzling or very hot plate and pour the sauce over each portion just before serving. Garnish with shredded scallion.

Cooking Rice

Malay style *¾ cup quality rice*	*1⅞ cups hot water* *salt to taste*

SERVES 3

Wash the rice very thoroughly in several lots of cold water. Place in a saucepan with water, and salt if liked. Bring to the boil, do not cover, and cook over a medium heat for approximately 10 minutes, until the majority of the water has either been absorbed or evaporated. Now cover with a tight fitting lid and place over the lowest possible heat. Cook for a further 10 minutes or until the rice is fluffy and tender.

Indian style *¼ cup good quality rice* *1 small onion, peeled and chopped*	*2 tablespoons cooking oil* *1⅞ cups boiling stock or water* *salt to taste*

SERVES 3

Wash the rice thoroughly and drain well. Fry the onion in hot oil until it browns. Add the rice and fry, stirring all the time until each grain is turning white. Pour in the boiling stock away from the heat. Stir well and add salt if wished. Cover with a tightly fitting lid and cook over a gentle heat for about 15 minutes when all the liquid will have been absorbed. Fork through gently. Remove from the heat and leave covered until required.

Fah Song Chok
(Chinese rice porridge)

Rice porridge is eaten at any time of day, but is especially popular at breakfast and, in fact, in its plain form, it is used to wean babies onto solids. The rice is first boiled with chicken broth and water to a moist, creamy consistency, then strips of stir fry pork and even pig's liver are added. A fresh egg is often stirred into the piping hot porridge at the table, then the other accompaniments are spooned on top.

½ cup short grain rice *¼ cup skinned, raw peanuts* *3 cups chicken broth* *⅔ cup lean pork* *1 teaspoon soy sauce* *1 teaspoon sesame oil* *2 teaspoons seasoned cornstarch*	**Accompaniments** *2 cloves garlic, cut into slivers* *6 small onions, peeled and finely sliced* *4 tablespoons oil* *2 red chilies, deseeded and finely chopped* *sprigs fresh coriander* *small dish light soy sauce* *1 fresh egg per person (optional)*

SERVES 4

Rinse the rice and put it in a large pan with the peanuts and chicken broth. Bring to the boil, cover and simmer gently for 35 minutes or until the mixture is a soft, creamy consistency. Slice the pork into fine strips; dip these in a mixture of soy sauce and sesame oil and then into seasoned cornstarch. Prepare the garlic and onions, then fry them separately in hot oil, drain and serve in small bowls. Fry the pork strips in the oil in the pan for 2-3 minutes. Add to the cooked porridge and cook for 2-3 minutes. Prepare the chilies, coriander and soy sauce. Spoon the porridge into serving bowls. A whole egg can be broken into the porridge and stirred around to cook it, before scattering some of each of the other accompaniments on top.

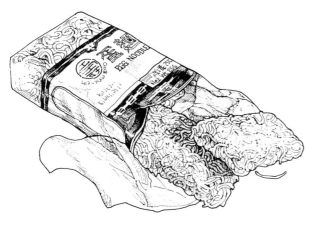

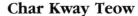

Char Kway Teow
(Fried noodles with pork)

This is a typical meal found at a hawker's stall — served in a bowl with chopsticks. These stalls provide an almost around-the-clock service, but especially in the evening as the light fades, a mass of these hawkers take over the space in the car park and in no time the scene is transformed to a bustling outdoor restaurant. Benches and fold-away tables are put up and usually a young boy will escort you round the various stalls selecting your meal. Miraculously it all arrives in stages in spite of the mêlée. There is something to be said for eating in such an informal way.

1lb/450g packet kway teow (sheets of white noodles, see page 26)	1 tablespoon dark soy sauce
a piece of pork fat	1 tablespoon oyster sauce
2 tablespoons cooking oil	1/2 cup bean sprouts
2 cloves garlic. crushed	1/4 cup cooked shrimp
1 red chili, deseeded and chopped finely	1/3 cup cooked pork,
1 tablespoon light soy sauce	Chinese chives or coriander leaves to garnish

SERVES 4

Cut the noodles into strips ½ in/1cm wide and set aside. Gently heat the pork fat in the wok until the fat runs out. Leave the liquid fat in the pan, but take out and cut the crisp fat into small pieces to add to the pan later. Heat the fat with the oil. Fry the garlic and chili without browning, then stir in the sauces. Pour boiling water over the noodles. Drain well and add to the wok with the bean sprouts, shrimp and pork and crisp fat. Taste for seasoning. Toss well and serve on a hot platter, garnished with Chinese chives or fresh coriander.

Sometimes a beaten egg is added: push all the mixture to one side in the pan just before serving. When it has set, which it will do very quickly, immediately pull the mixture back into the pan and stir well to incorporate the cooked egg.

Urap
(Green vegetable salad with coconut dressing)

Salad
4-6 cups prepared
  mixed green
  vegetables such as:
  beans
  Chinese cabbage
  bean sprouts
  $1/4$-$1/2$ cucumber

Sauce
$1/4$ cup desiccated
  coconut

5/8 cup water
$1/2$in/1cm blachan,
  prepared (see page
  18)
1 clove garlic, crushed
1 green chili, prepared
salt
juice $1/2$ lemon or 1
  tablespoon tamarind
  juice
sugar to taste
sprigs of mint to garnish

SERVES 4

Trim ends from the beans and blanch in boiling water for 2-3 minutes until just cooked. Rinse in cold water to retain the color. Wash the cabbage and shred, not too finely. Plunge the bean sprouts into cold water for a few minutes and drain. Cut the cucumber into 1in/2.5cm lengths and each chunk into 10 pieces. Cook the coconut and water together for 5 minutes. Cool. Pound the blachan with garlic and chili to a paste. Add to the grated coconut. Add salt, lemon or tamarind juice and sugar to taste. Transfer to a large bowl then add the prepared vegetables. Toss well and serve garnished with mint leaves. Do not keep overnight.

Chayote with Dried Shrimp

This unusual vegetable grows in great profusion in Fraser's Hill, a place where we used to spend cool weekends away from the sultry heat of Kuala Lumpur. The chayote is a member of the squash family and looks rather like a pear, but, in practice, it responds well to zucchini-type recipes. It is also popular in the Caribbean and South America and is known as *xuxu* in Brazil.

2 chayote
1 tablespoon dried
  shrimp, soaked in
  warm water for 20
  minutes

a little oil
juice $1/2$ lemon or lime

SERVES 4

Wash and cut the chayote into quarters through the seed. Steam for about 15 minutes in a bamboo steamer until tender. Remove the outer skin, although this is not essential, and cut it into even size pieces. Drain the shrimp. Heat the oil in a wok, add the shrimp and vegetable and toss altogether without browning. Add lemon or lime juice and taste for seasoning. Serve hot.

Sambal Blachan

2-4 fresh red chilies
salt

$1/2$in/1cm square blachan
  (see page 18)
juice $1/2$ lemon or lime

Prepare the chilies, removing the seeds and cut each one in half lengthwise. Pound in a pestle and mortar with a little salt. Add the prepared blachan and lemon or lime juice to taste.

Serve as an accompaniment to rice meals. It is best made in small quantities. Vary the amount of chili and blachan to your taste, but it will be hot and pungent nevertheless.

*Left Coconut graters
come in all shapes and
sizes in the east. You are
supposed to sit on this
one!*

Making carrot flowers
1 *Peel a carrot then place on a board. With a knife, make a V-shaped slit along the length of the carrot. Make four of these slits, at equal intervals around the carrot.*
2 *Then, cut across the carrot, slicing at a slight angle. Make fairly thin flowers for best effect. They are an attractive addition to many dishes, particularly* **Acar**.

Acar
(A vegetable pickle)

¼ cup peanuts	a selection of vegetables
4 macadamia nuts or almonds	and fruits to make up 3-4 cups, all peeled
3 small onions, peeled	and sliced: carrot,
2 cloves garlic, peeled	cauliflower, green
5 tablespoons oil	mango, cabbage,
1½ tablespoons powdered turmeric	cucumber, beans, small onions (leave
1¼ cups white vinegar	whole), fresh
3 tablespoons sugar	pineapple, green and
salt to taste	red chilies

MAKES 2lb 3oz/1kg

Roast the peanuts in a hot oven, at approximately 400°F/200°C, until brown, about 10-15 minutes. Rub off the skins and lightly pound; reserve. Pound the macadamia nuts or almonds. Pound the onion and garlic together. Heat the oil and fry the onion and garlic to give off a good smell. Add the macadamia nuts, fry, then add the turmeric. Stir in the vinegar, sugar and salt. Add the sliced vegetables and fruits. Cook briefly before adding the peanuts. Cool and transfer to a screwtop glass jar. Store in the refrigerator.

It is delicious served with curries or cold meats.

Left **Acar** *It is preferable with this dish not to chop up the vegetables too finely. It provides an excellent accompaniment to all types of curries.*

47

Gula Melaka
(Sago pudding)

This dessert is frequently called the 'three palm pudding': the sago from the sago palm, dark sugar from the nippah palm and coconut milk from the coconut palm. The sago comes from the sago palm (although, nowadays, much of the sago comes from the root of the cassava). The sago palm usually grows in a swampy spot, several in a clump, and takes up to 15 years to mature. It flowers, then promptly dies. The fallen tree is then split open and the starch scooped out of it. This is washed and then passed through fine sieves making the little grains or pearls as they are known. These are processed and dried. Huge quantities of sago came from Borneo where the palm grows profusely. Now it is cultivated in Indonesia.

The nippah palm produces the sugar for this pudding. Like the sago palm, it grows in a swampy place. The sugar is tapped from the crown of the palm giving the rich, dark brown sugar, which is formed into wheel-like cakes and wrapped in strips of palm fronds. The third palm is the coconut palm, which produces the coconut milk. We used to have coconut palms in our garden and, just as the coconuts were ready, an Indian man used to come on his vintage bicycle festooned in ropes. He would shin up the tree, with his *panga* (knife) and would skillfully cut away the coconuts still on the stem. This done he would then carefully lower his prize on his rope. It was carefully lowered so that he had a pulley effect with a huge bunch of coconuts at either end. He lowered himself, first, then loaded them onto his bicycle.

Above **Gula melaka** *The sugar syrup and coconut cream perfectly complement this dish.* *Serve separately for guests to help themselves and make up their own 'three palm pudding'.*

1¼ cups sago	slice fresh ginger
2 tablespoons coconut cream (see page 21)	1 pandan leaf (if available)
	1¼ cups thick coconut milk from 12oz/350g desiccated coconut and ⅝ cup boiling water
Syrup to serve	
½ cup palm sugar or dark brown sugar	
⅝ cup water	

SERVES 4

Bring a large pan of water to a boil. Wash the sago thoroughly in a sieve and immediately add it to the boiling water; cook until the granules become clear, stirring frequently. This will take 12-15 minutes. Strain through a sieve, washing well with cold running water until all the starch is removed. Drain well, then, turn the sago into a bowl, add the coconut cream and pour the mixture into 2½ cups/600ml mold or four individual serving dishes. Leave at least 6 hours in the refrigerator to set.

Prepare the syrup by dissolving the palm sugar with water in a pan. Add the pandan leaf and slice of ginger. Stir until the syrup thickens. Remove the pandan leaf and ginger and leave to cool. Prepare the coconut milk and stir before serving as the cream will have floated to the top. Unmould the pudding to serve or leave it in individual bowls. Each guest helps themself to the sugar syrup and coconut milk at the table.

Malaysian Coconut Ice Cream

3 × 8oz/225g packets unsweetened, desiccated coconut	10fl.oz/275ml can condensed milk
5 cups boiling water	pinch salt
	Gula Melaka syrup (see above)

SERVES 8

Add the water to the coconut and squeeze to make 3¾ cups/900ml of coconut milk. Blend with the condensed milk. Add a pinch of salt and pour into a shallow container then freeze. Twice during freezing stir well. Serve either in a scooped out coconut shell or a bowl, sprinkled with desiccated coconut. Hand around a jug of 'Gula Melaka' syrup to pour over each helping — it's superb.

Coconut Chips

1 fresh coconut (to open | *salt*
see below)

Select a fresh coconut, which sounds full of juice when it is shaken. This juice is quite pleasant to drink so, if you wish to save it, either pierce one of the 'eyes' of the coconut and drain off or open it carefully and collect the juice in a bowl.

When open use a palette or broad-bladed knife to ease the flesh away from the hard outer shell. Peel away the brown skin with a potato peeler. Slice the flesh into wafer thin shavings in the food processor, then scatter these evenly all over a couple of cookie sheets and sprinkle with salt. Crisp in a moderately slow oven (approximately 325°F/170°C) for about 30 minutes; but turn them over occasionally during this time. Cool and store in airtight containers.

Serve with drinks.

Opening a coconut
1 *Hold the coconut in the left hand, positioning it over a bowl to catch the juice.*

2 *Make sure the eyes are just above the thumb and, using the back of a cleaver, strike the top or crown of the nut.*

3 *The coconut will fall apart easily and the juice will be caught in the bowl, if you wish to drnk it.*

Making coconut chips
1 *Slit open the coconut and ease the two halves apart. Crack into smaller pieces if necessary.*

2 *Slide the blade between the white flesh and brown husk of the coconut to ease away the hard, outer casing.*

3 *Peel off the remaining brown skin with an ordinary potato peeler, leaving you with just the flesh.*

4 *Feed the peeled pieces of coconut into a food processor. Make sure you use the slicing blade attachment.*

5 *Switch the processor on and leave for a few seconds so that you are left with thin slices of coconut.*

6 *Place these slices on a cookie tray, sprinkle with salt and bake in the oven for 30 minutes. Cool before serving.*

Singapore

Singapore Island, set at the tip of the Malayan Peninsular with Java to the south, China to the east, India and Europe to the west, is aptly called the crossroads of the east. Raffles is a name synonymous with Singapore. Raffles is the hotel immortalized and patronized by the wealthy and well known such as Kipling, Coward and Conrad. Somerset Maugham, another famous and frequent guest said: 'Raffles stands for all the fables of the exotic East'. It is one of the few places in Singapore that has survived a massive rebuilding programme; you can't miss the low, rambling, old colonial building, which was constructed in 1866. For those who feel that a visit to Singapore would be incomplete without a look at Raffles, go along and enjoy a SINGAPORE SLING in the long bar and soak up the ambience and nostalgia of years gone by. Sadly, there is not a great deal of nostalgia left in the city itself, as shops and houses, which used to be such a feature of life, with their ornate, glazed, tiled fronts and red-tiled roofs, have been pulled down to make way for the high rise, Government-owned blocks, where about half of the predominently Chinese population live. Families are restricted to two children, which has kept population growth in check on this prosperous island.

Visitors flock to Singapore where anything and everything can be bought — it is a real shopper's Shangrila. As a port it has an enviable reputation and is one of the big four in the world. This is a far cry from its early beginnings as a fishing village spotted by Sir Stamford Raffles (he did not build the hotel) as a site for a great commercial empire for the East India Company, which was suffering greatly from Dutch competition in South East Asia. The island at that time was hot, humid, malarial and rat infested, inhabited by a few Malay, Indians and sea gipsys. The Chinese in their industrious way had cleared some areas and were growing peppercorns — others had set themselves up to supply passing ships plying from east to west and vice versa.

Malacca, a little way up the coast in Malaysia, had been, and, in fact, still was, a rich trading post with an immensely busy harbor. It was ruled by a sultan in the pay of the great Sultan of China, who recognized Malacca in 1400 as 'the fairest haven in the ocean'. The Portuguese at this time were desperate to wrest this pearl from the Venetians and, after a bloody battle, then usurped the island and adopted a policy to marry into local families. There is still a strong Portuguese presence even today. The Dutch drove them out in 1641 and the British captured this important port in 1795. At this time Raffles had just begun his first job as a clerk with the East India Company at the age of 14. Ten years later he took a six month journey to Penang, teaching himself Malay on the way. After several years and a meteoric rise in the East India Company, the death of his first wife, and postings in both

Java and Sumatra, he was asked to take charge of this new island development. By then he was a well-known figure in South East Asia and had a great rapport with the Malays, which was to stand him in good stead for this his most famous, although at first much criticized, venture. In Singa Pura — its original name meaning Lion City — he is still remembered for the town planning on the grid system, the Raffles Institute and the Botanical Gardens, which entranced Marianne North in 1876: 'The Botanical Garden at Singapore was beautiful. Behind it was a jungle of real untouched forest which added much to its charm. . . . One day we went to have tea with Mr Wampoa, the famous Chinaman, whose hospitality and cordiality to the English have been so well known for over half a century in the Straits. He showed us all his curiosities, but his garden was to me the greatest attraction, rare orchids growing in every tree'. The orchid is the national flower of Singapore and seems to thrive for even the least keen gardener.

Isabella Bird, another Victorian lady traveler, writes at about the same time: 'I almost fail to realize that it is an island; one of many; all, like itself, covered with vegetation down to the water's edge: about 27 miles long by 14 broad with the city at its southern end. It is only 70 miles from the equator, but it is neither unhealthy or overpoweringly hot. . . . Every oriental costume from the Levant to China floats through the streets — robes of silk, satin, brocade and white muslin emphasized by the glitter of 'barbaric gold'; parsees in spotless white, Jews and Arabs in dark rich silks; Klings in Turkey red and white; Bombay merchants in great white turbans, full trousers and draperies, all white with crimson silk girdles; Malays in red sarongs; Sikhs in pure white Madras muslin, their great height rendered nearly colossal by the classic arrangement of their draperies; and Chinamen of all classes, from the coolie in his blue or brown cotton, to the wealthy merchant in his frothy silk crêpe and rich brocade, make up an irresistably fascinating medley'. Even today the population of Singapore is made up of such diverse groups, although the forms of dress are not so exotic.

In 1877, a period of fantastic growth, rubber tree saplings were sent out to the east from Kew Gardens, which were to transform the livelihood of thousands of people. 'Rubber Ridley' as the Director of the Botanical Gardens became known, was immensely enthusiastic about the crop and succeeded in rearing these plants. Samples were also successfully grown in Perak and Kuala Kangsar in Malaysia, which marked the beginning of this highly profitable venture. Indian laborers were brought in to tap the rubber. Coinciding with this, tin mining boomed and even more Chinese came flooding in through the gateway of Singapore. For decades the Chinese traders and merchants had arrived, unaccompanied by their womenfolk. To resolve this they began taking Malay wives who would, of course, be Muslim. This resulted in a new ethnic group called the Straits Chinese who centered themselves in Singapore, Malacca and Penang — the area of the historic Straits settlement. The children of these marriages were called Peranakan who, in succeeding generations, were able to marry pure Straits Chinese as the population was growing so rapidly. The Nonyas, the Straits Chinese women — the men are Babas — then married newly arrived Chinese, creating a group whose unique contribution to the culture of this tiny cosmopolitan country is self evident.

Nonya food is a fascinating blend of both Chinese and Malay cooking. To produce food in the really traditional way is immensely time consuming with lots of chopping, pounding and grinding of ingredients. Pork, coconut milk, blachan, tamarind, fiery chillies, coriander, laos, screw pine and lime leaves are an integral part of Nonya cooking, as you will see from some of the recipes that follow. POPIAH is the Nonya answer to a spring roll — paper-thin pancakes are lightly annointed with hosein sauce and pounded chili and garlic. This is then topped with a lettuce leaf and small spoonfuls of a cooked filling, which has pork, salted beans and shellfish in it, as well as steamed Chinese sausages, hard-cooked eggs, shredded cucumber, bean sprouts and a host of other ingredients. The whole pancake is rolled up and served; it is enormous fun for a party.

To eat superbly and cheaply, try the Telok Ayer Market just near Raffles Quay. It used to be one of Singapore's main markets and now houses stalls run by Chinese, Nonya, Malay and Indians. Other popular stalls are at Empress Place on the bank of the river, Rasa Singapura in Tanglin Road, Newton Circus in Orchard Road and the Satay Club in Queen Elizabeth Walk. Here and throughout Singapore, you can take your pick of Chinese food with all its regional variations: Cantonese, Szechwan, Hainanese, Peking, Hakka and a host of others. Similarly, different groups of Indians are also represented from the lowliest stall to the most sophisticated restaurant, all there on that small island.

In the evening a trip to Fatty's in Albert Street is a never-to-be-forgotten experience. He produces a mouth-watering meal with such dexterity and skill — it is real entertainment to watch as the ginger, chilli, onions, meat, shellfish or whatever, is sliced exquisitely with a huge chopper on a thick, round board. The wok sits over a high flame — in go the various oils, ginger, garlic, meats and in a twinkling the food is garnished and brought to your Formica-topped table in hot bowls. The wok is speedily rinsed with water and is ready for more action. We sat and ate far too much quite captivated by the whole scene.

The food markets are immensely varied; there are dried frogs and live turtles, of which Isabella Bird wrote: 'the seas are so abundant that

The rich colors of the fruit and vegetables, soaked by the sun and rain, are what make the market displays so enticing. Eggplant, chilies and cucumber (above) are in abundance in Singapore. Live produce is also there for the choosing. Here (right) some ducks await their fate.

turtle soup is anything but a luxury and turtle flesh is ordinarily sold in the meat shops'. At any time of day you might find sellers offering monkey brains and python meat, or fruit hawkers with daintily cut pieces of papaya, mango, mangosteen, pomelo, pineapple, and numerous other succulent surprises. Eating is basically a round-the-clock affair, a characteristic shared by many of the oriental countries. It always seems to be 'time for a little something' and of course, it is all so cheap and spotlessly clean, a feature of Singapore not necessarily followed elsewhere; heavy fines are imposed on those who do not conform to the high standards. The cosmopolitan nature of the island brings such variety of foods — truly a gourmet's paradise.

Food and drink are supremely important to the Chinese and they will always check whether you have eaten so that they can have an

excuse to discuss food and if possible eat again! At a Chinese celebration 12 courses would always be served. A simple three-course meal would be considered an insult. The polite host will probably apologize for the poor food, even if it is superb. This is a compliment to the guests. It is polite for the guest on the other hand to enthuse about each dish as it is carried to the table and to speak glowingly and incessantly about the food.

The table setting is very simple. Each guest is provided with a pair of chopsticks and porcelain spoon, two bowls — one for soup, one for rice — one plate, perhaps a dish for bones or shells from fish (shrimp and crabs cooked in their shells are much enjoyed) and two tiny saucers for soy sauce and chopped chilies. Chinese tea or soft drinks will inevitably be served in a glass or cup and a napkin will be folded in a highly decorative shape. Chinese men generally drink brandy and beer with a meal — preceded by cups of tea to prevent them from getting inebriated.

Before beginning to eat you must always wait for the host to invite you to drink. This greeting signals the start of the meal and good fellowship to follow. The guest of honor sits on the left of the host, facing the front entrance so that he can protect his guest in case of trouble! When the host raises his glass it is polite for everyone to chant yam seng (cheers), which is repeated innumerable times. At the end of the meal place your chopsticks at the side of your dish, not across the dish, which would signify to your host that he had not provided enough food.

In many traditional Indian homes the wife will serve guests and then retire to some other part of the house. If you take a gift to an Indian household avoid black and white, plump for red, yellow or green and remember that they will not open your gift until you have departed. Unlike the Chinese, odd numbers are favored, so if a gift of money is made an extra dollar will be added to make it uneven. Offer gifts with the right hand supported with the left. Many Indians do not eat beef, nor any meat on Fridays. Some are vegetarians so you must establish this when inviting them to avoid offending anyone. They like their food well cooked and are not keen on salads. At the table food is usually placed in the center with a large plate or banana leaf for each person. Forks and spoons are normally provided. The devout Hindu will set aside a morsel of the food as a thanksgiving to God before beginning to eat. Hands must be washed before eating — the left hand for passing food or drinking.

The Malays make up a relatively small part of the Singaporean population — which accounts for only about 15%. When visiting their houses you would be advised to refer to the Malaysian chapter on do's and don'ts of table etiquette.

Singapore Sling

This drink was christened the Singapore Sling in 1915 by the head barman at Raffles, whose family are still represented in the long bar even today.

2 measures gin	few drops Angostina
1 measure cherry brandy	bitters
1 measure orange juice	few drops Cointreau
1 measure lemon juice	crushed ice cubes
1 measure pineapple	pineapple and
juice	maraschino cherry

MAKES 1

Shake all the ingredients with the ice then strain into a tall glass. Decorate with pineapple and cherry and serve at once.

Samosas
(Savory pastries)

⅓ packet spring roll wrappers, 10in/25cm square	½in/1cm fresh ginger, scraped and chopped
2 tablespoons flour, mixed to a paste with water	1 clove garlic, crushed
	2 tablespoons melted ghee or unsalted butter
oil for deep frying	½ teaspoon chili powder
Filling	1-2 teaspoons garam masala (see page 23)
1 large peeled and boiled potato	½ cup frozen peas, thawed
2oz/50g cooked cauliflower (optional)	1 tablespoon chopped coriander leaves and stems
1 small onion, peeled and chopped finely	squeeze of lemon juice
	salt to taste

MAKES 30

Let the wrappers thaw out. Make a paste from the flour and water and set aside. Prepare the filling by dicing the potato finely and evenly and cutting the cauliflower into small pieces. Fry the onion, ginger and garlic in ghee or butter. Do not brown. Add the chili powder and cook for a minute, then stir in the potato, cauliflower and peas. Sprinkle with garam masala and set aside to cool. Add the coriander and lemon juice. Taste for seasoning and add salt as required.

Cut the spring roll wrappers into 3in/7.5cm strips. Brush the edges of each piece with paste. Fold over one corner to make a triangle. Fill this with a small spoonful of the filling. Fold the whole strip over and over to make a triangular-shaped samosa. Seal any open edges with more flour and water paste, if necessary. You may have to add more water to this. Fry the samosas a few at a time in deep oil until golden and crisp. Drain well and serve hot, with a few slivers of carrot, cucumber and celery. If you are making these for a party, fry until they are cooked through, but not golden, and then plunge them into hot fat for a few minutes before serving. They go down very well at a party.

Left **Samosas** These are an excellent party snack. However they can also be served as an accompaniment to a main course in place of a vegetable.

Deep Fried Wonton with Apricot Sauce

1 packet wonton wrappers (40-50 approx), thawed
oil for deep frying

Filling
1 cup pork meat with a little fat
½ cup raw shrimp
2 scallions, finely chopped

1-2 teaspoon oyster sauce
salt and freshly ground black pepper

Apricot sauce
1⅛ cups apricot jam
3-4 tablespoons light vinegar
2-3 tablespoons hot water

MAKES 40-50

Keep the wrappers under a sheet of waxed paper and a slightly damp cloth to prevent drying out. Prepare the filling by blending meat and prawns in a food processor. Add scallions, oyster sauce and seasoning to taste.
Now you are ready to fill the wrappers.

Place the wrapper singly on a countertop, 10 at a time (leave the rest covered). Place a tiny spoonful of the filling onto the center of each wrapper. Damp two edges and fold over to form a triangle which is slightly off center. Now place two very small pieces of the filling onto either side of the centre mound. Draw the midpoints of the triangle over the filling and press down. The wings will then fall back. Deep fry for 1-2 minutes. Drain well and serve. Place the sauce in a bowl surrounded by the wonton puffs. To prepare the sauce, warm the jam, vinegar and water together, sieve and pour into a bowl.

If the wrappers are frozen leave them on a countertop to thaw. When thawed remove them from the package. Gently ease up the top one at a corner and slowly lift, pushing your hand between this and the next one to prevent tearing. Place each one on top of the other in a pile on the countertop, covered with a sheet of waxed paper and a slightly damp cloth to prevent drying out. Any torn wrappers can be used for patches, should you accidently damage any while filling them.

Filling and folding a wonton wrapper

1 *After laying out several of the wrappers, place a tiny spoonful of filling in the center of the first. Then, taking a brush, dipped in a flour and water paste, dampen the edges of the wonton.*
2 *Then fold over the corner facing you, but making it join up just off center with the opposite corner. Press down to make it stick.*
3 *Using a spoon, add a further two spots of filling one on the left and one on the right of the triangular shape.*
4 *Using your fingers, lift up both these wings and fold them over each dot, then turn them back on themselves and press down firmly. This will leave you with a butterfly shape — the finished, filled wrapper.*

1

2

3

4

Popiah
(Home-made wrappers)

Popiah are the Straits Chinese or Nonya version of the spring roll. They are an excellent party idea, especially for guests who don't know each other.

4½ tablespoons
  cornstarch
2 cups plain flour,
  sifted
2 cups water (approx)
6 beaten eggs
salt

Filling 1 (cooked)
1 onion peeled and
  finely chopped
2 cloves garlic, crushed
2 tablespoons oil
⅔ cup cooked pork,
  chopped
½ cup crabmeat or
  shrimp, thawed if
  frozen
1½ cup canned
  bamboo shoot, cut
  into shreds
1 yambean
  (bangkwang), peeled
  and grated, or 8-10
  water chestnuts, finely
  chopped
1-2 tablespoons salted
  yellow soybean
1 tablespoon light soy
  sauce
freshly ground black
  pepper

Filling 2 (fresh and arranged in separate bowls)
2 eggs, hard-cooked,
  shelled and chopped
2 Chinese sausages,
  steamed and sliced
1 square hard bean curd,
  deep fried and sliced
3 cups bean sprouts
  blanched in boiling
  water for 30 seconds
  and rinsed with cold
  water
½ cup crabmeat or
  shrimp
½ cucumber, shredded
small bunch scallions,
  chopped
20 lettuce leaves, left
  whole, rinsed and
  dried
sprigs fresh coriander

Sauces
1. 6 red chilies, seeded
  and pounded to a
  paste
2. 6 cloves garlic,
  pounded to a paste
3. 6 tablespoons hosein
  sauce

MAKES 20-24

Blend together the sifted flours with water, eggs and salt to make a smooth batter. Grease an omelet pan with lard to make the pancakes. They should not be thick so note how much batter you use for the first one or two. It is a good idea to use a measuring cup for pouring the batter into the pan. Pile the pancakes or wrappers on top of each other with a layer of waxed paper in between to prevent sticking. Stir the batter between making pancakes. Make the cooked filling (1) by frying onion and garlic in oil without browning. Add the pork and shrimp, bamboo shoots and grated yambean. Stir gently and cook for 2-3 minutes. Now

add the soy beans, light soy sauce and pepper to taste. Cover and cook gently for 20 minutes, checking from time to time that the mixture has not dried out. Add a little water before this happens. Turn into a serving bowl and allow to cool while preparing the other fillings.

Arrange the hard-cooked eggs, Chinese sausages, sliced bean curd, bean sprouts, crabmeat, cucumber, scallions, lettuce leaves and coriander either in piles on a large platter or in separate bowls. Similarly, spoon the chili and garlic into small bowls and also the sauce.

Each guest makes up their own popiah by spreading the minutest amount of chili or garlic or both and/or the hoisein sauce on the wrapper, followed by a lettuce leaf, cooked filling and a selection of the fresh ingredients. Do not overfill the wrapper. Roll it up tucking in the ends and eat at once. The popiah can be filled and rolled up before the guests arrive, but it is more fun for everyone to roll their own.

Curry Puffs

Along the beach, in the *kampongs* and down the streets you can hear the curry puff seller or *kueb* man ringing his bicycle bell. He has a pile of these delicious snacks in a huge aluminium box on the back of his bicycle.

14oz/400g puff pastry, thawed

Filling
½ onion, finely chopped
1 clove garlic, crushed
½in/1cm piece fresh ginger, pounded
1 chili, seeded and pounded (see page 19) or 1 teaspoon chili powder

2 tablespoons ghee or unsalted butter
½ cup ground fresh lamb or beef
½ teaspoon turmeric powder
½ teaspoon ground coriander seeds
small potato, grated
1 tomato, skinned and chopped finely
stock to moisten
seasoning to taste

MAKES 20-25

Leave the pastry to thaw while preparing the filling. Fry the onion, garlic, ginger and fresh chilies, if using, in hot fat without browning. Stir in the meat and cook until it changes color, stirring all the time. Add the turmeric and coriander. Stir in the potatoe and tomato and a little broth if necessary to just moisten. Cover and cook for 5 minutes, then taste for seasoning. Cook without a cover for a further 5 minutes. Set aside to cool.

Roll out the pastry thinly on a floured board and cut it into 4in/10cm circles. Put a spoonful of filling on one half avoiding the edges. Damp the edges and seal. Alternatively cut into 3½in/9cm squares and fold into triangles. Set on a cookie sheet and cook in a hot oven, at approximately 420°F/220°C, for 10 minutes or until they are puffy and golden brown. Serve as soon as possible.

Below **Popiah** *Spring roll wrappers can be used for this dish, although they are not as good as the home-made type. Any variety of sauces, dips and fillings can be substituted for those given.*

Murtabak
(Spice and meat-filled snacks)

Murtabak are quite a feature of both life in Singapore and Malaysia. There is little to beat the thrill of watching the Indian murtabak man flinging the dough in the air to get the finest sheet possible without tearing it. It would take years of practice to achieve this so we suggest you keep it simple by spreading the dough on the countertop!

Dough
3 cups plain flour
1/2 teaspoon salt
1 tablespoon oil
2/3 cup warm
    water (approx)
4 tablespoons extra oil

Filling
1 small onion, peeled
    and finely chopped
1 clove garlic, peeled
    and crushed

1/2in/1cm piece fresh
    ginger, finely chopped
2 tablespoons ghee or oil
1/2 teaspoon chilli powder
1/2 teaspoon ground
    turmeric
1 1/2 cups finely ground
    lamb
2 shallots, finely
    chopped
a little garam masala
    seasoning to taste
1 beaten egg

MAKES 24 SNACKS

Sift the flour and salt into a bowl. Add oil and water to make a soft dough. Knead for 1 minute in a food processor or 10 minutes by hand. Divide the dough into six balls, knead again and place in a shallow bowl. Spoon over some oil, cover them and leave for about 1 hour. Now prepare the filling.

Fry the onion, garlic and ginger in ghee or hot oil without browning. Increase the heat and add chili powder and turmeric. Stir all the time. Add the meat and cook until the meat changes color. Cover and cook gently for 10 minutes, adding a little broth or water if the filling looks like drying out. Add the scallions and garam masala. Taste for seasoning and cook for a few more minutes. Allow to cool. Remove the dough from the bowl. Lightly oil the countertop and gently spread the dough out into a round the size of the largest frying pan you have. Do not tear the dough. It is a good idea to remove rings as the dough is very fragile. Brush the surface of the frying pan with ghee or oil. Place the wafer thin piece of dough into this. Spoon a light covering of beaten egg over the dough and place a good tablespoonful of the filling in the center. Fold the sides to the middle once and then repeat so that you have a

square shape. Turn over and cook a further minute and serve hot. Cut into four portions if desired. Make in advance and reheat in a microwave oven before serving, or in a foil-covered dish in a hot oven for 10-15 minutes.

Mah Mee
(Noodle soup)

This is a typical Singaporean soup, which is a complete meal on its own.

Fish stock
1 fish head or shells and
    heads from the fresh
    shrimp (see below)
6 1/4 cups water
1/2in/1cm piece ginger,
    scraped and sliced
    (see page 24)
1 stick celery
1 small onion, peeled
salt and pepper

Soup
2 cloves garlic, peeled
    and crushed
1/2in/1cm piece fresh
    ginger, finely chopped
3 tablespoons oil

1 cup cooked pork,
    cut into shreds or
    small pieces
1 cup shrimp, fresh
    if possible or frozen
2 1/4 cups bean sprouts
broth
2/3 cup fine rice
    noodles (beehoon),
    soaked for 10 minutes
1/2 cup crabmeat or
    any white fish if liked
1/2 cup bamboo shoots
    (optional)

finely chopped scallions
    or coriander and
    slivers of chili to
    garnish

SERVES 6-8

Place all the ingredients for the broth into a large pan. Bring to a boil then cover and simmer for 20 minutes. Strain and reserve. Fry the garlic and ginger in oil without browning. Add the pork pieces, shrimp and bean sprouts and stir fry for 1-2 minutes. Strain in the broth and bring to a boil before adding the noodles. Cook uncovered for 3-4 minutes or until the noodles are just cooked. Place the crabmeat or white fish pieces in a warm serving bowl and top up with the soup. Garnish with scallions or coriander. Eat with chopsticks, to cope with all the pieces, and a Chinese soup spoon in warmed bowls.

Right **Mah mee** *This soup really is a meal on its own. In fact, it is more helpful to povide chopsticks as well as a soup spoon.*

Above right **Pork and shrimpwonton in chicken soup** *This soup can be garnished with greenery to complement the golden wontons.*

Pork and Shrimp Wonton in Chicken Soup

The wonton is prepared as in the recipe on page 57.

Chicken soup
2 cloves garlic, sliced
1 tablespoon oil
7½ cups chicken
  broth
a little sesame oil

Garnish
crisp fried onion flakes
  (see page 69)
2 scallions, finely
  chopped
fresh coriander leaves

SERVES 6-8

Prepare the wrappers. Cook in a large pan of boiling, salted water for 5 minutes. Drain and reserve. Meanwhile fry the finely sliced garlic in the oil without browning. Add the chicken broth and sesame oil. Pour the soup over the dumplings in a large tureen and garnish with onion flakes, scallions and coriander.

Nonya Pork Satay

1lb/450g pork fillet	1-2 stems lemon grass,
1 tablespoon brown	peeled and sliced (see
sugar	page 25)
½in/1cm cube blachan	½ teaspoon ground
(see page 18)	turmeric (optional)
2 medium-sized onions,	salt
peeled	1½ cups desiccated
3-6 red chillies, deseeded	coconut to make
2 teaspoons coriander	1¼ cups coconut
seeds	milk (see page 21)
6 macadamia nuts or	2 tablespoon coconut or
blanched almonds	peanut oil

MAKES 8-12

Soak 8-12 bamboo skewers in water for at least an hour to prevent them from burning under the broiler.

Cut the pork into even-sized pieces, about the size of your thumb nail, and sprinkle with sugar to help release the juices. Fry blachan in a foil parcel in a dry frying pan or on a skewer over the gas flame. Make the onions and chilies into a paste in the food processor with the blachan. First pound the coriander seeds, then add nuts and the bulb part of the lemon grass and grind using a pestle and mortar. Add turmeric and salt and then stir this into the onion mixture in the food processor. Pour in the coconut milk and oil. Switch the machine on and then off. Pour the contents into a shallow bowl containing the pork. Marinate for an hour or two. Thread five or six pieces of pork onto each skewer. Broil or cook over charcoal for an even more authentic flavor. Baste with the marinade. When tender, serve hot with cubes of cucumber.

As an island, fish is a great part of the Singapore diet. The markets are full of all sorts of exotic varieties (above right), which are creatively adapted to recipes. Fishing is therefore quite an industry, and there is always a boat to be seen on the horizon (far right).

King Prawns Cooked in Shells

1lb/450g whole,	3 tablespoons oil
uncooked prawns in	4 tablespoons tomato
shell (6-8 approx,	ketchup
depending on size)	1 tablespoon chili sauce
1 tablespoon sugar	or to taste
1in/2.5cm piece fresh	water
ginger, scraped and	salt and freshly ground
sliced	black pepper
1 tablespoon Chinese rice	coriander leaves and
wine or dry sherry	slices of cucumber to
1 tablespoon light soy	garnish
sauce	

SERVES 2

Rinse and dry the prawns in their shells. Sprinkle them with sugar then squeeze the ginger through a garlic press onto the prawns. Add the rice wine or sherry and soy sauce. Leave to marinate for 30 minutes. Heat the oil and fry the drained prawns for 3-4 minutes until the color changes, then add the marinade, tomato and chili sauces and water. Season to taste, adding more sugar if desired. Cook for 2-3 minutes and serve garnished with coriander and wedges of cucumber.

Fish in Bean Paste Sauce

1¹/₂lb/675g ikan merah, snapper or bream	oil for frying
¹/₂ medium peeled and chopped onion	1 teaspoon sugar
2 crushed cloves garlic	3 green chilis, seeded (see page 19) and roughly chopped
2 tablespoons bean paste	1¹/₄ cups water
1 tablespoon fresh ginger	seasoning to taste

SERVES 2-3

Wipe the fish, then make three incisions on each side with a sharp knife. Pound half the onion, one garlic clove and the bean paste together until creamy. Slice and shred the ginger. Half fry the fish in oil on both sides then lift out. Fry the reserved onion and garlic in the fat in the pan until just browning. Stir in the bean paste mixture and fry for 1-2 minutes to bring out the flavor. Add the sugar and green chilies. Cook until you can smell the aroma from the chilies. Pour the water. Bring to the boil then lower the fish into the sauce. Cover and cook for further 5-10 minutes or until the fish is cooked through.

Garnish with the chopped scallions or some fresh coriander leaves.

Chinese Chicken — Hainanese Style

Ah Moi introduced me to this Chinese-style chicken dish, which was always popular at supper parties. The chicken pieces are dipped into a little of the Hainanese chili sauce, eaten with rice cooked in the traditional way and the vegetables. Bowls of the clear soup are served at the same time as the chicken.

1 fresh, not frozen, chicken (2½lb/1.25kg)	2 cloves garlic 2-3 scallions or ½ small onion
1 tablespoon salt 1½in/3.5cm slice fresh ginger	1 tablespoon light soy sauce 1 teaspoon sesame oil

SERVES 4

Remove the giblets from the chicken and wash thoroughly. Bring a large pan of water to a boil. Meanwhile rub the chicken with salt. Bruise the peeled ginger and cloves of garlic and place them inside the body cavity of the chicken, together with the washed and sliced scallions. Place the chicken into the boiling water, cover with a lid and bring just back to the boil, then turn off the heat immediately. Twice during the next 30 minutes lift the chicken out of the water to empty the liquid from the body and replace in the water immediately. After 30 minutes bring the water almost to a boil and turn it off again. Repeat the lifting out process twice more during the next 30 minutes. After the hour remove the chicken from the pan onto a plate, drain well and leave to cool for a few minutes. Rub the skin with a mixture of soy sauce and sesame oil to impart some flavor and give a good color to the chicken skin.

To serve the chicken in the traditional way, cut the legs and wings away. Cut the whole of the breast away in a separate piece. You will then have only the back section remaining. This should be chopped right through the spinal bones and arranged on the plate with some care, with the breast section similarly chopped through and laid on top. Replace the wings and legs so that the bird is almost restored to its whole shape once again. (The chicken pieces are dipped in the Hainanese sauce, which is described below.) Serve together with the rice, soup and vegetables.

Hainanese chili sauce

3 chilies, deseeded (see page 19) 1 piece fresh ginger, bruised 1 clove garlic	1 small onion oil from chicken stock above salt lime or lemon juice

Pound the deseeded chilies with the fresh ginger, garlic clove and a small onion. Add a little oil from the stock pot to moisten. Stir in a little salt and fresh lime juice or lemon to taste. Serve in separate dishes in front of each person.

Hainanese rice

1 clove garlic, bruised 1in/2.5cm piece fresh ginger, bruised 2 tablespoons coconut or cooking oil	¼ cup washed rice 1⅞ cups chicken stock (from above)

Fry the garlic and ginger in oil, do not brown. Stir in the rice and fry for a minute. Add stock and seasoning, if required. Cook over a medium heat without covering for about 10 minutes. Reduce the heat to its lowest and cover. Cook for a further 10 minutes until all liquid is absorbed and the rice is fluffy and tender. Remove the ginger and serve.

The soup and vegetables

2 cups prepared, mixed vegetables: carrot, cauliflower, beans, leeks and peas	1½ cups well-washed spinach

While the chicken is cooling, boil the stock to reduce it and improve the flavor. Cut up the chicken and cook the rice. Transfer half the stock to a separate pan and cook a selection of vegetables in it, putting in those which require the longest cooking first. Strain the stock back into the soup pot when the vegetables are cooked and drained. Finally, add the spinach to the soup and cook for just 2 minutes. Taste for seasoning and serve in a bowl with the chicken, chili sauce and rice, with the vegetables put in a separate dish.

Right *Fresh vegetables are used in abundance in Singapore, where they are readily available. The soup for the* **Hainanese style chicken** *is stacked full of them.*

Babi Lemak

(Spiced pork in coconut milk)

This is a typically Nonya recipe, using pork, coconut milk, blachan and spices.

1lb/450g lean pork, cut into cubes	*1½-2 teaspoons chili powder*
1½ cups desiccated coconut and 1⅞ cups boiling water to make 1¼ cups coconut milk (see page 21)	*3 tablespoons coconut or vegetable oil*
	1 stem lemon grass
	salt to taste
	juice ½ lemon
½in/1cm square blachan (see page 18)	*pinch sugar*
2 medium-sized red onions, peeled and chopped	

SERVES 3

Set the pork on one side. Prepare the coconut milk. Dry fry the blachan. Pound the onions with the blachan and chili powder. Fry in oil without browning. Add the pork and fry until the meat changes color and is well covered with the spices. Stir in the prepared coconut milk over a gentle heat and the bruised stem of lemon grass. Slowly bring to a boil, stirring to prevent curdling. Add salt to taste. Simmer until the pork is tender. Remove the lemon grass stem. Add lemon juice and sugar to taste. Serve with plain boiled rice and a cucumber sambal.

Long Cook Pork Leg Stew

Cook the day before you wish to serve this pork leg stew, as this gives the dish a richer blend of flavors and a chance to skim off any excess fat which may collect. The trotters have a large proportion of bone so you will require this quantity for four people. It would be advisable to order them from the butcher in advance.

3½-4lb/1.5-1.75kg meaty pigs trotters	*2 tablespoons dark soy sauce*
1 tablespoon tamarind pulp, soaked in ⅝ cup water (see page 16)	*1 star anise*
	½in/1cm piece fresh ginger, shredded finely
6 red chilies, seeded (use red for good colour)	*2 teaspoons dark brown sugar*
6 cloves garlic, crushed	*just under 2½ cups water*
2-3 medium-sized onions, peeled	*salt*
8 tablespoons oil	*fresh coriander leaves or shredded scallion to garnish*
2 tablespoons soybean paste	
2 tablespoons light soy sauce	

SERVES 4

Ask the butcher to cut the trotters into chunky pieces through the bone. Prepare the tamarind juice. Set one whole chilli aside for garnish and pound the remainder with garlic and onions. Fry in oil for 2-3 minutes. Stir in the bean paste, then turn the trotters in this mixture to coat them on all sides. Add the soy sauces, prepared tamarind juice, star anise, ginger, sugar and water. Add salt if necessary, but go carefully as the bean paste is quite salty.

Cover and cook gently for at least 2 hours or until the pork is tender. Cool and leave overnight. Skim away any excess fat. Cover and cook in an ovenproof casserole in a moderate oven (approximately 325°F/ 160°C) for an hour or until the pork is cooked through and the sauce is bubbling. Scatter with fresh coriander leaves or scallion and the reserved chili, cut into rings.

This dish is a useful one to know as it can and, in fact, should be prepared in advance. It is well accompanied by plain rice.

65

Indian Mee Goreng
(Curry noodles)

This is a truly international dish combining Indian, Chinese and western ingredients. It is a delicious lunch or supper dish and is available in Singapore and Malaysia from a host of hawkers' stalls.

1lb/450g fresh yellow noodles	*2-3 tablespoons tomato ketchup*
4-6 tablespoons oil	*1 tablespoon chili sauce (or to taste)*
1 square bean curd, well drained, diced dice	*1 large cooked potato, diced*
2 beaten eggs, seasoned	
1 medium onion, peeled and sliced	*4 scallions*
1 clove garlic, crushed	*1-2 green chillies, deseeded and shredded*
1 tablespoon soy sauce	

SERVES 4-6

Cook the noodles in boiling water in a large pan for just 2-3 minutes. Do not overcook. Drain and rinse with cold water to halt cooking; set on one side. Heat two tablespoons of the oil and fry the bean curd until brown. Drain and set aside. Pour the beaten eggs into the pan. When it has set like an omelet roll it up on a board and chop finely. Spoon the remaining oil into the wok and fry the onion and garlic for 2-3 minutes. Add the drained noodles, soy sauce, ketchup and chilli sauce. Toss well over a medium heat. Add the potato, most of the scallion, some of the chili and all the bean curd. Keep tossing. When hot, add pieces of the cooked egg. Serve on a hot platter garnished with the remaining spring onion and chili.

Left Indian mee goreng
The rich color of the yellow noodles, complemented with the green and white of the scallions, chilies and and potato make this a tempting dish. It is relatively quick and easy to prepare and welcome at lunch or supper.

Nasi Lemak
(Coconut rice)

This is a very popular breakfast 'snack' taken at about 10.30am, and is available from stalls and coffee shops. It is usually served with deep fried ikan-bilis, chopped hard-cooked egg, a chili sambal and chunks of cucumber.

2½ cups coconut milk made from 1½ cups desiccated coconut and 3⅛ cups boiling water (see page 21)	1 stem lemon grass 1 cup long grain rice salt to taste ring of fresh chili and sprigs fresh coriander to garnish

SERVES 4

Prepare the coconut milk. Rinse a heavy-based pan with water then pour in the coconut milk. Add the bruised stem of lemon grass and allow to come to a boil. Lift off the heat, then stir in the rice and salt. Bring to a boil, stirring occasionally, then cover and cook over the lowest possible heat for 12 minutes or until the rice is tender. Stir with a chopstick or fork. Turn off the heat — leave still covered in a warm place until required. Remove the stem of lemon grass before serving. Garnish with rings of fresh chili and coriander.

Chow Fan
(Fried rice)

1⅔ cups cold, cooked rice 4 dried mushrooms 1 egg, beaten cooking oil 8 shallots, peeled and sliced 3 cloves garlic, crushed ¼ cup small shrimp, peeled ½ cup Chinese sausage (optional), steamed (see page 20) and sliced	½ cup cold roast pork (optional) 1-2 tablespoons light soy sauce salt and pepper few frozen peas chopped scallion and red chili shredded lettuce leaves, if desired

SERVES 4

Prepare the rice a few hours ahead or the night before. Soak the mushrooms in water for 1 hour then drain and chop. Fry the beaten egg in a little hot oil in a frying pan to make an omelet then remove it and shred finely. Set aside. Fry the shallots in a wok until they are crisp and brown, stirring all the time. Lift out and reserve. Fry the shrimp and garlic for just a few minutes. Set aside Fry the Chinese sausage, pork and mushrooms, then lift out and reserve. Fry the rice in sufficient hot oil so that the grains are coated, keep turning all the time. Add soy sauce and seasoning to taste plus half the cooked ingredients and mix well. Stir in the frozen peas and some of the scallion. Turn onto a warmed platter and garnish with the remaining cooked ingredients, chillies, omelet and lettuce.

Left Rice is cooked and served in a great variety of ways in the east. In Singapore, where so many races have converged, Nasi Lemak and chow fan are two favourites. This bamboo basket might be used to serve it from.

Bean Curd Salad — Nonya Style

3 pieces hard bean curd
   (taukwa)
oil for deep frying
1½ cups bean sprouts
   blanched
1½ cups Chinese
   cabbage, blanched
½ cucumber, sliced and
   sprinkled with salt
salt

Sauce
¼ cup juice made
   from 1 teaspoon
   tamarind paste
1-2 fresh chilies,
   seeded
small red onion, peeled
   and chopped
1 tablespoon thick soy
   sauce
1 tablespoon brown sugar
2 good tablespoons
   crunchy peanut
   butter

SERVES 4

Cut the bean curd into quarters or slices and fry in hot oil until crisp and brown. Drain and leave to cool. Blanch the bean sprouts in a pan of boiling water for just 30 seconds. Drain and put into a bowl of iced water for 2 minutes. Drain well. Blanch the cabbage in the same way. Slice the cucumber and sprinkle with salt. Leave while preparing the sauce, then rinse and dry. Arrange the cucumber slices on a platter. Top with bean curd and bean sprouts and cabbage.

Prepare the sauce. First make the tamarind juice, then pound the chilies and onion to a paste in a food processor. Add soy sauce, brown sugar and peanut butter. Add a little water if necessary so that the sauce pours. Just before serving, pour the sauce over the arranged salad vegetables or serve separately, if preferred.

Fried Onion Flakes

shallots or onions, peeled | *oil for deep frying*

Finely slice the shallots or onions. Dry on absorbent kitchen towels and leave in a dry place, preferably the sun, for an hour. Deep fry until golden. Drain on kitchen towels; do not add salt. When cold and crisp, store in an airtight jar. These flakes are used as an accompaniment to a multitude of dishes such as NASI LEMAK and MEE GORENG.

A great variety of sauces and spices are used in Singaporean cooking, as both Chinese and Indian influences take the fore: red bean curd sauce, dark and light soy sauce, yellow bean sauce and black bean sauce (below). *It is fascinating to see raw bean curd being sold, fresh from the markets* (below left). *It is laid out in these slabs and cut with a razor.*

Indonesia

Indonesia became a republic in 1945 and is made up of seven fairly large islands and literally thousands of others, which has resulted in an incredible amalgam of religions, dialects and food, frequently unique to their own immediate area. The main islands are Java, the largest with a population of 57 million, Sumatra, Bali, a tourist paradise, Borneo, which is divided by the mountainous range from its Malaysian neighbours Sarawak and Sabah, the Indonesian half called Kalimantan, Sulawesi (Celebes), Madura, Irian Jaya and Irian Barat.

This island nation, once known as the East Indies, is tropical and volcanic, which accounts for its lushness and fertility. Some 40 of the 400 volcanoes are still active, but the Indonesian farmer is very philosophical about this, as the ash, which is more frequently blown from the crater than the lava, fertilizes the land he so lovingly tills. Seventy five percent of Indonesians still work on the land, which is a blessing since the population is so enormous.

Influences on Indonesian cuisine began centuries ago with the arrival of Hindus and Buddhists from India, who left a legacy of vegetarianism. Bali, once referred to as the Morning of the World and where Hinduism is still the main religion, has its own special cuisine that includes pork in many dishes; a whole roast pig is a festive food. Arab and Indian Moslem traders were to bring Islam to these islands and the religion became firmly entrenched in Sumatra and Java. When the Portuguese came in 1498 and the Dutch in 1605 they discovered a highly sophisticated people with religious, cultural and trade links all over Asia. Art and music flourished and even today each area throughout these diverse islands has its own style of music, dancing and singing from the Hindu story of Ramazan to the folksongs and dance of the Batak of Northern Sumatra.

The Chinese have inevitably made their contribution to Indonesia and its cuisine too; they came in vast numbers early in the 1900s, some were there much earlier, and many of their basic ingredients and methods of cooking are used. Soy sauce, bean curd, noodles, mushrooms, sharks fin and vegetables were incorporated, as well as stir frying, which results in lightly cooked foods with bright colors.

The city which is called Jakarta today was laid out by the Dutch in the seventeenth century as a new town, which they called Batavia, complete with canals to remind them of home. These proved to be a disaster, however, as malarial mosquitoes bred in the stagnant waters and large numbers of people died. A breakfast in Batavia is referred to in a book Raffles of Singapore *by Emily Hahn: 'They got up very early at*

71

daybreak (about 5 o'clock) apparently summoned by five strokes on the gong. The company assembled dressed in sarong and kabaja (both men and women) to drink coffee and admire the view; later the house gong called the servants to work and the guests to their morning bath, which they took either in the river or in the bathroom attached to the building, using only cold water. Next came a big breakfast on the back verandah, of warm rice, curry, fish, beefsteak, dendeng (dried meat), Makasas fish, bacon, peppered small chow, greens, roast chicken, lavishly washed down with red wine, beer, Madeira, Rhine wine, brandy and seltzer water. The day at Pondok Gedeh began with this Lucullan meal.'

Breakfast in today's Indonesia is much simpler and, I am sure, more enjoyable — all drink Java coffee, eat boiled cassava root, steamed banana, fried or boiled sweet potato or, for those who can afford them, bread and eggs. The two other main meals of the day for most are based on rice and two or three vegetable dishes with a little meat, chicken or fish. In colonial times the Dutch adopted this essentially Indonesian style of serving a meal, referring to it as rijsttafel, or the rice table. When served as a buffet the rice table is called a prasmanan and is a sight to behold. NASI KUNING LENGKAP (festive rice) is a dish presented with the rice piled up into a cone shape, bearing no small resemblance in shape to the volcanoes of the region. The accompaniments should encompass as many different textures and flavours as possible whether there are 10 or 20, some sweet, some sour, crisp and soft, hot and cold, spicy and mild, meat, vegetable, fish and so on. As a festive dish it is produced for births, weddings, baby's weaning, and even, I am told, to celebrate the seventh month of pregnancy. Traditionally no women were allowed to help themselves from the rice cone, but nowadays it has become less imbued with rituals — garnishes can be as you will and everyone, male and female, helps themselves. Glutinous rice is immensely popular for snack food; LONTONG are made from glutinous rice, cooked in a square of banana leaf and made up into a parcel, which gives the rice a special flavor. (We must resort to boil-in-the-bag rice here, which is not as good as the real thing, but not a bad substitute.) Every town and village has its own food stalls selling Lontong, mee with pork, prawns or beef, sate — meat, fish or chicken are all popular sate foods — together with the glorious peanut sauce.

After lunch a siesta is routine, followed by Java tea and then much later dinner, with rice again as the main ingredient. It is small wonder that rice is the main crop in Indonesia — it is the number one food. Paddy-fields in the plains and terraces on the hillsides make up a wonderful mosaic and in this lush tropical climate two crops a year can be harvested. Other crops that are so important to the kitchens of the country are the coconut palms, which grow almost everywhere, providing drinks, coconut milk and oil. Java also has its own coffee plantations and tea gardens — like rice, tea is a neat and tidy crop, which always looks like a well-manicured lawn from a distance. Groundnuts (peanuts) are also grown . — an essential ingredient in some of the sate sauces as well as in dressings for salads such as GADO GADO. Many different spices are grown and exported.

Fruit is never in short supply: bananas, pineapple, papaya, mangoes, jackfruit, rambutan, oranges, avocados, starfruit and chico. Durian, when in season, is much sought after, perhaps because it is claimed to be an aphrodisiac. The smell is unusual to say the least and it does put hosts of people off before they have even had a chance to savour the fruit. It is an oval, ball-shaped fruit with a mass of spikes on the outside. When broken into, it reveals sections of creamy like flesh, which are custardy in texture. The smell has been described as an over-ripe Roquefort or worse — I will spare you the descriptions! No matter, as long as you don't drink alcohol at the same time as eating them, or eat too many (as some say this results in the pores of the body giving off a durian smell for days), they are well worth trying as a new experience.

As in every country of South East Asia, markets of all kinds are to be found, such as bird markets and hanging markets, where the local batik is displayed and sold. Some of the fabrics are quite exotic with gold and silver thread woven into them. In some parts of the country hand-beaten jewellery is a speciality using silver and gold. Fish markets and general markets are an essential of life, as the ingredients for Indonesian cuisine are immensely varied. For example, Javanese recipes will include sugar (which grows in profusion), laos or trasi *(blachan or* kapi *as it is known in Thailand). In fact these are basic ingredients also used in Thai cooking, marking a common bond between the two cuisines. Sumatran food essentially uses chili or pepper, turmeric, cinnamon, cardamom and ginger — hot, spicy, robust-flavored food to match anyone's apetite, and on top of this there are still all the regional variations, which will reward the adventurous chef with a real wealth of surprises.*

As this is a mainly Muslim country eating with the right hand is important; however a spoon and fork will always be provided if you ask. Most food is cut into small pieces before cooking to speed up the process as well as ensuring that the spices permeate the food more effectively. Chopsticks will only be used where the food is of Chinese origin. Contrary to the drinks mentioned in the Batavian breakfast chilled local beer, soft drinks or coffee would usually be served.

Selamat makan — *'good eating', as they say at the start of each meal!*

Rempeyek
(Peanut Snacks)

3 cloves garlic, crushed
$^1\!/_2$ teaspoon coriander
   seeds, pounded
$^1\!/_2$ teaspoon turmeric
pinch salt
6 tablespoons rice flour

6-8 tablespoons coconut
   milk (approx)
$^1\!/_3$ cup salted peanuts
   lightly crushed
oil for frying

MAKES 20

Mix the garlic, coriander, turmeric and salt together, then stir in the rice flour. Mix to a creamy batter with coconut milk. Add the peanuts — they should still be in fairly large pieces. Heat a little oil in a frying pan and spoon some of the mixture into a pan, about the size of a small pancake. Fry on both sides, then lift onto absorbent kitchen towels on a cooling rack. Leave until cold. Store any left-overs in an airtight container.

Sayur Lodeh
(Vegetable soup)

This soup is very popular served with a rice dish. Ladle onto the rice and top with some of the accompaniments we suggest with the NASI KUNING — the festive rice.

8oz/225g chicken breast,
   cut into dice

$^3\!/_4$ cup peeled shrimp
1 onion, peeled
2 cloves garlic, crushed
1 fresh red or green chili,
   seeded and sliced
$^1\!/_2$in/1cm terasi or
   blachan (see page 18)
3 macadamia nuts
$^1\!/_2$in/1cm laos root or 1
   teaspoon laos powder
1 teaspoon sugar
oil for frying

$1^1\!/_4$ cups coconut milk
5 cups chicken
   stock

Vegetables
1 eggplant, diced
   and sprinkled
   with salt
2 cups French beans,
   cut small
small wedge of crisp
   white cabbage,
   shredded
1 red pepper, seeded
   and cut finely

SERVES 6

Dice the chicken and set aside along with the shrimp. Cut half of the onion into slices; pound the remainder with garlic, chili, terasi, macadamia nuts, laos and sugar to a paste. Fry in a little oil in a wok until the mixture gives off a rich aroma. Add the sliced onion and chicken pieces and cook for 3-4 minutes. Now stir in the coconut milk and stock. Bring to the boil and simmer for a few minutes. Rinse the eggplant and dry. Add to the soup with the beans and cook for only a few minutes until the beans are almost tender. At the last minute add the cabbage and red pepper and shrimp. The vegetables should still be crisp when the sayur is served.

Soto Ayam
(Chicken soup)

2 fresh chicken breasts or
   quarters
1 medium size onion,
   peeled and sliced
seasoning
4 shallots or equivalent
   white onion, peeled
4 macadamia nuts or
   blanched almonds
3 cloves garlic, peeled
   and crushed
$^1\!/_2$in/1cm piece fresh
   ginger, scraped and
   sliced
$^1\!/_2$ teaspoon ground
   turmeric

$^1\!/_2$ teaspoon ground chili
   powder
3-4 tablespoons oil
1 tablespoon light soy
   sauce
$1^1\!/_2$ cups bean sprouts
   or Chinese cabbage

Garnish
1 large cooked potato,
   diced
oil for frying
4 scallions,
   shredded
1 hard-cooked egg,
   chopped

SERVES 6-8

Cover the chicken pieces with $7^1\!/_2$ cups/ 1.75liters water. Add the onion and seasoning. Bring to a boil and simmer for 40 minutes or until the chicken pieces are tender. Lift the chicken from the soup and, when cool enough to handle, remove the meat (discard skin and any bones) and shred or cut it into small pieces. Skim the stock and reserve. Meanwhile pound the shallots or onions and nuts with the garlic and ginger. Stir in turmeric and chili. Head the oil and fry this spice mixture. Add the chicken pieces and 5 cups/1.2liters of the reserved stock and soy sauce. Taste for seasoning and bring to the boil. Simmer for a further 8 minutes. Add the cleaned bean sprouts for the final 2 minutes of cooking. Serve hot.

While the soup is simmering and before adding the bean sprouts prepare the garnishes. Fry the diced potato until brown all over; drain on absorbent kitchen towels. Arrange portions of the potato, scallions and hard-cooked egg in large soup bowls. Each person helps themselves from a tureen set in the center of the table.

Beef Sate

1lb/450g rump steak, cut in a 1/2in/1cm slice	1 tablespoon brown sugar
1 teaspoon coriander	1 tablespoon thick soy sauce
1/2 teaspoon cumin	salt
1 small onion, peeled	
2 cloves garlic, crushed	**To serve**
1/2 teaspoon tamarind pulp to make 3/8 cup tamarind juice	Sambal Kecap (see page 84)
	wedges of lemon or lime and cucumber

MAKES 12 SKEWERS

Above **Beef and chicken sate** This Indonesian man is concentrating hard on the cooking and fanning of his skewered meat.

Cut the meat into neat, 1/2in/1cm cubes. Dry fry the spices, pound and mix them with the meat. Place the onion, garlic, tamarind juice, brown sugar and soy sauce in a food processor to make a marinade. Alternatively, pound the onion and garlic and add the remaining ingredients. Soak the meat in this marinade in a shallow glass or glazed dish. Leave for at least 1 hour. Meanwhile soak 12 bamboo skewers and thread meat onto them. Sprinkle the meat with salt. Place under a hot broiler, or even better, over charcoal, turning frequently until tender. Baste with the marinade as necessary. Serve with the prepared sambal, wedges of lemon or lime to squeeze over the meat, and slices or chunks of cucumber. Rice may also be served.

Sate Udang
(Prawn sate)

12 king prawns	oil for frying
	8 tablespoons coconut milk
Marinade	1/2 teaspoon tamarind and 2 tablespoons water to make tamarind juice
1/4in/5mm terasi (blachan)	
1 clove garlic, crushed	
1 stem lemon grass, lower 2 1/2in/6cm only	
3-4 macadamia nuts or almonds	**To serve**
1/2 teaspoon chili powder	Lontong (see page 80)
1/4 teaspoon salt	cubes of cucumber
	wedges of lemon

SERVES 3

Peel the prawns and remove the spinal cord if desired. Make an incision along the underbody without cutting the prawn in half. Open them up like a book and thread two onto each skewer. Prepare the marinade by preparing the terasi, then pound with the garlic, lemon grass, nuts, chili powder and salt to a paste in a pestle and mortar or food processor. Fry this paste in a little oil, stirring all the time, until it gives off a good aroma, then add the coconut milk and tamarind juice. Allow to simmer for 1 minute. Cool, then leave the prawns on six skewers in the marinade. Leave for 1 hour before cooking under a hot broiler for 3 minutes or until cooked through. Baste with any remaining marinade. Turn once. Serve on a platter with the Lontong, cucumber and lemon wedges to complement the flavor of the shellfish.

75

Dadar Isie
(Omelets with a spicy meat filling)

Filling

1/2in/1cm terasi or blachan	oil for frying
3 cloves garlic, crushed	1/2lb/225g ground beef
4 macadamia nuts or almonds	2 scallions, trimmed and chopped
1 teaspoon ground coriander	1/2 stick celery, chopped finely
1/2 teaspoon ground turmeric	2-3 tablespoons coconut milk
1 teaspoon laos powder	4 eggs, beaten with 4 tablespoons water
1 teaspoon salt	seasoning

SERVES 4

Prepare the terasi and pound to a paste with the garlic and the nuts. Add coriander, turmeric, laos powder and salt. Fry in hot oil for 1-2 minutes then stir in the ground beef. Stir until the meat changes color, then continue to cook for 2-3 minutes. Stir in the scallions, the celery and the coconut milk. Cover and cook gently for a further 5 minutes or so.

Meanwhile prepare the omelets: whisk the eggs with water, add seasoning. Make up four omelets in a frying pan. When almost cooked spoon a quarter of the filling onto each one and roll up. Cut in half or quarters if to be part of a buffet or serve one to each person for a light lunch with salad. Garnish with celery leaves.

Gule Udang Dengan Labu Kuning
(Sumatran-style shrimp curry)

1lb/450g fresh shrimp	1/2 teaspoon ground turmeric
1-2 chayote or 2-3 zucchini	1/8 cup water water squeeze lemon juice
2 fresh red chilies, seeded	salt
1 medium-sized onion, peeled	8oz/225g packet desiccated coconut and 1 1/8 cups boiling water to make 1 1/4 cups coconut milk
1/4in/5mm slice fresh lengkuas or 1/4 teaspoon laos powder	
1 stem lemon grass	

SERVES 4

Peel the shrimp and set them aside. Peel the chayote, remove the seed and cut into strips, or trim the ends from the zucchini and cut into strips, 2in/5cm long. Pound the chilies and onion to a paste with the lengkuas and the lower 2in/5cm part of the lemon grass. Add laos powder, if using, with the turmeric. Add water to the mixture with lemon juice and salt. Pour into a pan — add the of the lemon grass stem — bring to a boil and cook for 1-2 minutes, stirring all the time. Add the chayote or zucchini pieces and cook for 2 minutes, stirring all the time, then add the coconut milk. Taste again for seasoning. Now add the shrimp and cook until they are tender, which will only take 3-4 minutes. Remove the stem of lemon grass. Serve at once with plain rice.

Boemboe Bali of Fish

Cubes of chicken meat or shrimp could be substituted for the fish in this recipe. Allow the chicken pieces to cook longer than the fish or shrimp before adding to the spicy sauce.

2lb/900g cod or haddock fillet	2 teaspoons Sambal Ulek (see page 85) or 1-2 tablespoons chili powder
1/2in/1cm terasi or blachan (see page 18)	6-8 tablespoons oil
2 medium-sized red (or white) onions	1 tablespoon Indonesian sweet soy sauce
1in/2.5cm fresh ginger, scraped	1 teaspoon tamarind pulp, soaked in 2 tablespoons warm water
1/2in/1cm piece laos, peeled, or 1 teaspoon laos powder	1 cup water
2 cloves garlic	

SERVES 6

Skin the fish and cut into bite-sized cubes. Drain on absorbent kitchen paper and set aside while preparing the other ingredients. Pound the terasi, onions, ginger, laos and garlic to a paste in a pestle and mortar or food processor. Stir in the sambal ulek or chili powder and laos powder, if you are using it instead of the fresh laos. Cook this mixture in two tablespoons of the oil until it gives off a rich aroma. Stir all the time. Add the soy sauce, strained tamarind juice and water. Cook for 2-3 minutes. In a separate pan, fry the cubes of fish for 4-5 minutes. Do not turn too much or the flesh will break up. Lift out of the pan on a draining spoon and into the sauce. Cook for 3 minutes and serve with boiled rice. Garnish with a little chopped chili, if desired, or celery leaves.

Ikan Tjuka
(Vinegar fish)

2 small-medium size mackerel, filleted	1 teaspoon turmeric
2-3 fresh red chillies, seeded	3 tablespoons coconut or vegetable oil
4 macadamia nuts or almonds	3 tablespoons vinegar
1 red onion, peeled	⅝ cups water
2 cloves garlic, crushed	salt
½in/1cm piece fresh ginger, scraped	fried onion or finely shredded chili to garnish

SERVES 4

Wipe the fish fillets and set aside. Pound the chilies and nuts with onion, garlic, ginger, turmeric and one tablespoon of the oil to a paste. Fry the mixture in the remaining oil without browning, then stir in vinegar and water; season and bring to the boil. Place the fish fillets in the pan. Cover and cook for 10-12 minutes or until the fish is tender. Lift the fish onto a plate and keep warm. Reduce the sauce by boiling rapidly for 1 minute, then pour over the fish and serve. Garnish with fried onion flakes or shredded chili.

For a buffet, cut the fish into manageable size pieces and reduce the cooking time accordingly.

Indonesian Deep Fried Chicken

Cook the chicken a day ahead, leave in the spices, then deep fry and allow to go cold before taking on a picnic.

6 chicken drumsticks and 6 thighs	1 teaspoon chili powder
1 tablespoon sugar	1 teaspoon ground turmeric
2¼ cups packet desiccated coconut, blended with 1⅞ cups boiling water to obtain 1¼ cups coconut milk	1 teaspoon salt
	1 medium onion
	1 clove garlic
	½in/1cm piece fresh ginger, peeled
	1 stem lemon grass
2 teaspoons coriander seeds, dry fried	1-2 tablespoons flour
	deep fat for frying

SERVES 6

Sprinkle the chicken pieces with sugar and set on one side. Make the coconut milk. Grind the coriander seed and add it to the chili, turmeric and salt. Mix to a smooth paste with a little coconut milk. Finely chop the onion, garlic and ginger in a food processor. Fry these in a little oil in a deep pan for 1-2 minutes. Add the spice paste and fry, then stir in the coconut milk. When just boiling reduce the heat and add the chicken pieces and bruised stem of the lemon grass. Cover and cook very gently for about 30 minutes or until the pieces are tender. Transfer to a container and leave in the refrigerator or cool place overnight. Carefully lift the chicken pieces out of the spice mixture. Scrape off any excess mixture. Dust the chicken lightly with flour. Deep fry the pieces in hot oil until they are golden. Cool before taking on a picnic. Sprinkle with juice from wedges of lemon if desired, and eat with pieces of cucumber and crisp lettuce leaves.

Barbecued, Spiced Chicken

1 × 3lb/1.5kg chicken, cut into 4 pieces	1 teaspoon chili powder
8 shallots	4 tablespoons light soy sauce
2 cloves garlic, crushed	2 tablespoons sweet soy sauce
6 candlenuts (buah keras)	3 tablespoons oil
½in/1cm ginger, peeled and sliced	salt
1 stem lemon grass	oil for frying

SERVES 4

Slash the flesh of the chicken quarters several times. Finely chop the shallots and set aside. Pound the garlic, candlenuts, ginger, lemon grass and chili powder together. Mix with soy sauces and oil and pour onto the chicken pieces. Leave to marinate for 30 minutes. Heat oil in a wok, fry the onions without browning, lift the chicken pieces out of the marinade and fry on both sides to seal. Reduce the heat, cook for 10 minutes. Transfer to the barbeque to complete cooking. Add the marinade to the remaining ingredients in the pan. Fry, then add stock. Cook for 5 minutes and serve this sauce with the chicken.

Rendang Daging
(Spiced beef in coconut milk)

2lb/1kg good quality beef	½ teaspoon ground cinnamon
2 onions, peeled and chopped	1 teaspoon tamarind, mixed with 6 tablespoons water to make tamarind juice
4 cloves garlic, crushed	
3 tablespoons oil	
1 stem lemon grass (see page 25)	3 cups desiccated coconut and 1¼ cups boiling water to make just over 2½ cups coconut milk (see page 21)
4-8 red chilies, seeded or 2 tablespoons Sambal Ulek (see page 85)	
8 cardamom pods	
1 teaspoon coriander seeds	salt
1 teaspoon cumin seeds	crispy onions to garnish

SERVES 6-8

Cut the beef into neat cubes. Fry the onions and garlic in oil for 3-4 minutes in a large pan. Draw from the heat. Pound the lower part of the stem of the lemon grass with the chilies. Spoon onto the meat. Remove the seeds from the cardamom pods and dry fry with coriander and cumin. Pound or grind. Add cinnamon. Spoon this mixture onto the meat and mix thoroughly to impregnate the meat with spices. Prepare the tamarind juice and coconut milk, then pour these into the pan containing the softened onions. Allow to come to a boil, stirring all the time, then stir in the spiced meat. Add salt, bring back to a boil, then reduce to the lowest heat so that the rendang is just bubbling, and simmer for 2½-3 hours or until the meat is tender and the sauce greatly reduced. Taste for seasoning. Transfer to a warmed serving dish. Garnish with crispy onions or scallions.

Left **Barbecued, spiced chicken** *This is a deliciously spicy recipe, although the sauce can be served separately, so the guests can choose how much or how little they want.*
Right **Rendang daging** *This is another spicy dish, which is excellent served with rice. Chopped, fresh scallions can be used as a garnish to add variety to the color.*

Gulai Kambing
(Spicy lamb curry)

1¼ cups shallots
4 cloves garlic
8 chilies
5 candlenuts (buah
   keras)
¾in/2cm ginger
6 tablespoons cooking oil
½ tablespoon coriander
¼ tablespoon fennel
½ teaspoon nutmeg
   powder

¼ tablespoon cumin
4 cloves
1 cinnamon stick
2 pieces lemon grass,
   broken up
2lb 3oz/1kg shoulder of
   lamb, cut into cubes
3 cups lamb or
   chicken stock
1pt/600ml coconut milk
salt and pepper to taste

SERVES 4-6

Heat the oil in a wok. Meanwhile, pound together the shallots, garlic, chillies, candlenuts and ginger and fry them for 3 minutes in the oil. Then add the coriander, fennel, nutmeg powder, cumin and cloves. Add the lamb for browning, then the cinnamon and lemon grass. Pour on the stock and half the coconut milk. Cook for 1 hour until the liquid has reduced by half. Stir in the remaining coconut juice, simmer for 10 minutes. Taste for seasoning and serve with plain rice.

Lontong
(Cubes of Compressed Rice)

Lontong is a festive dish in Indonesia. In parts of Indonesia and Malaysia it is also known as *ketupat*. Traditionally it is cooked either in a packet made from banana leaves, which are first soaked in hot water to prevent splitting during cooking. The rice is sealed inside this parcel and takes on a certain flavor from the banana leaf. Leaves from the palm fronds are also used. As these are quite slim they can be woven into delightful little baskets or cushions and sealed with the rib of the palm frond (which is also used to make the skewers for sate).

1 x 4oz/100g packet
   boil-in-the-bag rice

boiling, salted water

Place the boil-in-the-bag rice in the water and boil for 1¼ hours or until the whole bag is puffy and firm and the rice fills the whole of it. The bag must be covered in water all the time. You can place a saucer or plate on top to weight it down if necessary. Allow to cool completely before stripping off the bag, leaving a cushion of rice which can then be cut into neat cubes and served with spiced and deep fried chicken or with sate.

Another alternative you might like to try uses short grain rice (pudding rice).

1 cup short grain
   rice

⅝ cup water
salt

Place the washed rice, water and salt in a pan. Bring to the boil, stir, cover and simmer for 30-35 minutes over the gentlest heat until the rice is tender. Cool, then turn into a 1in/2.5cm deep dish. Press down, cover with foil, a plate and a weight. Leave until firm. Remove the weights and foil and cut into cubes or diamond shapes.

Left **Gulai kambing**
*Lamb makes a change
from a beef or chicken
curry and the coconut
flavor blends very well
with it. It is a hot dish
and should be served
with plain rice.*

Nasi Goreng
(Indonesian fried rice)

You should cook the rice at least 3 hours before using, although I often cook it the day before, allow it to go cold, then place in a covered container in a cool place until the next day. It must be covered otherwise the grains of rice will dry out and become hard.

1¹⁄₃ cups rice, cooked and allowed to go cold *1 egg* *4-6oz/100-175g pork fillet* *¹⁄₄ cup peeled shrimp (optional)* *2 fresh red chilies, seeded and shredded* *¹⁄₄in/¹⁄₂cm square blachan, prepared (see page 18)*	*1 onion, peeled and sliced* *2 cloves garlic, crushed* *6-8 tablespoons oil* *2 tablespoons sweet soy sauce* *scallions and Krupuk (prawn crackers, see page 83) to garnish*

SERVES 4

Make an omelet with a beaten egg (or fry it whole when the dish is ready) in a tablespoon of fat in a wok or frying pan; roll up the omelet and turn out, then, when cold, cut it into fine strips and set aside. Trim and cut the pork into fine strips and set aside with the shrimp, if you are using them. prepare the chilies, pound the blachan with onion and garlic, then fry with the chilies in hot oil without browning. Add the meats and cook for 2-3 minutes stirring all the time. Add the shrimp, if using, and the rice. Turn all the time to prevent the rice sticking to the pan. Stir in soy sauce and taste for seasoning. Turn onto a hot platter, garnish with the omelet or fried egg, scallions and a few of the prawn crackers.

Right **Nasi goreng** *This dish provides quite a feast of colors and taste. A fried egg on top adds interest, but a chopped-up omelet is equally attractive. Acar, the vegetable pickle, makes a good accompaniment.*

Nasi Uduk
(Coconut rice)

Rice cooked in coconut milk is a wonderful accompaniment, particularly to chicken and pork dishes and curries.

¹⁄₄ cup long grain rice *1¹⁄₂ cups desiccated coconut and 2¹⁄₂ cups boiling water to make 1⁷⁄₈ coconut milk* *¹⁄₂ teaspoon ground coriander*	*1 stick cinnamon* *1 stem lemon grass, bruised* *1 salam or bay leaf (optional)* *salt* *fried onion flakes to garnish (see page 69)*

SERVES 4

Wash the rice if necessary, then place in a pan with the prepared coconut milk, coriander, cinnamon stick, lemon grass and salam, bay or pandan leaf. Add salt. Bring to the boil over a medium heat, stirring a few times. Cook over the lowest heat for 12-15 minutes or until all the coconut milk has been absorbed. Fork through carefully and remove the cinnamon, lemon grass and leaf. Cover with a tight fitting lid, then cook over the lowest heat for a further 10 minutes.

Garnish with crispy fried onions.

Nasi Kuning Lengkap
(Festive rice)

3 cups desiccated
  coconut and
  6¼ cups boiling
  water to make
5 cups coconut
  milk (see page 21)
2 cups long grain rice
4 tablespoons oil
2 onions, peeled and
  chopped
2 cloves garlic, crushed
1 stem lemon grass, cut
  in half and bruised
1 teaspoon powdered
  turmeric
1 pandan or 3 curry
  leaves (if available)

Accompaniments
2 eggs made into an
  omelet
1-2 fresh red chilies, 1
  made into chili flower
  (see below) and the
  other shredded
chunks cucumber
fried crispy onions (see
  page 69)
Serundeng (see page 84)
Rempeyek (see page 74)
Krupuk (shrimp
  crackers) (see page
  83)
Rendang (see page 78)
Ikan Tjuku (see page 76)
Sayur Lodeh (see page
  74)

SERVES 8

Prepare the garnishes, accompaniments and coconut milk and set aside. Wash the rice, drain well. Heat the oil, fry the onions and garlic without browning. Stir in the lemon grass, turmeric, pandan leaf and rice. Stir gently for 1-2 minutes. Pour in the coconut milk, stir, then leave to come to a boil. Stir once more, then cover tightly and cook for 15 minutes or until all the liquid has been absorbed and the rice is tender and separates. Fork the rice through and leave to cool for a few minutes. Remove the lemon grass and pandan leaf. If the rice looks sticky, rinse it quickly, then turn it into a colander or steamer and set over gently boiling water for 10 minutes. Meanwhile assemble all the accompaniments.

Line a large serving dish with washed banana leaves, if they are available. Pile the rice into the center and form into a cone, if desired, or a dome. Arrange strips of omelet and chili over the cone with the chili flower on the top. Place cucumber all around the base, then separate piles of crispy onions, Serundeng, Krupuk, Rempeyek around the base and carry to the table. The accompaniments could be taken to the table in separate bowls if wished.

Serve the Rendang, Ikan Tjuku and Sayur Lodeh separately.

Making chili flowers
1 Take a knife and slit lengthways along the chili, red or green, leaving an end section by the stalk uncut.

2 Having made several slits around the chili, place in a bowl of ice cold water, where it will open out into a striking, spider-like flower.

3 As an alternative garnish, slice off a piece of chili and place the resulting ring over a scallion, then slit this at both ends to make a double flower.

Krupuk
(Prawn crackers)

Even in Indonesia these are rarely made from scratch at home. Packets are readily available from Chinese Emporiums. To my mind the best are the pink-colored variety, which have a more distinctive shrimp flavor. It is a wise precaution to put them on a cookie sheet in a slow oven (approximately 140°C/275°F for 10 minutes to dry them out before deep frying. They will be much more puffy and crisp if this is done. In Malaysia we used to put them in the sun first.

8oz/225g packet prawn crackers	*oil for deep frying*

Heat up the oil and fry four to six prawn crackers at a time in the hot oil until they are puffy, but not colored. Drain on absorbent towels and serve as suggested in the recipe.

They are a good snack to serve with drinks and can be fried at least an hour or two before serving.

Gado Gado
(Cooked salad with hot peanut sauce)

Peanut sauce	Salad
¾ cup salted peanuts	*2 medium potatoes, peeled, boiled and diced*
1½ cups coconut milk (see page 21)	*1½ cups bean sprouts blanched, rinsed and drained*
1 teaspoon tamarind and 4 tablespoons water to make tamarind juice	*1½ cups cabbage, shredded, blanched and rinsed*
¼in/5mm blachan, prepared (see page 18)	*1 cup each green beans, and flowerets of cauliflower, boiled until just tender and drained*
1 clove garlic, crushed	
3 shallots or 1 small red onion, peeled	*piece cucumber in slices*
oil for frying	*1 small carrot, cut into matchstick-like pieces,*
1 teaspoon chili powder or Sambal Ulek (see page 85)	*Chinese cabbage, shredded watercress (optional)*
1 tablespoon brown sugar	*2 hard-cooked eggs*
1 teaspoon thick soy sauce	
salt to taste	

SERVES 4-6

Grind the salted peanuts until gritty but not a paste; set aside. Prepare the coconut milk, tamarind water and blachan. Pound the blachan with the garlic, shallots or onion. Fry in three tablespoons of hot oil without browning. Stir in the chili powder or sambal ulek and cook for 1 minute. Add the coconut milk and allow to come to a boil. Stir in the tamarind water, sugar and soy sauce, and the ground peanuts, which will thicken the sauce. Taste for seasoning. Allow to simmer until creamy in consistency. Set aside. Arrange the vegetables in piles on a large platter with egg quarters. Heat up the sauce and serve separately in a gravy boat.

Each person takes some of the salad, tops it with peanut sauce, crumbled krupuk and some extra sambal ulek, if wished.

Nasi kuning lengkap (above left) *This dish is served on special occasions, often piled high into a volcano shape, topped with a chili flower.*

Gado gado (left) *This is a very popular salad, which may either be eaten as a light lunch or served before or after the main course in the evening.*

Atjar Ketimun
(Cucumber pickle)

1 cucumber	*1 red chilli, deseeded*
salt	*and chopped*
1 tomato, skinned,	*3 tablespoons good*
seeded and diced	*quality vinegar*
1 small onion, peeled	*2 teaspoons sugar*
and finely sliced	*pinch salt*

Trim the ends from the cucumber, peel lengthwise but leave some of the skin on to make the salad look more attractive. Cut into thin slices and lay on a large plate. Sprinkle with salt and leave for 15 minutes. Rinse and dry. Meanwhile prepare the tomato, onion and chili. Arrange all the vegetables in a bowl and pour over vinegar, sugar and salt blended together. Chill before serving.

Sambal Kecap

This can be served as a dip for a sate instead of the peanut sauce and is particularly good with the beef sate or deep fried chicken.

1 fresh red chili,	*4 teaspoons lemon juice*
seeded and	*or 4 teaspoons*
chopped finely	*tamarind juice*
2 cloves garlic, crushed	*2 tablespoons hot water*
4 tablespoons dark soy	*2 tablespoons fried*
sauce	*onions (optional)*

Mix the chili, garlic, soy sauce, lemon or tamarind juice and hot water together. Stir in the fried onions, if you are using them, and leave for 30 minutes before serving. Place in a separate bowl in the centre of the table for guests to help themselves.

Serundeng
(Peanut and coconut accompaniment)

³/₄ cup fresh coconut,	*1 teaspoon coriander*
grated, or desiccated	*seeds, dry fried and*
coconut	*pounded*
1 cup salted peanuts	*¹/₂ teaspoon cumin seeds,*
2-3 tablespoons oil for	*dry fried and*
frying	*pounded*
¹/₄-¹/₂in/5-10mm blachan,	*¹/₄ teaspoon tamarind,*
prepared(see page 18)	*soaked in 2*
(optional)	*tablespoons water to*
1 small onion, peeled	*give tamarind juice*
2 cloves garlic, crushed	*1 teaspoon brown sugar*
	salt

Dry fry the coconut until golden and crisp, then allow it to cool and add half of it to the peanuts. Pound the blachan, if you are using it, with the onion and garlic. Fry in hot oil without browning. Add the coriander and cumin and the tamarind and sugar. Fry over a medium heat, stirring all the time until the mixture gives off a lovely aroma. Add the other half of the coconut, cool, then mix with the coconut and peanut mixture. Taste for

Deep frying coconut
1 *Place the correct amount of desiccated coconut into a wok or pan and put over a gentle heat to cook.*

2 *Use a spatula or slice to turn the coconut continuously, until it begins to turn a golden brown color It is important to keep tossing the coconut.*

3 *Place in a food processor and blend until oil begins to show. This is then ready to add to dishes such as **Rendang** to thicken and flavor.*

seasoning and use as required. Allow to go quite cold before storing in an airtight jar where it will keep for several months. This accompaniment may be used served together with rice to flavor, or it can be scattered over other dishes as a garnish.

Sambal Goreng

This is an accompaniment made from a basic sauce, to which a host of different ingredients can be added. Serve with rice.

Basic mixture	a little oil for frying
1/4in/5mm piece terasi or blachan	1 tablespoon tomato paste
1 onion, peeled	1 cup stock or
2 cloves garlic, crushed	water
1/4 teaspoon laos powder	1/2 teaspoon tamarind,
2 teaspoons Sambal Ulek (see page 85) or 1 teaspoon chili powder	soaked in 2 tablespoons water
	pinch sugar to taste
1/4 teaspoon salt	1-2 tablespoons coconut milk or cream

SERVES 2-3 AS A LIGHT LUNCH

Prepare the terasi and pound with the onion and garlic to a paste in a pestle and mortar or food processor. Add the laos powder, sambal ulek or chili powder and salt. Fry in hot fat for 1-2 minutes until the mixture gives off a rich aroma. Add tomato paste and stock or water. Cook uncovered for several minutes and add one of the following according to preference:

Sambal goreng tomaat
1/4 cup tomatoes, skinned, seeded and coarsely chopped (add before stock)

Sambal goreng udang
1/2 cup shrimp and 1 green pepper, chopped

Sambal goreng hati
1 1/3 cups fine strips of liver

Sambal goreng telor
3 hard-cooked eggs and 2 tomatoes, skinned and seeded

Sambal goreng tumis
2 cups blanched green beans

Sambal goreng hati ayam
1 1/3 cups chicken livers

Cook any of the above in the sauce for 3-4 minutes, then stir in the tamarind juice, sugar and coconut milk or cream.

Sambal Ulek
(Crushed chilies)

We used to buy small packets of *chili bo* (pounded chili) from shops or the visiting 'van man' so that we rarely had to resort to chili powder. This sambal will keep for a couple of weeks in a well-sealed jar in the refrigerator, or longer in the freezer, so its worth making up a reasonable quantity at a time if oriental cookery has captured your imagination. Use a stainless steel, plastic or egg spoon to measure it out.

1/2lb/225g fresh red chilies, seeded (see page 19)	2 teaspoons salt

Plunge the chilies into a pan of boiling water and cook for 5-8 minutes. Drain then pound in a blender without making the paste too smooth. Turn into a glass jar, stir in salt and cover with a piece of waxed paper or plastic wrap, then screw on the lid and store in the refrigerator. Spoon into small dishes to serve as an accompaniment or use in recipes where suggested. It is fiercely hot and should you get any of the chili on your fingers wash them well in soapy water immediately.

Pisang Goreng
(Banana fritters)

1/2 cup rice flour	4 bananas, depending on size
1/2 cup plain flour	
1 egg beaten	oil for deep frying
5/8 cup coconut milk, prepared (see page 21)	sugar sauce from Gula Melaka pudding (see page 48)

SERVES 4

Sift the rice and plain flours into a bowl. Add the beaten egg and mix to a thick coating batter with coconut milk. Set aside. Peel and cut the bananas in half diagonally. Dip in the batter and fry for 3-4 minutes in hot oil until the outside is crisp and golden. Drain on absorbent kitchen paper. Then, fry the remainder and serve together with the prepared Gula Melaka sauce.

The Philippines

Philippino food is truly international, as you might expect if you know just a little of the history of these 7,000 islands, which make up the only Christian country in South East Asia. The original people of the islands probably came from a Polynesian background; then there were the Malays, Indonesian and Chinese, but the greatest impact was made by the Spaniards, who arrived in the sixteenth century and stayed for 400 years, followed by 50 years of American occupation. The Spanish brought their religion, culture and cuisine, all of which are well integrated into the way of life even today. Unlike the other colonial powers, the Spaniards inter-married with the local people, who readily adopted and adapted a whole range of Mediterranean dishes now considered typically Philippino. Adobo is one such dish. It is not one particular dish, but a method of cooking where pork or pork fat is the constant ingredient along with vinegar, garlic and pepper.

The Philippinos love to cook different meats together (as in a French cassoulet), so often you might be served a chicken and pork adobo. Coconut milk might be added, or fish is used as in ADOBONG MUSIT, an adobo of squid. Pork is really their favourite meat and the highlight of any feast is the lechon — a 12-week-old, barbecued suckling pig. The piglet is filled with fragrant leaves and secured to a bamboo pole for cooking. A very rich sauce is made from the pigs liver to serve with the meat after everyone has eaten the crackling. To be offered the first slice of crackling means that you are the most honoured guest. They love pork fat, too, and tuck into it with great relish. Unlike most other countries of the region, dinuguan, pigs' innards and blood, is a delicacy not to be missed. Another delicacy is balut, which takes some courage to eat. This is a fertilized duck egg (the duckling is partially formed inside); the top is taken off and the contents, beak and all, eaten in one gulp as you would an oyster. By some it is considered an evening pick-me-up! A festival even celebrates this curious and doubtful gastronomic experience — 29 July is the River Festival at Pateros, in the Province of Rizal, center of the balut industry. This is in honor of Santa Maria who saved the town's ducks from a marauding crocodile.

Being devout people, festivals are numerous. Every town has a patron saint who is honored on their particular feast day each year. These festivals are an integral part of Philippino life; bands play while processions, parades and feasting are enjoyed. Christmas is a special time. Between the 16 and 25 December cock-crow masses are faithfully attended. All the family will go to the last mass on Christmas Eve, Notte Bueno, and follow it with a traditional meal. Food for Christmas might be roast ham, sliced and served with sweet potatoes and a salad of the banana flower. Rellenong Manok is a favorite. It is a boned, whole

Above *Terraced paddy-fields are common throughout the Philippines. The fields are surrounded by levees or bunds and then submerged in water. The water is present practically right through the rice-growing period and is then harvested by hand.*

chicken, marinated in soy sauce then stuffed with pork, chorizo, ham, eggs, stuffed olives, pickles and raisins.

Three meals a day are the norm — plus two meriendas, *which are similar to morning and afternoon coffee breaks. At* meridenda *time, however, you will be presented with more than just a snack — it is more like high tea or light supper and can be quite an elaborate spread of both sweet and savory dishes.* UKOY, *shrimp and sweet potato fritters,* PANCIT GUISADO, *a stir fry noodle dish,* ENSAIMADAS, *cheesy, brioche-type buns,* BOMBONES DE ARROZ, *coconut and rice fritters, might feature as well as hosts of sandwiches and tiny sweet cakes with coffee and hot chocolate to drink.*

Breakfast might consist of rice with garlic and fish or sausages. Some people are very fond of scrambled eggs with garlic! Little hot rolls pain de sol *are available in towns and cities. Hot, milky coffee or chocolate are the usual drinks. Lunch and dinner are both substantial meals for the wealthy. Served buffet-style, these meals are more typically Philippino and the food may well be warm rather than hot. For the poor, however, it's a different story. They cook a huge pot of rice first thing in the morning. The clay pot* (palayok) *is first lined with banana leaves to prevent sticking and also to give some flavor. They then take out the cooked rice as they need it during the day. Often a sardine or sprat-like fish is fried until it becomes crisp. This is then crumbled on top of the rice, bones and all, and perhaps some bagoong is stirred in. Sometimes green mango and salt are eaten as accompaniments to the rice, or a kind of swamp spinach called* kang kong *or yardbeans, cooked and served with the fish and rice. Whatever, it is always a very simple fare, with the wok and a charcoal stove used throughout the islands.*

The most well-known soup is SINGEGANG, *which is soured with tamarind. This recipe uses shrimp, but chicken or meat can also be used and the vegetables and fruits varied according to the season and availability.* ESCABECHE, *pickled fish, is one of the most popular ways of preparing fish in the Philippines and can be served hot or cold.* PUCHERO *is immensely popular as Sunday lunch, combining pork, chicken and the spicy sausages as well as garbanzos, plantain and sweet potato.* TINOLA OF CHICKEN *or* ADOBO MANOK BATANGAS *may be less substantial, but they typify this cuisine in the use of green papaya in one, and a marinade of vinegar and use of coconut milk in the other.*

Two types of fish sauce are used to give saltiness and pungency to a host of Philippino dishes. These are bagoong — *a paste of fermented fish, which used to be made by treading the mixture with bare feet! A jar of this coarse-textured sauce, a rather lurid, pink color, is automatically placed on the table with each meal so that everyone can stir in as much or as little as they like.* Patis *is a pale golden to dark brown, clear liquid, which is added liberally to many soups and meaty dishes and is often placed on the table as extra seasoning.*

Philippinos have a reputation for having a sweet tooth; sweet fritters are popular, coconut and mango ice creams, milk jellies and LECHE FLAN, *made with evaporated milk and limes. All over South East Asia fresh food is in abundance, but the Philippinos have a high regard for canned food, an inheritance from the 50 years of American occupation, which began in 1898.* HALO HALO, *a mixture of fruits and legumes, topped up with evaporated or coconut milk and shaved ice, served up in a tall glass and eaten with a long spoon, is available around-the-clock from the cafés and wayside restaurants.*

Some of the world's most exotic coral gardens can be seen off the coasts of this archipelago. Beautiful shells can be bought from beach girls — centuries ago these shells would have been used for barter in trade with the Chinese. Fishing from the hundreds of miles of coast around the chain of islands is a flourishing business. The results of these labors can be seen at local markets, where garishly decorated lorries and jeepneys, the Philippino open jeep, wait to transport the catch to the customers. In fact, one lasting memory of the place is the abundance of fresh fruit and fish of every shape, size and description available in these markets.

89

The Philippines is still a fairly rural country, where a large number of the people live in villages that nestle between the endless hills of terraces (top). This lady, sorting through her beans (far left), is from a village in the north of Luzon, the largest of the islands. The terraces pictured here (above) are also located in Luzon, an area where much rice is farmed. Coconuts and bananas (left) also account for a large amount of the produce grown.

91

Empanadas
(Patties with savory meat fillings)

12oz/350g prepared puff or short crust pastry milk or beaten egg to seal deep fat for frying or see baking instructions **Filling** 1 tablespoon oil ½ small onion, peeled and chopped ½ cup ground pork 4oz/100g minced pork	½ chorizo, finely chopped ½ tablespoon tomato paste 1 hard-cooked egg, choppd 1-2 tablespoons raisins 4 stuffed olives, cut into rings 1 little chopped gherkin seasoning

MAKES 20

Make the pastry or thaw if you are using frozen. Cover and leave to rest in the refrigerator while preparing the filling. Heat the oil and fry the onion and garlic without browning. Add the ground pork and stir until the meat browns. Add the sausage and tomato paste. Cover and cook very gently for 10-15 minutes. Draw from the heat and leave to cool, then stir in the hard-cooked egg, raisins, olives, gherkin seasoning to taste. Leave to cool completely.

Roll out the pastry on a floured board and cut into 4in/10cm rounds. Divide the filling between these rounds. Damp the edges half-way round, then fold into a half circle. Seal the edges by knocking up with the back of a knife then flute, or mark with the prongs of a fork, to seal. When the empanadas are ready, fry in hot oil for 10 minutes until golden and cooked through. Drain thoroughly on absorbent kitchen towels and serve hot or warm. An alternative to frying is to bake them in a preheated hot oven (425°F/220°C) for 12 minutes.

Lumpia na Carne
(Fried meat spring roll)

8oz/225g pork meat, finely minced ⅛ cup onions, chopped finely 3 cloves garlic, crushed ½in/1cm ginger, scraped and shredded 2 red chilies, shredded oil for frying salt and pepper 1 teaspoon turmeric powder	10 spring roll wrappers, cut in half flour and water paste to seal **Sauce** ½ cup vinegar 1½ cloves garlic salt and black pepper 6 pieces chili, sliced

MAKES 20

Set the pork meat on one side. Fry the onions, garlic, ginger with the chillies and oil. Add the pork, cook for 5 minutes, stirring until the meat changes color. Add green pepper, seasoning and turmeric. Cook for 2 minutes and cool. Fill rolls, sealing with flour and water paste. Then deep fry in hot oil until they turn crispy and brown. Mix together all the sauce ingredients and serve in a small bowl as a dip for the rolls.

Right **Lumpia na carne**
These spring rolls are excellent as a starter or a snack, served together with the spicy vinegar dip.

Far right above **Ukoy**
These fritters are a truly mouth-watering snack, and should be served together with the tangy sauce.

Sinegang
(Sour soup with shrimp and vegetables)

1½ cups raw shrimp
  with shells and
  5 cups water
¼ cup cooked, shelled
  shrimp and
  5 cups prepared
  fish stock
1 level tablespoon
  tamarind pulp and
  ⅝ cup warm
  water to make
  tamarind juice (see
  page 16)

½ sweet potato, peeled
  and finely diced
1 cup green beans,
  trimmed and cut into
  ½in/1cm lengths
2 tomatoes, skinned,
  deseeded and
  chopped
½ cup spinach leaves,
  stems removed and
  leaves torn
salt and pepper

SERVES 6

Rinse the shrimp and place in a large pan with the water. Bring to the boil and gently cook uncovered until they are tender. Lift them out then strain the stock into another pan. Alternatively, use the cookd shrimp together with a ready made up pot of fish stock.

Meanwhile prepare the tamarind juice and shell the shrimp. Discard the shells. Add the sweet potato to the stock in the pan and cook for 5-10 minutes. Add the beans and cook for 5 minutes. At the last minute add the tamarind juice, tomato and spinach. Just before serving, stir in the shelled shrimp to reheat, and season to taste.

Ukoy
(Shrimp and sweet potato fritters)

16 medium-sized fresh
  shrimp
water to just cover
2¼ cups plain flour
1 teaspoon baking
  powder
½ teaspoon salt
1 egg, beaten
small sweet potato,
  peeled (4oz/100g
  approx)
1 clove garlic, crushed
2 handfuls of bean
  sprouts, soaked in

cold water for 10
  minutes and well
  drained
1 small bunch scallions,
  shredded
oil for shallow and deep
  frying

Dipping sauce
1 clove garlic, crushed
3 tablespoons good
  quality vinegar
1-2 tablespoons water
salt to taste

MAKES 16

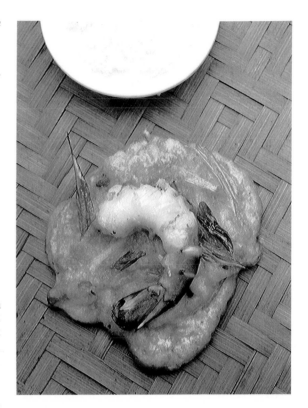

Place the whole shrimp in a pan of water. Bring to the boil, then simmer for 4-5 minutes or until the shrimp are tender. Lift the shrimp from the pan with a draining spoon. Discard the heads and the body shell, but leave the tails on if desired. Strain and reserve the cooking liquid and allow to cool. Sift the flour, baking powder and salt into a bowl. Add the beaten egg and sufficient of the cooked stock to make a batter, the consistency of whipping cream. Grate in the sweet potato, (this discolors on standing so add only at the last minute), stir in garlic and bean sprouts. Chop the scallions. Heat the oil, ¼in/5mm in depth, in a large frying pan and put more oil in a large pan for deep frying. Spoon a good tablespoonful of the mixture of a large small pancake), top with a few chopped scallions and one shrimp in the center. Cook spring onions and one prawn in the centre. Cook over a medium heat until almost cooked through. Transfer to the hot (375°F/190°C) oil in the large pan, flip over when crisp and brown, then drain on absorbent kitchen paper. Fry several at a time and serve hot or warm, garnished with a little more chopped scallions. Mix all the ingredients for the dipping sauce and divide between tiny dishes.

Jnihaw na Pusit
(Broiled squid with lime)

2-3 large squid
  1½-2lb/750-900g
  uncleaned weight,
  cleaned (see page 40)

salt and pepper to taste
oil
6-10 pieces lemon or
  lime

SERVES 3-4

Season with squid then brush with oil before broiling over a barbecue for 8-12 minutes. They can also be cooked under a grill or in a frying pan with oil. Slice them into rings after cooking and serve with the lemon or lime.

Adabong Musit
(Squid cooked in marinade)

2lb/900g fresh squid,
  cleaned (see page 40)
8 tablespoons cider
  vinegar
4 tablespoons light soy
  sauce
4 cloves garlic, peeled
  and crushed
4 tablespoons butter or
pork fat

2 onions, peeled and
  chopped
1½ cups tomatoes,
  skinned and seeded
water if necessary
seasoning
4 scallions, cleaned
  and finely sliced

SERVES 4

Slice and prepare the squid into rings or ribbon-like pieces and place in a shallow glass or glazed earthenware dish. Pour over the vinegar, soy sauce and stir in the crushed garlic. Leave to marinate for at least 30 minutes. Melt the butter or pork fat, and fry the onion until it is soft. Push to one side. Turn heat to high and stir in the drained squid. Reserve the marinade. Cook over a brisk heat for 1-2 minutes. Reduce the heat, add the tomatoes and marinade. Cook over a gentle heat without a cover until the squid are tender. Taste for seasoning and serve with white rice.

Right **Jnihaw na pusit** *This is quick to cook and looks very appetizing laid out on a platter simply surrounded by lemon or limes. It can be accompanied with a vinegar sauce, but this is not absolutely necessary.*

Escabeche
(Pickled fish)

1½-2lb/675-900g red
  snapper, bream or
  white fish fillets
3-4 tablespoons seasoned
  flour
oil for frying

Sauce
1in/2.5cm ginger,
  scraped and shredded
2-3 cloves garlic, crushed
1 onion, peeled and cut
  into thin rings

½ large green pepper,
  seeded
½ large red pepper,
  seeded
1⅞ cups water
1 rounded tablespoon
  cornstarch
3-4 tablespoons herb or
  cider vinegar
1 tablespoon brown
  sugar
patis to taste, if available
seasoning

SERVES 6

Wipe the fish and cut into serving portions. Pat dry on kitchen towels then dust lightly with seasoned flour. Fry in shallow, hot oil in a frying pan until golden brown and almost cooked through. In a separate pan fry the ginger, garlic and onion in clean oil until soft and transparent, but not browned. Add the green and red pepper, cut into cubes and cook for just 1 minute. Lift out and reserve. Blend a little water with cornstarch to a paste. Add the remaining water, vinegar and sugar. Stir into the pan in which the vegetables were cooked and stir until the sauce is smooth and thickens a little. Add the fish sauce and seasoning to taste. Pour the sauce over the fish and reheat without stirring. Transfer to a warmed serving platter and pour over the sauce. Serve hot or cold.

Puchero

This dish is the Philippino answer to the French *pot au feu* — the complete meal. Sometimes it is separated into two courses, soup first followed by meats and vegetables with rice, but it can quite happily be served as a whole on a liberal helping of rice in a wide soup bowl. Either way it is a very satisfying meal and a siesta afterwards is to be recommended. It is especially popular as a family meal on Sunday — the ingredients can be and are much varied according to the cook, with recipes handed down from one generation to the next. There tend to be regional variations, and this is just one of them.

1⅓ cups garbanzos,
  soaked in water
  overnight
1 × 3lb/1.4kg chicken,
  cut into 8 pieces
1⅞ cups pork fillet, cut
  into cubes
2 chorizo (Spanish
  sausages)
1 onion, peeled and
  sliced
salt and pepper
water (approx
  10 cups)
4 tablespoons oil
1 large onion peeled and
  chopped

2 cloves garlic, crushed
3 large tomatoes,
  skinned and seeded
1 tablespoon tomato
  paste
1-2 sweet potatoes,
  peeled and diced
  (½in/1cm cubes)
1-2 plantain (cooking
  bananas), peeled and
  sliced
½ Chinese cabbage,
  shredded
chives or scallions to
  garnish

SERVES 8

Place the garbanzos with the prepared chicken pieces into a large pan with pork cubes and sausages cut into chunks. Cover with water. Add the onion and seasoning. Bring to a boil then simmer, cover and cook for 1 hour or until the meat is just tender when tested with a skewer. Heat the oil, fry the onion and garlic until soft but not brown, stir in the tomatoes and tomato paste. Add this mixture to the large pan with the diced sweet potato and banana, if using. Cook over a gentle heat until the sweet potato is cooked through, it will not taste good if it is not cooked properly.

Add the Chinese cabbage at the last minute with a little of the chives or scallions. Boil rapidly. Serve the liquid as soup and the meat and vegetables with rice separately, if liked; otherwise, you can serve everything together.

Adobo Manok Batangas
(Chicken casserole with coconut milk)

3lb/1.4kg chicken or 4
  chicken quarters
4 cloves garlic, crushed
⅞ cup cider
  vinegar
½-1 teaspoon black
  peppercorns, crushed
sprinkling annatto seeds
  (see page 16)
1⅞ cups chicken stock
  or water
1¼ cups prepared
  coconut milk, made
  from 8oz/225g

desiccated coconut
  and 1⅞ cups hot
  water
1 chayote, peeled, seed
  removed, cut into thin
  slices then blanched
  and drained
oil or pork fat for frying
1 tablespoon light soy
  sauce
cucumber and tomato
  matchsticks to garnish

SERVES 4

Rinse the prawns and place in a large pan with the water. Bring to the boil and gently cook uncovered until they are tender. Lift them out then strain the stock into another pan. Alternatively, use the cooked prawns and fish stock.
the garlic, vinegar, peppercorns and annatto seeds. Mix well then leave to marinate for 1 hour. Meanwhile prepare coconut milk and chayote.

Turn the marinaded chicken pieces into a pan with the stock or water. Bring to the boil, but do not cover, then simmer for 25-30 minutes adding a little extra water if necessary to keep the chicken moist. When the chicken is tender lift out and reduce the cooking liquid to ⅝ cup/150ml and set aside. Clean the pan, add oil and fry the chicken pieces until they are brown all over. Keep warm on a serving dish. Add the coconut milk and chayote to the reduced sauce in another pan. Add soy sauce. Cook for 4-5 minutes until the chayote is just tender. Pour over the chicken pieces and garnish with cucumber and tomato sticks. Serve with freshly boiled rice.

Right **Adobo manok
batangas** *Adobo is really
a method of cooking,
which inevitably includes
garlic, vinegar and
pepper. Pork, beef and
fish are other adobo
ingredients.*

Tinola of Chicken
(Chicken casserole with ginger)

1 × 3lb/1.4kg chicken
1in/2.5cm piece fresh
  ginger, scraped and
  chopped
1 large onion, peeled
  and sliced
2 cloves garlic, crushed
4-6 tablespoons oil or
  pork fat
2¼ cups water or
  chicken stock

1 unripe papaya
  (paw-paw)
2 tablespoons patis (fish
  sauce) or to taste
1 good handful of
  washed spinach leaves
a few fresh chili leaves if
  available
salt and pepper

SERVES 4-6

Cut the chicken into eight or more pieces, dry on absorbent kitchen towels and set aside. Fry the ginger, onion, and garlic in hot oil or pork fat until soft and tender, but not colored. Lift out and reserve. Reheat the fat in the pan and fry the chicken pieces on all sides until golden, turning frequently. Add water or stock and seasoning. Stir in the onion, garlic and ginger. Cover and cook over a gentle heat until the chicken pieces are almost cooked — about 35-45 minutes depending on the size. Wash and cut the papaya in half, remove the seeds and outer skin. Slice evenly and add to the chicken. Cover and cook until the papaya is tender — about 5 minutes. Bring up to a rapid boil, add the fish sauce, spinach and chili leaves if using. Cover and cook for 1 minute. Taste for seasoning and serve.

97

Crispi Pata
(Crispy pork knuckle)

1-2 pieces pork knuckle
salt to taste
oil for frying

Sauce
½ cup vinegar
1½ cloves garlic
salt and black pepper to
    taste
5-7 pieces chili, sliced

SERVES 1-2

Allow 14-18oz/400-500g (raw weight) pork knuckle per person. Cook the pork knuckle in salted water over a low heat until tender (1-1½ hours, depending on their size). Remove and pat dry with kitchen towel. Then fry in medium hot oil for 15 minutes until they have acquired a crispy consistency. Mix together all the vinegar sauce ingredients and serve as an accompaniment.

Bombones de Arroz
(Rice fritters)

½ cup long grain rice
2 eggs beaten
¼ cup sugar
few drops vanilla extract
¾ cup plain flour
1 tablespoon baking
    powder

salt
¼ teaspoon ground
    cinnamon
⅓ cup desiccated
    coconut
oil for deep frying
icing sugar for dredging

MAKES 25

Cook the rice and cool. Turn it into a bowl, add the beaten eggs, sugar and flavoring. Mix well. Sift in the flour, baking powder, salt and cinnamon with the coconut. Mix thoroughly. Drop teaspoonfuls into hot oil and cook until golden brown. Cook three or four fritters at a time, draining them on absorbent kitchen towels. Dredge with icing sugar. Serve hot at *merienda* time.

Right **Crispi pata** *These pork knuckles can be rather off-putting to look at, but their crispy outside and succulent inside make them irresistable.*

Morcon
(Stuffed rolled beef)

3¹/₂lb/1.5kg brisket of beef in one piece, suitable for rolling 1 tablespoon Japanese soy sauce 1 tablespoon lemon juice 2 cloves garlic, peeled and crushed salt and pepper	a few stuffed olives 2 whole large gherkins, cut in half lengthwise
Filling 2 slices cooked ham 1 chorizo (Spanish sausage) skinned and then chopped finely 2 large carrots, peeled and cooked in boiling water for 3 minutes 2 hard-cooked eggs 1-2 tablespoons raisins	**For cooking** 4 tablespoons oil 1 large onion, peeled and chopped 1¹/₄ cups canned, crushed tomatoes 1 tablespoon tomato paste 2 tablespoons vinegar 1 bay leaf ⁵/₈ cup beef stock or water few chopped scallions to garnish

SERVES 8

Order the beef a day or two before you need it so that the butcher can select a good piece of meat. Sprinkle the meat with soy sauce, lemon juice and garlic. You can then leave it to marinate while you are preparing the filling. It should then soak up plenty of flavour.

When ready, season the meat then arrange the ham and finely chopped sausage over half the meat. Lay the carrots along from end to end and the hard-cooked egg left whole. Scatter with raisins and olives and, finally, place the gherkins on top. Now roll up very carefully like a jelly roll and tie securely with string to make a firm roll; otherwise you will find that it unravels during cooking.

Fry the roll in hot oil until brown all over. Add the onions, cook until soft then add the tomatoes, tomato paste, vinegar, bay leaf and stock or water. Taste for seasoning. Cover and cook in a moderate oven (325°F/160°C) for 2¹/₂-3 hours or until tender. Lift the meat onto a serving dish and keep warm. Pass the vegetables and stock through a vegetable mill. Return to the pan and taste for seasoning. When hot serve with the Morcon, cut into neat slices, and scattered with scallions. It may be accompanied with rice or noodles.

Pansit Guisado
(Fried noodles with shrimp, meat and vegetables)

3-4 cups egg noodles, fresh or dried 3 cups whole, fresh shrimp, or 3 cups thawed, frozen shrimp 1¹/₃ cups cooked chicken breast 1¹/₃ cups cooked ham or lean pork 4 tablespoons lard or 4-6 tablespoons cooking oil 1 medium onion, peeled and chopped 2 cloves garlic, peeled and crushed	¹/₂ small Chinese cabbage, finely shredded or 3 cups bean sprouts ⁵/₈ cup fish stock from shrimp or chicken stock 2 tablespoons fish sauce (see page 23) seasoning chopped scallions bagoong, served in a separate dish at the table

SERVES 8

Cook the fresh noodles in boiling water for 1-2 minutes, rinse with cold water and drain thoroughly, or cook dried noodles according to packet directions and drain in the same way. Cover the fresh shrimp, if using, with cold water. Bring to a boil and cook gently for 5 minutes. lift out with a slotted spoon, remove the heads and shells and reserve the shrimp. Discard the shells. Strain the cooking liquid. if using frozen shrimp, thaw well. You will need to substitute the shrimp stock with chicken stock later in the recipe. Using a very sharp knife, finely slice the chicken meat and ham or pork.

Heat half the oil in a wok and fry the drained noodles for 2-3 minutes, stirring. Lift out of the pan onto a platter and keep warm. Heat the remaining oil in the pan, fry the onion and garlic until soft and just beginning to turn golden. Add the cabbage or bean sprouts, cook for 1-2 minutes, mix well, then stir in most of the chicken, ham or pork and shrimp, reserved fish or prepared chicken stock and fish sauce. Turn the mixture all the time. Return the noodles to pan, taste for seasoning and serve on a hot platter garnished with the reserved shrimp, the chicken, ham or pork and the scallions. Serve the bagoong separately. It can be served at lunch or supper and is greatly enhanced by the accompaniment of wedges of lemon or lime.

Ensaimadas
(Sweet bread-rolls)

4½ cups bread flour
  (a strong flour is
  necessary if
  available)
1 teaspoon salt
1 tablespoon sugar
⅝ cup lukewarm water
1½ tablespoons fresh yeast
  or 1 tablespoon dried
  yeast

½ cup softened butter
4 egg yolks
6-8 tablespoons warm
  milk, approx (this will
  depend on type of
  flour used)
2 tablespoons butter
1 cup grated cheese
extra sugar for sprinkling
  on the buns

MAKES 10-12

Sift the flour and salt into a large bowl. Dissolve one teaspoon of the sugar in the warm water, then crumble in the fresh yeast or sprinkle in the dried yeast. Stir, then set aside until it is frothy, which will take about 10 minutes. Meanwhile cream the remaining sugar with the softened butter until fluffy, then beat in the egg yolks and a little of the sifted flour. Stir in the remaining flour with the frothy yeast mixture to the creamy mixture and sufficient milk to form a soft but not sticky dough. Transfer to an oiled plastic bag and close the bag with a tie, leaving plenty of room for the dough to rise. Allow about 1 hour until the dough doubles in size. Punch down, then roll out into a large rectangle. Brush over the surface with melted butter, scatter with cheese, then roll up from the long end into a jelly roll shape. Divide into 10-12 pieces. Now roll each piece into a long, thin, sausage shape and form into a neat coil on greased baking sheet, or place eight of the pieces of dough, coil-side uppermost, into a 10in/25cm cake pan and the rest into a 6in/15cm cake pan. Allow to rise in a warm place until they are double their size. Bake in a hot oven (approximately 425°F/220°C) until golden and cooked through, about 15-20 minutes. Brush immediately with melted butter and sprinkle generously with sugar. Serve them warm.

Right **Buto maya** These sticks of coconut are quite delicious and typically Philippino. These people have a very sweet tooth and make the most of their vast coconut supplies. The sweet rice may be eaten as a snack or as a dessert.

Buto Maya
(Sweet rice with coconut)

2¼ cups thin
  coconut milk
1 cup glutinous rice
½ tablespoons salt
⅔ cup brown sugar

½ cup coconut cream
1 teaspoon anis seed
4 tablespoons grated
  coconut

SERVES 4-6

Bring the thin coconut milk to a boil and add the rice and salt, cooking gently until the rice is soft, about 1 hour. Add two-thirds of the brown sugar and stir it into the rice. Pour the rice into a 2lb/900g loaf tin. Pour over the coconut cream and the remaining sugar, together with the anis seed. Bake in the oven at 400°F/200°C for 30 minutes. Leave to cool over night. Cut into long, square-shaped sticks and roll in shredded coconut. Arrange on a platter.

Halo Halo Supreme
(Iced coconut milk desert)

1 tablespoon each:
jackfruit
coconut flesh
sweet kidney beans
garbanzos
plantain or yam
leche flan (see page 101)
kernel corn

crushed ice
7fl.oz/200ml evaporated milk
ice cream (optional)

maraschino cherries to garnish

MAKES 1 LARGE SUNDAE GLASS

Spoon the fruits, beans and so on into the base of a tall sundae glass. Add the crushed ice and then top with evaporated milk, ice cream, if using, and maraschino cherries to garnish. Eat with a long sundae spoon.

Napalet a Chocolate
(Thick chocolate drink)

¹/₂ cup plain chocolate
⁵/₈ cup boiling water

⁵/₈ cup evaporated milk
sugar to taste

SERVES 1-2

Break the chocolate into small pieces and dissolve in the boiling water in a saucepan. Draw from the heat and add evaporated milk and sugar to taste.

Serve hot in mugs.

Leche Flan
(Caramel and lime custard)

Serve hot or cold with cream and a quarter of a fine lime slice on top. The lime makes all the difference to this caramel custard-type dish.

Caramel
1 cup sugar
8 tablespoons water

Custard
1¹/₄ cups canned evaporated milk

1¹/₄ cups fresh milk
5 large eggs
1 tablespoon sugar
few drops vanilla extract
a little lime rind, finely grated

SERVES 8

Place the sugar and water in a heavy based pan. Stir over heat until the sugar has dissolved. Bring to the boil and boil until the caramel turns a deep golden brown. The caramel will continue to cook even when it is removed from the heat so speed is essential. Remove it from the heat and immediately pour it into eight individual custard cups and rotate each one so that the caramel coats the sides of the dishes as well as the base. Leave on one side. Meanwhile heat the evaporated and fresh milk without boiling. Pour the mixture onto the beaten eggs, sugar and vanilla extract. Stir well, then strain into a large jug and pour into the custard cups when the caramel is set. Any extra custard can be cooked in a separate ovenproof dish and used up as an extra quantity.

Place in a roasting pan of warm water that comes half way up the sides of the dishes. Set in a moderately hot oven (approximately 320°F/160°C) and cook for 35-45 minutes or until it is quite set. Serve hot or cold with cream. If serving cold, I recommend piping a whirl of cream on top of each and a piece of lime, or spiking with a little caramel, which you can make at the same time as the caramel for the base of the custard cups (that is 1oz/25g sugar, 1 tablespoon water). Pour onto a piece of foil. Leave to set and crush with the end of the rolling pin when required. Store the caramel in the refrigerator for several weeks, wrapped in foil. If you prefer one large crème caramel instead of the individual servings, use a 5 cups/1.5 liters ovenproof soufflé dish and cook for about 1 hour in the water bath or until set. It is quite delicious served in either dish!

Thailand

Bangkok, the capital of Thailand, is often spoken of as the 'Venice of the East' referring, of course, to the klongs *(canals) that divide up the city. These* klongs, *which spread out in a network from the Chao Praya river, were built 200 years ago to separate the Royal Palace and magnificent temples from the rest of the city. These buildings certainly do stand out as they dazzle and twinkle in the sunshine, the most famous temple being the Temple of the Reclining Buddha.*

The Thai people were originally forced to migrate from Southern China by the expanding Mogul empire and finally settled in the city, which they called Bangkok — city of angels. Thailand (Siam as it was called) is unique in the Far East in that it was never colonized by Europeans. King Bhumibol Adulyadej has ruled for the past 37 years as a constitutional monarch.

The country is well known for its silk, made even more famous by Jim Thompson, whose disappearance in the Cameron Highlands in Malaysia is still an unsolved mystery. Thai rice is equally famous and much sought after. It is of superb quality and in the rich, fertile Chao Praya basin as many as three crops a year can be grown and harvested. The rice has a special fragrance, which is lost if salt is added when cooking. Everything and anything grows in Thailand. The abundance, quality and variety of goods on display is mesmerizing and the people are perhaps some of the best fed in South East Asia.

Getting about in present day Bangkok is a hazardous business as traffic is heavily congested. The local buses, which are called baht *(a coin's worth), and* tuktuks, *three wheel taxis, are seen everywhere. Crossing the road is to take your life in your hands yet, in contrast, around a corner and away from the seething, pulsating bustle, you are likely to find a temple glistening and glittering, bedecked with flowers and fruit or even a simple family shrine just as lovingly tended.*

Most Thai men at some time have been Buddhist monks and with shaved heads will have dressed in the traditional saffron robes. Each day during his stint as a monk (which is believed will put him in good favor with the gods in the next world) he will have gone out to beg alms of rice in the local neighbourhood. A family celebration is usually held to mark the start of this period of meditation and austerity in the life of sons and grandsons.

The markets provide a fascinating place to study the people and capture a flavor of the country. The floating market is an unique feature of Thailand, encapsulating a world of its own. Sampans, *loaded with produce of all kinds, rice barges, houseboats, fishing boats and floating restaurants ply up and down the* klongs *selling their wares on the busy waterway. Along every sidewalk, as well as in the markets, are women and shy little girls braiding flowers into beautiful garlands. People love to wear flowers: in the hair, around the neck or wrist, or all three. Flowers are also used for cooking and in salads, as well as offerings at wayside shrines to the gods. Plants and flowers — bougainvillaea, orchids, jasmine, gardenias — festoon themselves around doorways, paying homage to a shy charm and elegance that is so much part of the Thai identity.*

Descriptions of Thai food are mouth-watering. The appeal lies in the skilful blend of hot chilies (the smallest variety, prik khee noo, *being the hottest), garlic,* kapi *(blachan), lemon grass, ginger, coriander, mint, basil,* khaa *(lengkuas), fish sauce and sugar. In many ways Thai cooking shares some of the characteristics of Indonesian cuisine. The fish sauce corresponds to soy sauce, which lends a saltiness as well as its own special flavor — to some people an acquired taste. It is made by placing sea or freshwater fish in vats layered with salt and left to ferment for several months. The vats are then tapped and the fermented liquor, which can be golden to dark brown in color, is drawn off. Sometimes this sauce is further matured before being sold.*

Coriander is another essential ingredient and, unlike other countries in the region, the stem and root are employed in the make-up of the wet curry paste, which is another facet of Thai curries. Many housewives, as in Malaysia, will buy these pastes ready pounded in the market. One characteristic in the making of Thai curries is that the meat is cooked in the coconut milk first. Then a ladleful or two of this cooking liquid is spooned into the clean wok and, when hot, the wet spices are fried until they give off a rich aroma. The meat is then returned to the pan with any remaining ingredients. This is quite different to the usual technique of frying off the spices in oil before adding the meat, as would be done in Malay cooking. Coriander leaf is scattered over almost everything.

The invitation to a meal rappatan arhan *means 'come and eat rice'. Even for breakfast, a kind of* congee *or rice porridge is served; at midday perhaps a light meal of rice or noodles. Rice is certainly the basis for the main meal of the day with a minimum of five dishes, perhaps a mixture of one soup, then fish, beef or chicken curry and vegetable dishes. These all come under a heading of* kaeng *(pronounced kang), which means something with soup, sauce or gravy.* Krueng kieng *are side dishes, which come to the table dry or in a thick sauce. A vegetable or salad,* yam *(meaning to mix with the hands), will almost certainly be part of the meal, along with a* NAM PRIK SAUCE, *a kind of sambal, which sounds as hot as it tastes! There are as many recipes for*

this sauce as there are cooks; the Thais hate to be pinned down to specific quantities of this and that; they love to taste and add. This sauce is served as an accompaniment to vegetables, as well as plain boiled rice or fish, and is often added to soups, rice or noodles. No self-respecting Thai will survive without his daily dose of Nam Prik Sauce.

To eat Thai style is to recline on pillows or cushions set around a low table. A spoon and fork (sometimes chopsticks) are used for eating, although in the past people would have used their fingers. Knives are not necessary as all Thai food is cut into small morsels before cooking or serving. All the food is laid out at once and placed in the centre of the table. Everyone has their own portion of rice and eats this to complement the spicy, sour, crisp or soft medley of flavors and textures that make up a real Thai meal. An essential is the three-way appeal, which is an inborn and unwritten law for the Thai cook — man or woman: food must please the eye, nose, and taste buds. When you witness the sculpting of vegetables and fruit, you will begin to appreciate the consummate skill required in the Thai kitchen. Girls are schooled in this from a

Above *Often the best way to get about Bangkok, the capital of Thailand, is along the many* klongs. *Men and women can be seen traveling up and down these canals at all hours of the day. (The flat-topped hat is typically Thai.)*

105

tender age and produce near perfect specimens of crabs from pieces of ginger; melons to look like baskets or even birds with feathers. Thai food being so highly spiced is complemented by iced water, tea such as lapsang souchong or crysanthemum. Keep tea fairly weak and pop an ice cube into the glass or cup. Chilled beer is preferred by some people.

At home in a Thai household a charcoal stove would be the usual mode of cooking, although in the cities now people are turning to bottled gas and a gas ring. A wok is standard equipment for all cooking, as in Malaysia, its neighbor. Bamboo steamers, which rest over a wok filled with water, are also used. The food is frequently wrapped in bamboo leaf as their substitute for aluminium foil, but it is better because it adds its own special flavor to the food. A granite pestle and mortar is essential here where wet curry pastes are so important. The pitted inside surface grips the wet ingredients while they are being pounded, although a food processor does the job almost as well.

Throughout Thailand waterways are used to convey fresh fruit and vegetables straight from the land to the markets (left). The Thais even cook on board their boats (above). Food stalls are in abundance on land as well. This one (far right) is from Hang Dong market, near Chang Mai in northern Thailand. The rural population throughout the country is large, farming the land, and often the huts are built on stilts (right), particularly in waterlogged areas. Fishing is another type of farming, both from the rivers and sea. This type of net (above right) is used by the Thais both in rivers and canals to catch small fish.

Kai Kra Tong Thong
(Cocktail cups)

Batter
½ cup rice flour
½ cup plain flour
⅝ cup coconut
   milk
oil for deep frying

Filling
1⅓ cups cooked
   chicken meat
1oz/25g rice, cooked
   weight
1-2 red chilies, seeded
   and finely chopped
juice ½ lemon or lime

seasoning
½ cup salted peanuts,
   lightly crushed
a few water chestnuts
   (optional), chopped
1 small onion, peeled
   and finely chopped
1 clove garlic, crushed
½in/1cm piece fresh
   ginger, scraped and
   finely chopped

fresh coriander leaves to
   garnish

MAKES 12

Prepare the batter by mixing the rice and plain flours together. Pour in the coconut milk to make a smooth batter, the consistency of whipping cream. Heat oil to 400°/200°C, dip the outside of a small metal ladle or cup-shaped mold into the hot oil then into the batter, almost to the top edge, and back into the hot oil until crisp and golden. Leave for a few seconds, then gently ease off the mould and repeat until all the batter is used up. A small, stainless steel sauce ladle is perfect for this, although a dariole mold will suffice, using a pair of tongs to lift it in and out of the batter and into the oil. Drain the cups on absorbent kitchen towels while preparing the filling. Chop the chicken finely with the rice — you could do this in a food processor. Add the chilies, lemon or lime juice and seasoning. Mix the peanuts with the water chestnuts, if you are using them, onion, garlic and ginger and divide them between the cups. Top with the chicken mixture and garnish with fresh coriander leaves to provide an interesting colour combination.

The cups and fillings can be made up in advance. Fill 10 minutes before serving. Cover with foil and reheat in a moderate oven (350°F/180°C) for 8-10 minutes. Garnish and serve.

The cups can be made and stored in the freezer, but remember to allow them to thaw before filling and warming through in the oven.

Ma Hor
(Galloping horses)

Make up the filling just before using — it binds together better when still warm.

¼ cup pork with a reasonable proportion of fat to lean, finely ground	1 tablespoon nam pla (fish sauce) (see page 23)
1½ tablespoons peanut or vegetable oil	1 tablespoon brown sugar or to taste
1 clove garlic, peeled and crushed	freshly ground black pepper
1 red chili, seeded and chopped (see page 19)	pieces of fresh pineapple mandarin segments, cut almost through vertically and opened out like a book, skin-side down
a few stems fresh coriander, stems chopped and leaves reserved	fresh rambutans with stone removed, or canned lychees, well drained
¼ cup salted peanuts, crushed coarsely with pestle and mortar	crackers or croûtons, if liked

MAKES 16

Prepare the pork and set aside. Heat the oil in a wok, fry the garlic and chilies without browning, then add the coriander stems. Now add the meat and cook until the color changes. Add the peanuts, fish sauce, sugar and pepper. Continue cooking, stirring occasionally, for 10 minutes or until the mixture is cooked but not too dry. In my experience the mandarins are more difficult to pick up and eat elegantly than the pineapple, so you might like to set each one on a small cracker or croûton of the same size.

Arrange the pieces of prepared fruit on a serving dish and top each one with a spoonful of the pork mixture. Lightly press with fingers to bind the mixture. Garnish decoratively with reserved coriander leaves and serve as an hor's d'oeuvre or cocktail snack.

Left **Kai kra tong thong**
These cocktail cups are a sumptuous party idea. The light batter and tasty filling go extremely well together. Fresh coriander provides a color contrast.

Kaeng Chued
(Clear soup with stuffed mushrooms)

7½ cups home-made clear, beef or chicken stock	2 cloves garlic, peeled and crushed
18 small, dried Chinese mushrooms	4 stems coriander, finely chopped with leaves chopped separately
1 small piece of winter melon or ½ chayote, peeled, sliced and cut into cubes	salt and freshly ground black pepper
	2 teaspoons soy sauce
Stuffing for mushrooms	1 scallion root, trimmed and chopped
1 cup finely ground pork with a little pork fat	6 water chestnuts, peeled and chopped
	few coriander leaves to garnish

SERVES 8

Prepare the stock or use a bouillon cube with a little soy sauce for color. Soak the mushrooms for 30 minutes until soft. Remove the stalks and set aside on absorbent kitchen towels. Peel and cube the melon and set aside; if using chayote sprinkle with salt then rinse before cooking. Meanwhile prepare the stuffing for the mushrooms. Mix pork, garlic, coriander stems and leaves, seasoning, soy sauce, spring onions and water chestnuts together. Divide the mixture between the soaked mushrooms. Place the stuffed mushrooms in a bamboo steamer over a wok with a lid on a sheet of waxed paper. Cook for 20 minutes. While this is happening bring the stock to a boil, then add the cubes of melon or chayote and cook until they are just tender.

Place the stuffed mushrooms and a few cubes of melon or chayote in each serving bowl. Pour on the soup and scatter with a few coriander leaves.

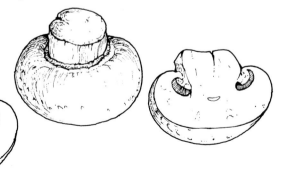

Tom Yam Kung
(Shrimp soup)

1lb/450g raw shrimps, head and shell removed
5 cups cold water or use alternative below
2 stems lemon grass, bruised, or 1 teaspoon serai powder (see page 25)
1 teaspoon salt
3 lime leaves, reserve one for garnish

3 chilies, seeded and two bruised, using pestle and mortar, the other cut into rings for garnish
1 tablespoon fish sauce (see page 23)
juice 2 large lemons or limes

SERVES 4-6

Reserve the shelled shrimp and put the head and shells into a pan with water. Add lemon grass or serai powder, salt and two of the lime leaves, and the chilies. Bring up to a boil (do not cover) and simmer for 15 minutes. Strain off the stock and return it to the rinsed pan. Allow it to come to the boil, add the raw shrimp and simmer for 3-4 minutes or until the shrimp are pink and cooked. Stir in the fish sauce and enough lemon or lime juice to make the soup taste sharp. Taste for seasoning. Pour into a serving bowl or tureen and scatter the top with sliced chili and torn lime leaves if using.

In the absence of fresh shrimp make up a fish stock (see page 36). Strain and reheat with lemon grass, salt, lime leaves and pounded chilies. When this has cooked for 15 minutes, lift out the lemon grass, add 1-1½ cups/175-225g cooked shrimp and other ingredients. Serve almost at once.

Kaeng Chued Pla Muek
(Stuffed baby squid in a broth)

1lb/450g baby squid, cleaned (see page 40), but left whole for stuffing. (I used 6 x 4in/10cm squid as smaller ones were unavailable)
1 cup raw pork meat, ⅔ meat, ⅓ fat, finely ground
4 stems coriander, leaves reserved for garnish
1-2 cloves garlic, peeled and crushed

salt and freshly ground black pepper
6¼ cups prepared fish stock (see page 36)
2 stems lemon grass, bruised
2 or 3 lime leaves
2 tablespoons nam pla (fish sauce) or lime juice
1-2 chilies, seeded and cut into rings

SERVES 6-8

Prepare the squid by removing the heads, rubbing off the purplish skin and pulling out the quill. Turn inside out and wash well. Turn back to the original side and drain well. Cut the tentacles from the head and squeeze out the center bone. Wash and reserve the tentacles. Mix the pork, finely chopped coriander, garlic and seasoning together. Stuff the squid with this mixture, but do not overfill. Replace the tentacles at the opening of the squid. Secure with wooden cocktail skewers if liked.

Bring the fish stock to the boil with the lemon grass. Cook for a few minutes. Drop in the squid with torn lime leaves and cook gently for 10-15 minutes. Remove lemon grass and lime leaves. Taste for seasoning and add fish sauce or lime juice. Serve in bowls topped with slices of chili and coriander

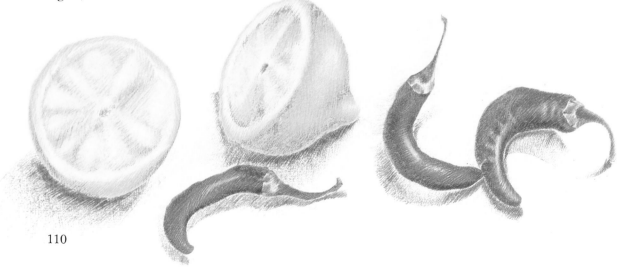

Above *Greens are readily available in Thailand, from cabbage to Chinese leaves. The recipe for* **Lettuce mouthfuls** *demonstrates how imaginatively they use their vegetables.*

Lettuce Mouthfuls

6-8 lettuce leaves, medium size, rinsed and dried
1 small lemon
1 red chili, seeded and chopped finely

½in/1cm fresh ginger root, scraped and chopped finely
a few salted peanuts
12-16 cooked shrimp or more, depending on size

MAKES 6-8

Leave the lettuce leaves to dry on a tea-towel while preparing the fillings. Cut the lemon in half, setting one half aside, cut the other into thin slices, each of which should then be quartered. Place these and the following ingredients in small bowls or on a platter in separate piles, the chili, ginger, peanuts and shrimp. Ask each guest to place a little of each of the fillings onto the lettuce leaf. Squeeze over a little lemon juice from the half lemon and roll up the leaf and contents into a neat parcel. Eat it at once. If, on the other hand, you know your guests' chili and ginger tolerance level, then the lettuce mouthfuls can be made up just before they are needed, but it is much more enjoyable for everyone to make up their own. They are an enjoyable way to start a meal.

Pla Tod Mak Ham
(Fried fish with tamarind)

1 whole fish (2lb/900g) bream or red snapper, cleaned and scaled
2-3 tablespoons seasoned cornstarch
oil for frying
1 tablespoon tamarind pulp, soaked in ⅝ cup warm water
2-3 cloves garlic, chopped
4-6 scallions, root removed and the white bulb cut from

green tops, make tops into curls (see page 39)
½in/1cm fresh ginger, scraped and shredded
1 tablespoon soy sauce
1-2 tablespoons dark brown sugar
1-2 tablespoons fish sauce
1-2 fresh red chilies, seeded and shredded

SERVES 4

Ask the fishmonger to leave the fish head and tail on. Rinse and pat dry on absorbent kitchen towels. Dredge with seasoned cornstarch and fry on both sides in a large pan for 10-15 minutes in all, or until cooked through. Set aside and keep warm.

Meanwhile strain the tamarind juice through a sieve, then discard the seeds and pulp. Fry the garlic, white bulbs of the spring onion and ginger in a little oil in the cleaned pan without browning. Add soy sauce, sugar and fish sauce, along with the tamarind juice. Stir well. Pour over the cooked fish and garnish with the red chilies and the reserved, chopped scallion tops or curls.

Krueng Kaeng Phed
(Red curry paste)

1 tablespoon coriander seeds
1 tablespoon cumin seeds
½ teaspoon each ground mace and nutmeg
10-20 seeded red chilies or 1-1½ tablespoons chili powder
12 shallots or ¼ cup red onions, peeled and chopped
4-6 cloves garlic, peeled and crushed

3-4 stems lemon grass, lower part only (see page 25), sliced
½in/1cm khaa or lengkuas root, peeled and sliced
6 stems coriander, leaves removed
1 teaspoon grated magrut (see page 20) or bitter orange or grapefruit peel
1in/2.5cm square kapi (blachan) (see page 18)
1 tablespoon salt

Dry fry the coriander and cumin seeds for 2-3 minutes over a medium low heat until they give off a spicy aroma. Pound finely and add to the mace and nutmeg. Drain the chilies and pound them with the shallots or onion, garlic, lemon grass and khaa, coriander, magrut, kapi (blachan) and salt. Add spices. This can be done very efficiently in a food processor. Pound to a fine paste. If you want a fiery hot paste leave some of the seeds in the chilies. Store any left-over paste in a screwtop jar in the refrigerator. It will keep for 1-2 weeks. Place a piece of plastic wrap over the jar before putting on the lid to keep fresh.

This makes enough red curry paste for the KAENG PHED GAI (Red curry chicken) and the MUSAMAN CURRY (note the extra ingredients for the latter, given in the Musaman Curry recipe).

Kaeng Khieu Wan
(Green curry paste)

Use the same ingredients as for the red curry paste, but use fresh green chilies, instead of the red ones. To improve the color use the coriander leaves as well as the stems and root, or substitute chili leaves or spinach, if desired. Any left-over paste can be stored in the freezer for another occasion. This is extremely useful as it is time consuming to prepare fresh every time.

Kaeng Khieu Wan Kung
(Green curry of shrimp)

3 cups raw shrimp
1⅞ cup coconut milk from 12oz/350g desiccated coconut and 1pt/600ml water

4 tablespoons green paste (see page 112)
1 tablespoon nam pla
coriander leaves to garnish

SERVES 4

Wash and shell the shrimp. Put the shells in the coconut milk and slowly bring to a boil, stirring. Cook for 5-10 minutes then strain through a sieve and lift out the shells and heads and discard. Spoon a quarter of the strained coconut milk into a clean pan. Heat it, then add the prepared curry paste. Cook over a moderate heat until the mixture gives off a rich aroma, adding more and more of the coconut milk until it is all incorporated into the sauce. Cook for 5 minutes then add the fish sauce and the shrimp to the curry and continue cooking for a further 5 minutes. Remove from the heat and leave for several hours, if possible, for the flavors to blend. Reheat just before serving.

Kaeng Phed Gai
(Red curry chicken)

Above **Kaeng phed gai**
*This curry chicken can be
cooked using either red* *or green curry paste.*
Kaeng khien wan pla
uses shrimp (above left).

If red chilies are not available, you can make a green curry chicken by making a green curry paste, but this will not give such a rich color to the finished dish.

1 × 3lb/1.4kg chicken, cut into 8 portions	*2-3 lime leaves*
3¼ cups coconut milk (see page 21)	*1 tablespoon fish sauce a few basil leaves, deep fried and drained, or*
3-4 tablespoons red or green curry paste (see page 112), or to taste	*shredded chili and coriander leaves to garnish*

SERVES 4

Prepare the chicken. Pour off the top one-third of the coconut cream from the rest and reserve. Put the remainder into a pan, bring to a boil, stirring, then add the pieces of chicken. Allow to simmer for 40-45 minutes or until the chicken is tender. Lift out the chicken and allow it to cool a little. Remove the meat from the bones and cut into bite size pieces that can be picked up easily with chopsticks. Meanwhile put a cupful of the coconut milk from cooking the chicken into another pan or wok. Add the curry paste and cook fairly rapidly so that the liquid evaporates and the spices fry, giving off a rich aroma. Add the remaining coconut milk in which the chicken was cooked and cook for 5 minutes. Now add the chicken pieces, lime leaves and fish sauce. Taste for seasoning and cook for 5-10 minutes. Just before serving stir in the coconut cream. Serve in a bowl scattered with crushed, deep-fried basil or chili and coriander, and a bowl of rice. This is fairly strong-flavored dish so you would be advised to serve refreshments.

113

Water buffalo (below) *roam wild in the northern region of Thailand. Forestry is farmed here, particularly teak, and these beasts of burden are used to transport the logs* (far right). *Coconuts are carried from the plantations* (right) *on the canals and all sorts of* *fresh vegetables* (below far right) *This lady* (bottom) *is busy frying up Pla Tod (Fish with tamarind) in the Hang Dong market in the north. This stall in the middle of a 'weekend' market is selling shrimps and prawns of varying sizes and prices* (below center

Musaman Curry

The ingredients for the traditional Musaman curry paste are the same as for the red curry paste (KRUENG KHAENG PHED) with the addition of three cardamom pods, bruised then roasted or dry fried with the coriander and cumin seeds. Remove the cardamom seeds from their pods and pound, adding half a teaspoon each of ground cloves and cinnamon. The wet ingredients for the curry paste should be fried whole in a little oil in a pan for several minutes, turning over all the time. Transfer to a food processor and pound finely before adding the dry fry spices. Blend altogether until smooth. It is now ready for use. This curry should taste sweet and sour for it to resemble the authentic Musaman Curry.

2lb/900g beef, cut into slices and then pieces, 2in/5cm square (approx)
oil for frying
3¼ cups coconut milk
1lb/450g potatoes, peeled and cut into large dice
4 cups small onions, peeled and left whole

4-6 tablespoons Musaman curry paste (see above) (approx ½ the prepared quantity)
2 tablespoons tamarind pulp, soaked in ⅝ cup warm water
2-3 tablespoons dark brown sugar
bay and cardamom leaves to garnish (optional)

SERVES 4-6

Prepare the curry paste. Fry the beef in hot oil on all sides until it starts changing color, stirring all the time. Pour off ¼ cup/300ml coconut cream and reserve. Cook the meat for 5 minutes, then stir in the remaining 2½ cups/600ml coconut milk, bring to a boil, cover and cook for 45-60 minutes or until the beef is tender. Lift out the meat and reserve. Meanwhile fry the onion and potatoes in a separate pan until they are brown all over, then lift them out and reserve. Add curry paste to ⅝ cup/150ml of the coconut milk in which the meat was cooked and cook rapidly without a cover for 5 minutes, slowly adding the remaining coconut milk. Reduce the heat, return the beef, potatoes and onions to the pan with tamarind juice and sugar. Cook for a further 30 minutes or until the vegetables are tender. Add the reserved coconut cream. Taste for seasoning and serve with garnishes.

Top **Lahp isan** This is a type of curry, which is delicious served with sticky rice.
Above **Musaman curry** This is a popular curry in Thailand. It is a hot, spicy dish with a definite coconut flavor.
Right **Mee krob** The garnishes supply a red, yellow, white and green combination of colors for this dish.

Lahp Isan

A favorite northern Thai dish, it has a near relation 'lap' in Laos, the bordering country. The quantity of chili used can be varied according to taste.

1 tablespoon long grain rice	3-4 green chilies, seeded and chopped
4 small red chilies or 1 teaspoon chili powder	1-2 stems lemon grass, lower bulb only (see page 25), chopped
1lb/450g best quality ground beef	1 green pepper, seeded and chopped
⅝ cup water	nam pla (fish sauce) to taste
juice large lemon	lemon slices or wedges to garnish
1 handful mint or basil leaves	
1 onion, peeled and chopped	

SERVES 4-6

Dry fry the rice in a pan until it is pale yellow in color, then pound it to a coarse texture with a pestle and mortar. Repeat the dry frying and pounding with the red chilies, then mix these ingredients together. Add the beef to boiling water and stir until the meat changes color. Remove and drain off the stock, which can be used on another occasion. Turn the meat onto a serving platter and squeeze over the lemon juice. Stir in the coarsely ground rice and chilies and half the mint leaves, which have been chopped. Stir in the remaining ingredients and season with fish sauce. Garnish attractively with the remaining mint leaves and lemon. Serve with rice.

Mee Krob
(Crisp fried noodles)

Sauce
2¼ cups finely chopped, raw chicken breast
⅓ cup cooked pork, sliced
¾ cup cooked, shelled shrimp
6 shallots, peeled and chopped
2 cloves garlic, peeled and crushed
oil for frying
1 square bean curd, yellow or white, cut into neat cubes
1 cup canned salted soya beans
4 beaten eggs
2 tablespoons cider or wine vinegar
1-2 tablespoons icing sugar
nam pla (fish sauce) to taste

Noodles
1¼ cups rice vermicelli (lai fan or beehoon)
deep fat for frying
¼ teaspoon chilli powder

Garnish
scallions
2-3 red chilies, seeded and finely sliced
fresh coriander leaves chopped, pickled garlic or fried garlic flakes
rind of lime or a strip of grapefruit peel, cut into fine shreds
2¼ cups bean sprouts tails removed for best effect

SERVES 6-8

Prepare the chicken breast, cut the cooked pork into fine slices and set aside with the shrimps. Fry the shallots and garlic in hot oil in a wok; do not color. Add the chicken and stir for 3-4 minutes, then stir in the pork and shrimp. Turn the ingredients all the time. Add the bean curd cubes and salted soy beans and cook for 2-3 minutes. Then add the beaten eggs little by little, stirring throughout and adding extra oil if necessary to the sauce. At this stage stir in the vinegar, icing sugar and fish sauce. Toss in the pan for 1-2 minutes, then check the flavor. It should have a sweet, salty taste. Set aside. Heat oil to 375°F/190°C in a large pan and deep fry the noodles for just a few seconds. This is best done in several stages in a frying basket or wok. The noodles will become puffy and crisp. Remove them from the fat, drain and keep warm. Just before serving, put half the sauce and a sprinkling of the chili powder in a large wok or pan with half the noodles. Toss together without breaking up the noodles too much. Repeat with the remaining sauce, chili and noodles. Pile onto a large serving platter and garnish attractively with scallions, chilies, coriander, garlic and lime rind or grapefruit shreds. Arrange the bean sprouts all around the base.

Khao Phad Kra Ree
(Curried fried rice)

1½-2 cups cooked meats,
    chicken, pork and/or
    shrimp
2½ cups cold, cooked
    rice from 1 cup
    long grain rice
½ cup green beans or
    French beans,
    cut into 2in/5cm
    lengths and blanched
nam pla (fish sauce)
    and sugar to taste

Curry paste
3-5 dried red chilies,
    seeded and
    pounded or 1-2
    teaspoons chili
    powder

6 shallots, peeled and
    chopped finely
2 cloves garlic, peeled
    and chopped
2 stems lemon grass, use
    bottom part of bulb
    (see page 25), sliced
½in/1cm khaa
    (lengkuas) root, sliced
    finely
4 stems coriander,
    chopped, leaves
    reserved for garnish
a little grated lime peel
6-8 tablespoons vegetable
    oil

SERVES 4-6

Cut the meats into fine slices and leave the shrimp, if using, whole. Set the rice on one side. Prepare and blanch the beans. Meanwhile pound the chilies with shallots, garlic, lemon grass, laos and coriander stems and peel. This can be done in a food processor. If using the chilli powder add it to these pounded ingredients. Heat the oil and fry this paste until it gives off a fragrant aroma. Add the cooked meats then the rice, stirring all the time until the fried rice is well mixed. Add more oil if necessary. Season with salt, fish sauce and sugar, if liked, to taste. Finally add the green beans. Serve garnished with coriander leaves.

To take on a picnic, put portions of rice into a banana leaf or foil parcel. Steam until the banana leaf softens and carry to the picnic in a plastic box.

Right **Khao phad** *This is the basic Thai fried rice, to which a multitude of things can be added and stirred in. The wok is an excellent piece of equipment for this type of recipe.*

118

Khao Neung
(Steamed rice)

1 cup long grain rice | *2½ cups cold water*

SERVES 4

Rinse the rice in a sieve then place it in a pan with water. bring to a boil, lower the heat and cook uncovered until the water has been absorbed and a series of holes appear in the surface of the rice. Line the base of a steamer within ½in/ 1cm of the edges with foil and raise the edges into a shallow, bowl-like shape. Puncture all over base with a skewer. Turn the rice into the foil in the steamer and place over a pan of fairly fast-bubbling water. Cover and cook for 30 minutes until the rice is just tender and fluffy. Refill the base pan with boiling water as necessary. You will notice that no salt is added to this recipe — this is quite traditional as the real Thai rice is of such excellent quality, with a fragrant flavor, that salt detracts from this.

Above **Khao neung**
Steaming the rice after boiling separates out each grain. It is a traditional way of cooking Thai rice and makes it very light and fluffy. It is delicious served with any type of curry.

Khao Tang
(Crisp fried rice)

This is proof of a thrifty people. The hard, caked layer of rice, which sometimes forms in the bottom of a pan that has been left to cook too long, can be removed by soaking the hot pan in a bowl of water for 10 minutes; the water should come half way up the outside of the pan. Use a spatula to release the rice, as a whole or in pieces. Allow these to dry out completely. Break into small pieces and deep fry. Use as a cocktail snack or in smaller pieces in lieu of *croûton* in a soup.

Nam Prik Sauce for Raw Vegetables

½in/1cm square kapi (blachan)	4-5 fresh red chilies, seeded and chopped
4 tablespoons (2oz/50g) dried shrimps, soaked for 15 minutes until soft, then drain	1 root coriander, stalks and leaves
4 cloves garlic, peeled and crushed	nam pla (fish sauce) to taste
4 tablespoons (1-2oz/25-50g) freshly cooked shrimp (optional)	1 tablespoon brown sugar
	juice of ½-1 lemon or lime

Dry fry the shrimp paste. Pound it with the drained, dried shrimps and garlic to a paste. Add freshly cooked shrimp if you are using them and pound again. Add the chilies and repeat. Bruise the coriander stems and leaves with the mixture. Season with fish sauce, sugar and lime or lemon juice. More chilies can be added, but try these quantities first.

This nam prik goes well with raw vegetables or plain ·boiled rice.

Yam Chomphu
(Salad of tart fruits)

	Dressing
2 green apples	2-3 tablespoons lemon juice
2 green mangoes	2 teaspoons sugar
½ small pineapple	1 tablespoon fish sauce or to taste
¾ cup cooked pork, cut into strips	mint or coriander leaves to garnish
⅓ cup cooked shrimp	

SERVES 4-6

Peel and cut the apples and mangoes into even-sized pieces. Slice the pines from the pineapple, remove the core and cut the flesh up into bite size pieces. Arrange these attractively with the pork and shrimp on a serving dish. Blend the dressing ingredients together and pour over the salad. Garnish with mint or coriander leaves.

Taeng Kwah Ah Jad
(Fresh cucumber accompaniment)

1 medium-sized cucumber	1 small onion, peeled and cut into fine slices
1 tablespoon salt	1-2 fresh red or green chilies, seeded and chopped
2 tablespoons distilled vinegar	
2 teaspoons caster sugar	

Wash the cucumber and score the flesh lengthwise with a fork. Then, slice it finely and put the slices into a glass dish. Sprinkle with salt and leave for 15 minutes. Drain off the juices, rinse with cold water and drain thoroughly. Arrange them in a serving dish and sprinkle over vinegar and sugar. Scatter with onion rings and chopped chilies. Serve with curry of your choice.

Far left **Nam prik sauce**
If you use this sauce as an accompaniment to raw vegetables and crisp fried pork rind, as here, then place it in a bowl in the middle of the dipping ingredients.

Left **Taeng kwah ah jad**
This is a refreshing side salad. It need not be too hot despite the chilies, provided the seeds are removed.

121

China

Centuries ago the Chinese called their great country the Middle Kingdom. Life has never been easy for the majority of the people and day-to-day living, even now, is spartan and frugal by our standards. The Chinese thrive in such circumstances and out of this have produced a cuisine that is one of the greatest in the world. They are passionate about food — they live to eat. Food has always been a great topic of conversation. A greeting from a friend or stranger will not be 'How are you?' but 'Have you eaten?', 'Have you taken rice?'

The countless numbers of cookbooks on Chinese food sold every year show that there is immense interest in the food of the most populous nation of the world. Where we in the west are increasingly keen to eat and experiment with other cuisines, the Chinese are content with their own, so wherever they go restaurants and take-outs flourish. It would take a lifetime of study and eating to fully understand the cooking of the whole of that vast continent; the regional cooking styles are so different. Much of this variety stems from the climatic extremes from north to south, from the availablity of fuel, from the suitability of crops to region and from the traditions of the people.

There was very little movement of people from one area to another until comparatively recently. Family ties were, and still are, of paramount importance. Wherever there are Chinese a business will always be a family affair. They are extremely astute people, hence their success in setting up restaurant and food shops worldwide, not to mention all the other trades and professions in which they excel. Once the immediate family are employed, members of the extended family are drawn in — this applies from street vendor to restaurant magnate. A friend who recently visited the country vividly relayed her view of it. 'I think my main impressions of China were (1) the people and their good manners, (2) the numbers of people and bicycles, (3) the gigangic problem of feeding so many, (4) the miles and miles of market gardens growing vegetables and rice, all so neatly kept without any hedges or trees, (5) the washing hanging out to dry from every possible window or tree, and, lastly (6) the beautiful children, so well cared for and proudly displayed.

Many festivals punctuate the Chinese calendar. There is the Moon Festival, held in September to mark the end of the harvest. Gay, colorful lanterns abound in the shape of a butterfly or turtle for longevity — the Chinese obsession — or a carp for success. Boxes of moon cakes are exchanged, which look like miniature 'black buns' and are about the size of cup cakes; they have a Christmas cake-like filling in a sweet pastry. New Year is the celebration of the year; the buzz of activity is like

123

our own preparation for Christmas. It is considered bad luck for the housewife to cook during the first few days of the New Year so preparations are elaborate as many guests will call at that time and everyone must be fed handsomely. On New Year's day itself floors must not be swept, fires lit or water poured out and children wear new clothes, all traditions which have been faithfully followed through the centuries.

The Chinese are extraordinarily fond of proverbs and two I thought very apt were: 'If you want your dinner nicely cooked don't offend the cook!' and 'Those nearest the government official get the honor and those nearest the kitchen get the food!' The Chinese preoccupation with food is rivalled only by the French — in fact many top French chefs choose to eat Chinese when they eat out. But how did it all begin and why is the cooking of China so universally popular?

The Chinese are inherently practical people and have learnt many things through the ages from their forebears, who lived a meagre existence. For example, fuel was hard to come by so speed in cooking was essential. Early records show that the wok was being used as far back as 500AD, as the shape was ideal to sit cradle-like above the fire, absorbing heat over a large area. Not only was fuel scarce, but meat, poultry and fish too, which resulted in the ingenious Chinese evolving cooking methods to stretch those ingredients to the maximum. The clever combinations of fish and meat, meat and vegetables in stir fry illustrate this skill perfectly. Not just any fish or meat is used, however. Care will be taken that the ingredients complement each other — the ying *and* yang *(balance) that comes from being at one with nature is faithfully followed. The scarcity of fuel led naturally to the stir fry method, although the Chinese are also renowned for their long cook stews, tasty broths and soups.*

Nothing is thrown away, even chicken feet are used in recipes. Similarly half a dozen mange tout (snow peas), a few shrimp or a slurp of rice wine might be used to transform a dish into something special. That being said, the Chinese are in no way as preoccupied with the appearance of the dish as, say, the Japanese — the appearance matters, but it is of secondary importance to the taste. Pickling, drying, smoking and preserving are skills used to provide the diet with variety during the winter months, adding flavor and texture to a host of classic dishes. Flavor or taste and texture are two vitally important features of the Chinese cuisine: sweet, sour, hot, bland, bitter, salty. Frequently the two are experienced in one particular dish; notably sweet and sour.

Ingredients for Chinese cooking are, in the main, familiar to us and easy to come by, The soybean crops up in a variety of guises — rich in protein, it became an important part of the diet. As light (thin) and dark (thick) sauce, used in hosts of dishes, it is salty, so take care when

Left *The Chinese are very imaginative with eggs, selling both fresh and preserved ones. Their 'hundred year old eggs' are covered in lime and rice husks, then left for several months. Needless to say there is a strong sulphurous smell, which is often played down with pickled ginger.*

adding extra salt. Hoisin sauce is soya based and then there are the salted yellow soybeans, black beans, bean sprouts and bean curd, fresh or fried, all of which will be found in the recipes of China or countries where there is a strong Chinese influence on the cuisine.

In the north, wheat, maize and corn are grown and as a consequence much more bread is eaten than rice. The rolls may smell like our bread and taste delicious, but look rather pale and insipid by our standards as they are steamed not baked. Noodles made from the wheat are very popular and in the north will be served as a main meal. Spaghetti is an acceptable substitute for northern noodles, but where the Italians just boil their pasta the Chinese then go a stage further and fry them too. Rice is eaten steamed or boiled or as a congee, *the rice porridge which is so popular at breakfast.*

'Though you add a guest you needn't add another chicken'; this is another apt proverb. Two or three different dishes can be prepared from the one bird, the breast for stir frying, the legs and thigh for stewing and the rest for a wonderful stock. Chicken and pork are the two most popular meats. Up in the north however lamb, mutton and beef are consumed from the great herds that graze the Inner Mongolia region. Carp is one of the most famous fish for cooking whole, such as BRAISED CARP. Much of the fish eaten in China is freshwater fish, including river shrimps and freshwater crabs which are found in rivers and lakes. But the east and south coastal regions provide an immense variety of sea fish and the cooks of those areas produce some exquisite dishes using them. You are bound to find eel, bass, squid, millet, bream, perch and tuna, lobsters, crabs, shrimp, clams, to name but a few.

Selecting recipes to include here was extremely difficult as it is not what you take, but what is left out that matters. I decided to offer sugges-

There is a universal belief in ancestor worship; filial duty really does extend beyond the grave (above left). For a living, many of the people work on the land (top). Rice, silk and tea are major crops. The fresh produce tilled from the land is sold, as so often in the east, at the bustling markets (left). However, it is not only fresh food that is for sale, but also the preserved eggs with their sulphurous smell (above). In fact, a great variety of goods are on offer, such as these hand-woven baskets (below left).

tions from the areas roughly north, south, east and west. These regions have their own culinary characteristics not only in the ingredients, but in the style of cooking employed. From Peking, the capital in the north, came the sophisticated food of the Chinese emperors, known as the Imperial Cuisine. With the capital in its midst, the mandarin or northern style of cooking has adopted many dishes brought by visitors and dignitaries from other regions over the centuries resulting in a very cosmopolitan range of food. Notable characteristics are the use of wine and noodles, and dishes such as PEKING DUCK, HOT AND SOUR SOUP and the MONGOLIAN HOTPOT, using thin slices of lean lamb that are cooked in a bubbling stock at the table in front of the guests.

The Yangtze River flows through the east to the sea just north of Shanghai. This is the rice-growing area of China where two or three crops a year are harvested and the best rice wine and vinegars are made. From the hills silk and tea are produced and kaolin for the famous China porcelain. Slow cooking is quite a feature and red cooking is popular, the soya marinade being used again and again, gaining in flavor each time. Sugar is added to balance the saltiness.

Szechwan, in the west, is renowned for its generous use of hot peppers, unique in Chinese cooking. This spectacularly beautiful region is very fertile; huge quantities of rice are grown on hillside terraces. Wheat, corn, sugar cane, tea, cotton and citrus fruits grow in profusion, as well as potatoes and fungus. The Szechwan shrimp come from freshwater fish ponds. Tangerine peel is a characteristic addition to chicken dishes. Frequently a dish might have three complementary flavors — hot, salty and sour. The Szechwan peppercorns should be dry fried and crushed before using.

Cantonese cuisine from the south is perhaps the most widely known, due to the mass emigration to the other countries of South East Asia, Europe and America. The climate is tropical with sugar and rice as the main crops, along with silk. Citrus fruits grow freely, pineapples, bananas and lychees, too. On the hillsides paddy-terraces are a common feature. With such a long coastline fish features in the food of this southern region and some would say that the Cantonese cuisine is the best in China. Stir frying is especially popular — ginger, sugar and light soy or oyster sauce giving flavor. The juices are lightly thickened with a little cornstarch, which gives a beautiful gloss to the food. Sweet and sour dishes and chicken, to our standards undercooked (the bones being red), are typical Cantonese fare. Snacks of all kinds such as dim sum *are very popular.*

A Chinese meal does not consist of set courses as we know them, which adds greatly to a relaxed atmosphere for the diners, but not for the cook/hostess! Usually at home there will be up to four dishes and one

or two soups brought to the table together. Everyone helps themselves. A lazy susan or dumb waiter (a small revolving table) is a common feature at Chinese dining tables, making it easier for everyone to sample all the dishes.

At a party or celebration it is traditional to serve the food at a round table with seating for 10 guests. A dozen or more different dishes, including soups, may be served. The first few dishes frequently consist of lighter food and are eaten at a faster pace than subsequent dishes, which might be whole fish, casseroles and meat dishes. Generally speaking, there would be three or four stir fry dishes, two or three fish dishes cooked in different styles, two or three soups (one may be sweet, adding another dimension to the meal), then there may be two, three or four main course dishes: beef, pork, poultry or offal and vegetable dishes, plus rice or noodles. After that you can see how essential it is to learn to pace yourself at one of these banquets — you will be expected to sample a little of everything! It is considered impolite to leave any food in your bowl, even a grain of rice. Rice may well be served at the end of the meal as a filler or, more frequently, with the more substantial dishes.

Tea is not traditionally served with the Chinese meal and is not necessary when soups are served and drunk during it. However, if you like to have tea, choose a green, jasmine or crysanthemum rose, lychee or, my favorite, lapsang souchong.

Above *An abundance of fish can be found in the rivers and lakes of China as well as the sea. This market stall is not only selling, but also cooking, a whole range of delicious shellfish.*

Northern China — Peking

Suan-la T'ang
(Hot and sour soup)

6 cloud ears and 12
  golden needles or
  4 Chinese dried
  mushrooms, soaked in
  warm water for 30
  minutes
1 cake fresh bean curd,
  neatly diced
²/₃ cup pork fillet
3 tablespoons cornstarch
⁵/₈ cup water
1-2 tablespoons oil
1 small onion, peeled
  and chopped

6¼ cups home-
  made beef stock
  or consommé
4 tablespoons rice wine
  vinegar
1 tablespoon light soy
  sauce
freshly ground black
  pepper and salt
1 egg beaten
1 teaspoon sesame oil
2-3 scallions,
  shredded

SERVES 6

Drain the cloud ears and golden needles or the mushrooms, which should be nicely plump. Cut into thin shreds and set aside with the bean curd. Finely slice the pork into matchstick size pieces and dust with cornstarch. Blend the remaining cornstarch with water and reserve. Heat the oil in a Chinese claypot or wok over a gentle heat and cook the onion until soft. Turn up the heat slightly and fry the pork slices until they change color. Pour in the stock, cloud ears, needles or mushrooms, cook for 10-15 minutes, then thicken with the cornstarch paste. Add bean curd, vinegar, soy sauce and black pepper and salt to taste. Lower the heat and drizzle in the beaten egg from a balloon whisk or your finger tips so that it forms threads of mixture. Add sesame oil just before serving. Garnish with the scallions if desired.

Mu Hsu Jou

(Scrambled eggs with mushrooms)

1½ tablespoons golden
    needles and cloud ears
    or Chinese mushrooms,
    soaked in warm
    water for 30 minutes
1 tablespoon thick soy
    sauce (optional)
1 tablespoon Chinese rice
    wine or dry sherry
freshly ground black
    pepper
2-3 scallions, finely
    chopped

¼ cup lean pork, cut
    into fine strips
1½ cups bamboo shoot,
    finely sliced
2-3 tablespoons peanut
    or corn oil
small piece ginger,
    scraped and sliced
4 eggs, beaten
dash sesame oil
mandarin pancakes (see
    page 134)

SERVES 4

Drain the golden needles and cloud ears or Chinese mushrooms and slice into fine strips. Mix together the soy sauce, if using, wine or sherry, pepper and scallions. Prepare the pork and bamboo shoots. Heat one tablespoon of oil and fry the ginger for 30 seconds without browning. Now add the beaten eggs and scramble them until they are just firm. Lift out and break up. Clean the wok and heat the remaining oil. Add the pork and stir over a brisk heat for about 1-2 minutes until it changes color. Add the bamboo shoots then stir in the mushrooms and the flavoring mixture Toss continuously for 1 minute then add the scrambled egg and toss again. Draw from the heat, stir in the sesame oil and taste for seasoning. Reheat the mandarin pancakes meanwhile. Each person places a portion of the egg mixture on a pancake and rolls it up before eating.

Left **Suan-la t'ang** *This
hot and sour soup is a
classic Chinese dish. Both
these flavors are
prominent at the same
time as complementing
each other.*

Right *Chinese
mushrooms, as used in*
Mu hsu jou, *need
soaking in water before
using. The dry
mushrooms, Fragrant or
Winter mushrooms,
actually grow on trees,
whereas the canned
variety, Straw
Mushrooms, are grown
on a bed of straw.*

Braised Carp

1 carp (2lb3oz/1kg) or bream, gutted and scaled, but head and tail left on	1 tablespoon light soy sauce
	1¼ cups fish or chicken stock
salt	1 tablespoon cornstarch
deep fat for frying	rice wine or dry sherry to taste
1in/2½cm fresh ginger, scraped, sliced and cut into slivers	seasoning to taste
2 cloves garlic, crushed	1 red chili, seeded and cut into fine strips
6 scallions, roots removed, white part left whole and tops cut into strips	coriander leaves

SERVES 2-3

Slash the flesh of the fish at ½in/1cm intervals on each side, dry on paper towels and rub lightly with salt. Lower carefully into the hot fat and cook for 5 minutes, then lift out onto a platter lined with paper towels. Pour off all except three tablespoons of the oil and fry the ginger, garlic and white parts of the scallions. Stir in soy sauce and stock. Replace the fish in the pan and cook for a further 15-20 minutes or until tender. Lift the fish onto a serving platter. Blend the cornstarch to a paste with water and stir into the pan to thicken the sauce. Add rice wine or sherry and seasoning to taste. Pour this sauce over the fish and garnish with the scallion tops, chili and coriander.

Chih pao chi
(Paper wrapped chicken)

2 fresh chicken breasts, skin and bone removed	1½in/1cm fresh ginger, scraped and sliced, then crushed in garlic press
3 tablespoons light soy sauce	1 small bunch scallions, washed and dried
1 tablespoon Chinese rice wine or dry sherry	⅔ cup cooked ham
1 tablespoon sugar	oil for deep frying
freshly ground black pepper	stir fried snow peas or brocolli to garnish

MAKES 15

Cut the chicken into pieces the size of your little finger. Marinate in a mixture of soy sauce, wine or sherry, sugar, black pepper and ginger. Meanwhile cut the scallions into 2in/5cm lengths and the ham into small pieces. Prepare 7in/18cm squares of waxed paper to make the parcels. Brush the paper with oil, then lay a piece of marinated chicken in the middle, top with a few of the scallions, ham and another piece of chicken. Fold the paper up almost corner to corner to make a triangle. Fold sides to middle to make an envelope shape, then tuck the flap in to form a neat parcel. (Seal with a staple if you prefer, but do warn your guests when they open their parcels). Repeat with the remaining ingredients. Fry several parcels in hot oil for 2-3 minutes. Do not overcook or let the paper turn brown. Serve garnished with snow peas or brocolli and any remaining scallions. Serve this dish hot.

Right **Drunken chicken**
It is small wonder that this chicken is so named! However, the alcohol is not overpowering and the dish is not unlike the French Coq au vin *in flavor. A green vegetable complements the pale color of the chicken.*

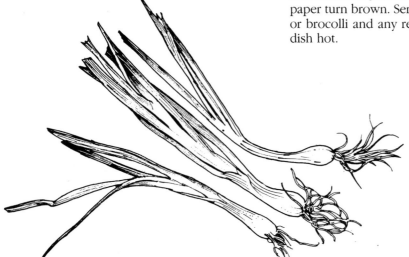

Tsui Chi

(Drunken chicken)

1 × 3lb/1.4kg fresh
   chicken
$\frac{1}{2}$in/1cm fresh ginger,
   scraped and sliced
2 shallots
7$\frac{1}{2}$ cups water or to

1 tablespoon salt
1$\frac{1}{4}$ cups dry sherry
few tablespoons brandy
   (optional)
scallion curls to
   garnish

SERVES 4-6

Wipe the chicken inside and out. Place the ginger and the scallions in the body cavity. Set the chicken in a large pan or oven-proof casserole and cover with water. Bring to a boil, skim and cook for 15 minutes. Turn off the heat and allow the chicken to stay in the cooking liquid for 3-4 hours, by which time it will be cooked. Lift out and drain well. Reserve 1$\frac{1}{4}$ cups/300ml the stock. Cool and skim.

First of all remove the leg joints — divide each into a drumstick and thigh. Now cut away the wings to include some of the breast. Cut away the breast still on the bone and divide it into two pieces. Arrange these chicken portions in a shallow glass or glazed dish (only use enamel if it is unchipped). Rub salt into the skin of the chicken, leave for several hours or overnight. Next day mix the sherry and brandy, if you are using it, with an equal amount of chicken stock and pour over the chicken pieces. Cover with plastic wrap or a lid and leave in a refrigerator or cool place for at least 2 or 3 days; turn over occasionally. When ready to serve, cut into chunky pieces through the bone and arrange on a serving platter garnished with scallion curls.

Peh-ching K'ao Ya and Po-ping
(Peking duck with mandarin pancakes)

4lb/1.75kg duckling
3 tablespoons honey
2 tablespoons water
salt
1 bunch scallions
½ cucumber, cut into
   thin, finger-like strips

12 mandarin pancakes
   (see page 134)

Dipping sauce
¼ cup hoisin sauce
a little thick soy sauce to
   taste

SERVES 8

Bring a large pan of water to the boil and plunge in the duckling to scald the skin. Carefully lift out and drain thoroughly. Secure the legs with string and leave to drip over a bowl overnight in a cool dry place. Blend the honey, water and salt together and use to brush over the duck skin. Hang up again and leave for 2-3 hours. Repeat and leave to dry completely for a further 3-4 hours. Set the duck on a rack over a roasting pan and place in the center of a hot oven (450°F/230°C). Immediately reduce the oven temperature to moderate (approximately 350°F/180°C) and cook for 1¼ hours. Check that the skin is crisp (do not baste the duckling) and, if you think it necessary, increase the oven temperature for the last 15 minutes. Meanwhile remove the root from the scallions, then cut in half lengthwise and cut in half again. Pop in ice cold water.

Prepare cucumber, drain and dry on paper towels. Prepare the mandarin pancakes and the sauce. Carve the duckling at the table; traditionally only the skin was eaten, but these days most people carve the skin and meat together into 1½in/4cm pieces. This is then dipped into the prepared sauce and deftly rolled up together with some of the scallions before eating.

Mandarin pancakes
2¼ cups
   flour
¼ teaspoon salt

⅞ cup boiling
   water (approx)
3 tablespoons peanut or
   sesame oil

MAKES 20

Sift the flour and salt into a bowl or food processor. Gradually add sufficient boiling water and one tablespoon of the oil to form a soft but not sticky dough. Knead for 2-3 minutes or 30 seconds

in the food processor. Allow to rest for 30 minutes. Divide the dough into 20-24 pieces. Roll out each evenly into a 5in/13cm or 7in/18cm rounds. Brush the surface of half the rounds with oil and sandwich pairs together, matching the size as near as possible. When the pancakes are ready, brush the surface of a heavy frying pan sparingly with oil. Even better, have two pans to speed up the process. Place the pancakes in the pan one at a time and cook over a gentle heat until the pancake is puffy but not colored. Turn over and cook a further 2-3 minutes.

Lift out and pull the two pancakes apart. Pile up on a plate while cooking the remainder. Keep hot covered with foil. Serve hot or, alternatively, place the plate of pancakes, covered with foil, in a bamboo steamer over a wok until they are soft and heated through.

Any left-over pancakes can be frozen for use on another occasion. Simply wrap up frozen pancakes in a foil parcel and steam for 10 minutes before serving.

Above **Peking duck** *This is probably the most famous Chinese dish. A true Peking duck differs to the common duck; it is pure white in color and is force-fed to the correct weight. Elaborate slaughtering and preparation exercises are carried out before the actual cooking can commence. Carving and presentation are then as important as any of the previous treatment. To do traditionally really does require some ceremony! However you can just prepare as the recipe says.*

135

Shua Yang Jou

(Mongolian hotpot or fire-pot)

2lb/900g boned leg lamb
   (ask the butcher for
   the bones to make
   4 cups stock)
½lb/225g lambs liver or
   kidney
3¾ cups prepared
   chicken stock
½in/1cm fresh ginger,
   scraped and sliced
a little dry sherry
seasoning to taste
½ Chinese cabbage
   (bok choy),
   washed and shredded
few young spinach leaves
2 squares sliced, fresh
   bean curd (optional)
¼ cup transparent
   noodles

Dipping sauce
¼ cup red wine
   vinegar
½-1 tablespoon thick soy
   sauce
½in/1cm fresh ginger
   root, scraped and
   shredded
2 tablespoons finely
   shredded
   scallions
2. A range of other
   bottled sauces can be
   arranged such as:
tomato sauce
chilli
mustard of your choice
sesame oil
3. Steamed rolls (see
   page 148) to eat with
   the hotpot

SERVES 6-8

Set the lamb aside and prepare a good stock from the bones. Trim the calves liver and remove the skin and core from the kidneys. The meats can be popped in the freezer for a while before slicing to make the meat easier to cut finely. At any rate you require a sharp knife and a steady hand or ask the butcher to do this for you. Blend equal quantities of the lamb and chicken stocks together to fill the 'moat' of the hotpot or fondue dish. Reserve some of the remaining stock just in case the moat has to be replenished. Add the ginger, sherry and season. Cook for 15 minutes in a large pan and transfer to the 'moat' just before eating.

Meanwhile slice the meats finely and arrange attractively on a platter, the Chinese cabbage, spinach and bean curd on a separate platter. Leave the noodles to soak until required. Prepare the dip (1) by blending all the ingredients together. The other sauces should be spooned onto small dishes on a serving tray with a basket of steamed flower rolls. When the stock is simmering each guest cooks his own portions of meat in the hot stock, using chopsticks. Dip the meat in the sauce of your choice or accompaniments, before eating with a roll. When all the meat is used up, add Chinese cabbage and spinach and noodles to the moat and cook for a minute or two.

Ch'a Yeh Tan
(Tea eggs)

6 eggs, gently boiled for 20 minutes
2 tablespoons thick soy sauce
1 teaspoon salt
½ star anise
2 tablespoons tea or 2 teabags

MAKES 6

Allow the eggs to cool in the water then gently crack the shells to mark them without removing any of the shell itself. Return the eggs to a pan of cold water with the soy sauce, salt, anise and tea. Bring to the boil, cover and simmer for 1½–2 hours. Check the pan from time to time and add more boiling water as necessary to keep tne eggs covered. Allow them to cool in the liquid overnight. Remove the shells. The surface of the eggs will be covered with a maze of fine lines. Cut into quarters and serve as part of a meal.

Left **Shua yang jou** *The hotpot* (below left) *is a common way of cooking meat and vegetables and even fish. However, the northern hotpot is traditionally meat, with a range of vegetables and sauces* (above left).

Below **Chinese toffee apples** *These are not toffee apples as we know them. The apple pieces are dipped into iced water by the guests at the table to harden the caramel. They are a fun party idea.*

Chinese Toffee Apples

Fritter batter
1 cup flour
a good pinch salt
½ cup water

2 tablespoons cooking oil
2 egg whites

4 crisp eating apples

1 tablespoon flour
good quality oil for deep frying
1 cup granulated sugar
4 tablespoons water
a few toasted sesame seeds
ice cold water

SERVES 8

To prepare the batter, sift the flour and salt together. Slowly stir water and oil into it to make a smooth batter. Set it aside with egg whites at room temperature until required. Peel, core and cut the apples into eighths, and dust these with flour. Whisk up the egg whites and fold them into the batter. Holding the apple pieces on a skewer dip each one in the batter and then fry in hot oil until golden brown. Drain on kitchen paper. Heat the sugar and water in a heavy pan, stirring all the time until the sugar dissolves. When the caramel becomes pale golden, remove from the heat. Dip the fritters in this and transfer to oiled serving bowls. Sprinkle with sesame seeds. Take a bowl (or individual bowls) of iced water to the table so that guests can dip each fritter in it to harden the caramel.

Eastern China, Shanghai and Fukien

Shanghai Spring Rolls

6 Chinese mushrooms,
    soaked in warm
    water for 30 minutes
2 cakes bean curd
1 cup finely ground
    pork
peanut or corn oil for
    frying
1 1/2 cups cooked
    shrimp, chopped
    coarsely
1/2 teaspoon cornstarch,
    mixed to a paste with
    1 tablespoon light soy
    sauce

1/2 cup each bamboo
    shoot and water
    chestnuts, sliced finely
1 1/4 cups bean sprouts
6 scallions, finely
    chopped
a little sesame oil
12 spring roll wrappers,
    thawed and
    separated, covered
    with damp cloth
deep fat for frying
hoisin sauce for dipping

SERVES 12

Drain the mushrooms, remove stalks and cut into fine matchstick-like pieces; slice the bean curd similarly. Fry the ground pork in a little hot oil until it changes colour, stirring all the time. Cook for 2-3 minutes. Add the shrimp then the cornstarch paste and keep breaking up the mixture with a slice. Now add the bamboo shoot, water chestnuts, bean sprouts and scallions over a high heat stirring all the time. Add the mushrooms and bean curd. Taste for seasoning and stir in the sesame oil away from the heat. Allow to cool before filling the spring roll wrappers exactly as described below. Deep fry in the same way and drain one by one on absorbent kitchen towels. Serve hot with hoisin sauce for dipping.

Right **Shanghai spring rolls** These rolls are world famous and are popular everywhere.

Folding spring roll wrappers

1 Use a palette knife to separate out each of the spring roll wrappers. Then keep them under a slightly damp cloth so that they do not dry out.
2 Position the first one in a diamond shape in front of you. Place a spoonful of the filling just inside the corner nearest to you.
3 Then, fold over this corner to cover the piece of filling. Take a brush, dipped in flour and water mix, and dab this around the further two sides.
4 Fold in the two outside corners, tucking them against the roll.
5 Continue to roll up the wrapper and press down so that it sticks. The completed roll is now ready for cooking.

Wonton Soup

20 ready prepared
   wonton wrappers (see
   page 57)
1/2 cup lean pork,
   finely ground
1 teaspoon finely
   chopped ginger
2 teaspoons light soy
   sauce

salt to taste
1/2 cup spinach,
   washed and dried

Soup
6 1/4 cups chicken
   stock
1-2 tablespoons dry
   sherry or rice wine

SERVES 6-8

If the wonton wrappers have been frozen, thaw
then separate carefully and leave under a slightly
damp cloth to prevent them drying out while
preparing the filling. Mix the pork, ginger, soy sauce and salt together. Place a tiny teaspoon of the filling into the center of each wonton, positioned like a diamond in front of you. Take the nearest point over the filling and tuck it in. Roll up to within 1/2in/1cm of the top peak of the triangle. Damp the edges very lightly then pull the side wings under the wonton and seal to form 'a little hat'. Repeat with the remaining filling and wrappers. Remove the stems from the spinach, tear into shreds and leave aside. Heat the chicken stock and pop the wontons in the soup. Cook for 3-5 minutes or until the wontons are almost cooked. Now add the spinach and cook for 1 minute. Add sherry if using and taste for seasoning. Serve the soup very hot.

Below **Wonton soup**
Wontons are particlarly
good in a soup. They are
filling, but delicious.

Crab with Eggs

4 eggs, beaten
$\frac{1}{2}$-$\frac{3}{4}$ cup
    crabmeat
1 teaspoon sugar
1 small piece ginger,
    scraped and crushed
    in garlic press

2 teaspoon light soy
    sauce
seasoning
a little oil for frying
4-6 scallions, finely
    chopped

SERVES 4

Set the beaten egg on one side, pick over the crabmeat to remove any shell or cartilage. Stir in sugar, ginger and soy sauce and season to taste. Add this to the beaten eggs and scramble in fat in a pan for 1 minute. Add the scallions and serve at once.

Red Cooked Chicken

1 × 3lb/1.4kg fresh
    chicken
1 clove garlic, peeled
    and crushed
$\frac{1}{2}$in/1cm fresh ginger,
    scraped and chopped

$\frac{7}{8}$ cup chicken
    stock
$\frac{7}{8}$ cup each light
    and dark soy sauce
1 star anise
1 tablespoon sugar
2 tablespoons sherry

SERVES 4-6

Plunge the chicken into a pan of boiling water to completely cover it. Cook for 3-4 minutes. Carefully lift out and drain. Place, breast-side down, in another large pan or ovenproof casserole and add the garlic, ginger, chicken stock, soy sauces, star anise, sugar and sherry. Allow to come to the boil, cover and simmer for 45-60 minutes or until the chicken is tender, turning it over two or three times so that it is evenly cooked in the rich sauce. Turn by inserting a roasting fork into the body cavity to prevent damage to the skin on the breast. Allow it to cool slightly, then lift out and chop into bite-size pieces to serve. You can cut it in a traditional Chinese way so that when the portions are reassembled on the plate, it looks like the whole chicken again. Serve scattered with scallion curls.

The sauce can be used again, several times in fact, with the flavor improving on each occasion as it gets stronger and mature.

Anita Wong's Duck

1 × 4lb/1.75kg fresh
    duckling
2 cloves garlic, chopped
4 tablespoons cooking oil
1in/2.5cm piece fresh
    ginger, sliced thinly
3 tablespoons bean paste
2 tablespoons light soy
    sauce

1 tablespoon dark soy
    sauce
1 tablespoon sugar
$\frac{1}{2}$ teaspoon five spice
    powder
3 points star anise
$1\frac{7}{8}$ cups duck stock or
    water
salt to taste

SERVES 4

Use the giblets to make a duck stock; strain and reserve $1\frac{7}{8}$ cups. Heat the oil, fry the garlic without browning, then add the duck. Fry, turning frequently until the outside is slightly brown. Lift out the duck. Add the ginger, then bean paste to the pan. Cook to bring out the flavors. Add light and dark soy sauces, sugar and five spice powder. Return the duck to the pan and fry in this mixture to coat the outside of the duck. Add the star anise, duck stock and seasoning to taste. Cover and cook over a gentle heat until the duck is tender, stirring occasionally. Allow 2-2$\frac{1}{2}$ hours. Skim off any fat or oil, then leave in sauce to cool. Cut into serving portions. Serve with the skimmed sauce poured over the portions, which will set like jelly. Garnish with scallions. Eat with rice.

Above *The chemicals that preserved eggs are coated in, penetrate the shell and affect the color of yolk and white — but do not be put off by this!*

Shih Tzu Tou
(Lion's head)

*1lb/450g lean pork,
    ground finely with a
    little fat
4-6 water chestnuts
    (from a can), finely
    chopped
1 teaspoon finely
    chopped ginger
1 tablespoon finely
    chopped onion
2 tablespoons soy sauce
seasoning to taste*

*sufficient beaten egg to
    bind mixture
2 tablespoons cornstarch
a little peanut oil for
    frying
1¼ cups chicken stock
a little sugar
seasoning
1½ cups each Chinese
    cabbage and spinach
    leaves, washed, dried
    and shredded*

SERVES 2-3

Mix the pork, water chestnuts, ginger, onion, one tablespoon of the soy sauce and seasoning together. Bind with sufficient beaten egg and form into eight balls. Toss in a little of the seasoned cornstarch and make a paste with the remaining cornstarch and water. Fry the balls in the hot oil to brown all over then transfer them to another pan or ovenproof casserole. Add stock, sugar, seasoning and the remaining tablespoon of soy sauce. Cover and simmer for 20-25 minutes then increase the heat and add the Chinese cabbage and spinach. Cook for 3-4 minutes. Lift out the vegetables with a slotted spoon onto a serving platter. Arrange the lion's heads on top and keep warm. Thicken the gravy with the cornstarch paste and pour over just before serving.

Left **Shih tzu ton** *Lion's head is an apt description for these meat balls. The Eastern region of China, where this dish originated, has some fascinating sites. The tranquil countryside just outside Shanghai, for example, has changed little over the years; this is a scene on the Yangtze River delta (above). Inside Shanghai, the traditional tea-houses are still very much part of life (right).*

Western China — Szechwan

Szechwan Shrimps

1½lb/675g fresh shrimp
1 teaspoon sugar
2 tablespoons tomato
   ketchup
1 tablespoon chili sauce
1 tablespoon thick soy
   sauce
2 cloves garlic crushed
½in/1cm ginger, scraped
   and finely chopped
oil for frying

1-2 teaspoon Szechwan
   peppercorns, dry fried
   and crushed
1 tablespoon rice wine
   vinegar
2fl.oz/50ml stock or
   water
salt to taste
a few chopped
   scallions

SERVES 6

Remove the heads and body shells from the shrimp, but leave on the tails. Sprinkle with sugar and set aside. Blend the ketchup, chili and soy sauce together. Fry the garlic and ginger in oil without browning. Add crushed peppercorns and the shrimp. Toss well and when the shrimp are firm and pink add the sauce mixture. Cook for 1 minute, then add vinegar, stock or water and salt to taste. Cook again for 1 minute, stir in most of the scallions. Serve on a warmed platter, scattered with the remaining scallions.

Below **Szechwan shrimp** *These shrimp are coated in a thick* *sauce, which is best accompanied with plain rice.*

144

Szechwan Chicken with Tangerine Peel

1 × 3lb/1.4kg chicken
3 tablespoons light soy
  sauce
3 tablespoons dry sherry
salt
3 scallions
3 tablespoons seasoned
  cornstarch
deep fat for frying
1-2 dried red peppers (or
  more if you like this
  dish hot), dry fried
  then crushed

$\frac{1}{2}$ teaspoon Szechwan
  peppercorns, crushed
1 piece dried tangerine
  peel, crushed
2 tablespoons rice wine
  vinegar
$\frac{5}{8}$ cup chicken stock
  (approx)
salt to taste

SERVES 4-6

Cut the chicken into eight pieces first and then each of these into a further two or three pieces. Marinate for 3-4 hours in soy sauce together with sherry, salt and one chopped scallion. Chop the remaining scallions and then set aside for garnish. Drain the chicken pieces and reserve the marinade. Dust the chicken with cornstarch and deep fry in two or three lots for about 7 minutes or until golden and crisp. Lift out and keep warm. In another pan, heat a little oil and fry the pepper, peppercorns and crushed tangerine rind for a minute. Add the cooked chicken pieces and toss all together. Pour in the vinegar and cook over a higher heat until the vinegar evaporates. Keep moving the chicken around in the pan. Add sufficient stock to the marinade to make up to $\frac{7}{8}$ cup. Pour into the pan. Do not cover and cook for 15 minutes or until the liquid evaporates, stirring occasionally. Serve at once sprinkled with scallions.

Left The western school or Szechwan style of cooking is generally considered to be fairly hot. This is not always the case and they usually like to blend hot, sweet, sour and so on. As a landlocked region they do not have any sea-water fish, but there are inland lakes to provide some fish. As seen here, these lakes also provide the necessary water for growing rice around the edges.

Hui Kwo Juo
(Twice cooked pork)

2lb/900g belly of pork, rind and bones removed after weighing	*¹/₂-1 tablespoon sugar a little oil for frying*
4 tablespoons black beans from a can, rinsed	*2 cloves garlic, peeled and crushed*
1 tablespoon soybean paste	*¹/₂in/1cm ginger, peeled and finely chopped*
2 tablespoons soy sauce	*¹/₄ cup chicken stock*
1 tablespoon tomato purée	*2 tablespoons sherry few drops sesame oil*
1 tablespoon hoisin sauce	*few pieces bamboo shoot, finely sliced*
2 teaspoons chili sauce	*scallion curls to garnish*

SERVES 6

Place the pork into a pan of boiling water and cook for just over 30 minutes or until tender. Lift out, drain, cool a little and cut into slices, a finger width, and then each slice into four pieces, and set aside. Drain the beans. Blend the soya bean paste with soy sauce, tomato paste, hoisin and chili sauce. Stir in sugar. Mash the black beans to a paste. Heat the oil in a wok, and fry the garlic and ginger, add the mashed beans, stir well, then add the meat and the mixture of sauces. Toss the meat well to coat each piece with the sauce. Add stock and extra water if the sauce is too thick. Cook for 5 minutes. Increase the heat, add the bamboo shoot slices, sherry and the sesame oil. Serve on a warm platter garnished with scallion curls.

Above **Hui kwo juo** *Red or green peppers can be* *added to this pork for some color contrast*

Beef with Black Bean Sauce

1lb/450g best steak	*oil for frying*
1 tablespoon cornstarch	*¹/₂-1 tablespoon red peppercorns, dry fried then crushed*
1 egg white, lightly whisked	*1 teaspoon brown sugar*
1 tablespoon light soy sauce	*1 piece bamboo shoot, shredded*
3 tablespoons black beans, soaked in water for 30 minutes	*1 leek, or 2-3 spring onions, cleaned and shredded*
¹/₂in/1cm ginger, scraped and pounded	*3-4fl.oz/85-120ml chicken or beef stock*
3-4 cloves garlic, peeled and crushed	*sesame oil*

SERVES 6

Cut the beef into thin slices and then into strips, 1in/2.5cm wide. Blend the cornstarch with egg white and soy sauce. Marinate the beef in this while preparing other ingredients. Drain the black beans and pound in a pestle and mortar with the ginger and garlic. Heat the oil in a wok, add the beef and toss well until the meat changes color. Lift out and reserve. Clean the pan, add a little more oil then fry the black bean paste until it gives off a rich aroma. Add the peppercorns and sugar. Cook for 1 minute, then add the bamboo shoot and leek or scallions. Toss well, add the stock, then return the beef to the pan. When the meat is hot turn it onto a serving dish and sprinkle over a little sesame oil.

146

Szechwan Noodles with Peanut Sauce and Vegetables

*3 cups fresh egg
    noodles or dried
    noodles, cooked
    according to packet
    directions
4 tablespoons oil for
    frying*

Sauce
*2 large tablespoons
    crunchy peanut
    butter
1 tablespoon hot oil and
    1 teaspoon sesame oil*

Garnish
*a handful of dry fried
    peanuts, lightly
    crushed
2 scallions,
    shredded
1¹/₂ cups bean sprouts,
    blanched in boiling
    water for 1 minute,
    rinsed in cold water
    and drained
¹/₄-¹/₂ cucumber, cut into
    small chunks
a few radishes*

SERVES 6

Plunge the noodles into boiling water for 1 minute. Rinse with cold water and leave on one side to dry. Meanwhile prepare the sauce by blending the peanut butter with hot oil and sesame oil to a smooth paste. Prepare the garnishes. Now fry the noodles in two or three lots in hot oil. Flatten out on one side and, when hot, turn over and fry on the other side. Keep warm while cooking the other noodles. Pile onto a large platter and pour over the sauce — mix lightly then scatter with peanuts and scallions. Arrange the bean sprouts, cucumber and radishes either around the noodles or in separate bowls.

This is an original way of serving noodles and a very tasty one. If you like peanut-tasting food, I highly recommend it.

Southern China — Canton

Steamed Buns

The basic dough

3 teaspoons sugar (use only 1 teaspoon for flower rolls)	1½ tablespoons dried yeast
1¼ cups warm water (approx), depending on the flour used	4½ cups strong or plain flour
	1 teaspoon salt
	1 tablespoon lard

MAKES 16

Dissolve the sugar in half the water then sprinkle into the yeast. Stir and leave for 10-15 minutes until the mixture is frothy. Meanwhile sift the flour and salt together in a bowl and leave in a warm place or put into a food processor. Stir in the yeast mixture with sufficient of the remaining water to make a soft but not sticky dough. Knead for 1 minute in the food processor, or on a floured board by hand for 10 minutes. Pop into a large, oiled plastic bag, seal the top and leave in a warm place until it doubles in size. Knock out air bubbles and knead again for 5 minutes or 30 seconds in the food processor. Now make into one of the following.

Steamed Flower Rolls

Dough prepared as above	1 tablespoon sesame seed oil

MAKES 16

Divide the dough into two. Roll each piece into a rectangular shape, 12 × 8in/30 × 20cm. Brush the surface of one with sesame oil and set the other piece on top. Roll up like a jelly roll, trim the ends and cut into 16 even-sized pieces. Take the 'rolls' one by one and press down firmly on the rolled side with a chopstick. Now place the roll on the countertop, coiled side uppermost, and pinch the opposite ends with fingers of both hands, and then pull the ends underneath and seal. The dough should separate into petals. Place, sealed-side down, on lightly greased trays or on waxed paper that will fit into the steamer. Allow them to rise until they are double in size, then steam over fast bubbling water for 35 minutes.

Pork–Stuffed Steamed Buns

dough prepared as above	2 tablespoons chopped scallions
Filling	½ tablespoon yellow bean sauce, crushed
8oz/225g roast pork, very finely chopped	½ tablespoon sugar
a little oil for frying	1 teaspoon cornstarch mixed to a paste with water
1 clove garlic, peeled and crushed	

MAKES 16

Prepare the dough. While it is rising for the first time prepare the filling. Place the pork on a plate. Heat the oil and fry the garlic, then add pork, scallions and crushed bean sauce (this can be done in a pestle and mortar). Add sugar and thicken slightly with cornstarch paste. Draw from heat and cool. Divide the dough into 16 pieces; roll each out into 3-4 in/7.5-10cm rounds. Place a spoonful of filling into the center of each and gather up the sides and cover the filling. Twist the top to seal. Set on cheesecloth or some waxed paper in a steamer and leave to double in size. Cook over fast-boiling water for 30-35 minutes or until cooked.

Date Filling for Steamed Buns

dough prepared as above	½ cup red or yellow bean paste
Filling	¾ cup red dates or prunes, soaked and chopped
2 tablespoons pork fat or lard	

MAKES 16

Prepare the dough and then the filling. Render the pork fat or heat the lard. Stir in the bean paste and the chopped, soaked and drained dates or prunes. Cool before filling the buns as in the above recipe, but place in steamer, sealed-side down. The traditional Chinese way to denote a sweet filling is to dip the end of the chopstick into red colouring and mark a dot on top of each.

Right Dim sum *is a classic Chinese delight. These small snacks are, in fact, a Cantonese invention.*

You can try any of your own fillings, using the basic dough recipe.

Southern China or the Cantonese region grows plenty of rice. The water buffalo have been the farmers' companions for many years, and can be seen circling the paddy-fields daily (right). Their dim sum snacks include steamed rice, or glutinous rice, wrapped up in lotus leaves. Chicken is usually mixed in with the rice, and it is served as just a part of the dim sum lunch (above). People help themselves; there are generally no fixed portions.

Above right *This is a typical Cantonese store, selling a great assortment of dried foods, pencils, towels and so on.*

Cantonese Egg Foo Yung
(Chinese omelet)

6 Chinese mushrooms,
   soaked in warm
   water for 30 minutes
⅓ cup cooked, roast
   pork, cut into fine
   strips
¾ cup bean sprouts,
   rinsed and drained
6 water chestnuts, cut
   into fine strips

1 handful of Chinese
   cabbage or spinach,
   rinsed and shredded
a little cooking oil
4 eggs, beaten
salt and freshly ground
   black pepper
few pinches sugar
dash dry sherry

SERVES 4-6

Drain the mushrooms and dry them, then shred into matchstick-like pieces. Set on one side with the pork, bean sprouts, chestnuts and cabbage or spinach. Heat a little oil in a pan. Toss in the meat and vegetables and turn over all the time. Lift out, cool, then stir into the egg mixture. Clean and reheat a little more oil in the pan, then turn in the egg mixture. When the omelet sets on one side sprinkle with seasoning and sugar. Turn over and cook for a further minute. Drizzle the sherry over the top and serve the omelet immediately, while the flavor of the sherry is still strong.

Chen Chu Jou Wan
(Shrimp and noodle balls)

¾ cup Chinese rice
   vermicelli (bee-
   hoon)
1½ cups peeled shrimp
½ teaspoon sugar
4 tablespoons pork fat

few slices fresh ginger
salt and pepper
very little, lightly beaten
   egg white
oil for deep frying

MAKES 15

Crush the beehoon finely and leave in a dry place. Grind the shrimp (use a food processor for this), sprinkle with sugar. Grind the pork fat with fresh ginger, add the shrimp with seasoning and bind together. Use wetted hands to form into even, bite-size balls. Chill well, and roll in crushed beehoon just before frying in hot oil. Cook for about 3-4 minutes until cooked through, or steam in a bamboo steamer over hot water for 30 minutes.

Canton is on the edge of the South China Sea, from where it reaps a great haul of fish. This is either sold fresh or dried (right). Shrimps and prawns are also sold in abundance (above).

Fish with Sweet and Sour Sauce

A whole fish such as
  bream or red snapper
  (2lb3oz/1kg) or fish
  steaks
4 tablespoons flour
shallow oil for frying

Sauce
3 tablespoons tomato
  ketchup
1 tablespoon sugar
2 tablespoons Chinese
  rice wine or dry
  sherry
1 tablespoon soy sauce
2 tablespoons vinegar
2 teaspoons cornstarch
⅞ cup water
salt

2 tablespoons oil
1 clove garlic, crushed
1 small onion, peeled
  and sliced
½in/1cm piece fresh
  ginger, scraped and
  cut into shreds
1-2 slices pineapple, cut
  into fine chunks
few water chestnuts, cut
  into wedges, or lychees
¼ each red and green
  pepper, deseeded and
  cut into strips
1 red chilli, deseeded
  and cut into fine
  shreds
fresh coriander to
  garnish

SERVES 4-6

If using steaks or fish make sure that they are of uniform thickness for even cooking. Make sure that you gut the fish, leaving the head and tail on, but trimming off the fins. Clean and dry, then dust the steaks or whole fish with seasoned flour and fry in hot oil for 5 minutes on each side or until cooked through. Set aside and keep warm while preparing the sauce.

Blend the tomato ketchup with sugar, rice wine and sherry, soy sauce and vinegar. Blend the cornstarch with some of the water to a paste. Stir into the tomato mixture and add the remaining water. Add a pinch of salt. Heat the oil, fry the garlic and onion without browning for 1 minute. Fold in the cornstarch sauce mixture and stir until the sauce is smooth and thickens. Reduce the heat, stir in the ginger, pineapple, water chestnuts or lychees, red and green pepper and chili. Pour over the fish, laid out on a serving platter, and garnish attractively with fresh coriander leaves.

Fish markets abound in this southern area. You can be sure you are buying it in tip-top condition and absolutely fresh (left). All fresh fish and shellfish has to be kept on ice to protect it from the tremendous heat. The shrimp are generally weighed out on little hand-scales (above). Skinned, dried fish is also sold (top). This man is busy skinning his fish for his customers.

155

Left **Chicken buried in salt** *This is precisely what happens to this chicken. It is rich in vitamins and generally comes out a white color because no direct heat reaches it. Pigeon can be substituted for chicken.*

Chicken Buried in Salt

The Chinese claim that this method of cooking ensures that the bird is full of vitamins and is especially good eaten on its own just before going to sleep!

1 × 2lb/900g fresh chicken	*salt and pepper*
2in/5cm piece fresh ginger	*15 cups coarse salt (depending on size of casserole)*

SERVES 4

Remove the giblets from the chicken; dry inside and out with kitchen paper. Tie at the neck with a piece of string and tie up over a bowl so that the chicken will drain and dry. Peel and bruise the ginger; place inside the body cavity of the bird and wrap the chicken in a sheet of oiled waxed paper. Tie with a piece of string. Cover the base of an ovenproof casserole with some of the salt. Set in the chicken and spoon the remaining salt over it to completely cover. Cover with a tight fitting lid or foil.

Set in a hot oven (approximately 400°F/200°C) and cook for 1½ hours. Cool a little then lift the chicken parcel out of the casserole carefully spooning out some of the salt first; it will be hot. Unwrap the parcel and serve the chicken on a platter. Cut up into small portions.

Cantonese Chicken

1 × 2½lb/1.25kg chicken	*oil for deep frying*
salt	*scallion curls and*
1 tablespoon cornstarch	*pieces of cucumber to*
2 tablespoons sherry	*garnish*
2 tablespoons liquid honey	

SERVES 3-4

Rinse the chicken inside and out thoroughly. Plunge it into a large pan of boiling water for 1 minute. Lift out carefully, drain and dry thoroughly. Tie up by the feet and dry out for 3-4 hours. Rub the skin with salt and suspend overnight in a cool, dry place. Blend the cornstarch and sherry, then stir in the honey. Rub the skin of the chicken with this mixture and leave for several hours or overnight. Lift the chicken into a frying basket and lower into a large pan of deep fat, lifting out several times to allow the fat to regain heat. The chicken will be cooked in 50-60 minutes and the skin will be crisp and golden.

The traditional way of cooking this chicken is called 'splash frying' where the chicken is placed into the frying basket, but ladlefuls of hot oil are constantly poured over it. Drain thoroughly and cut into even size, smallish pieces. Serve garnished with scallions and cucumber and perhaps a hoisin sauce for dipping mouthfuls.

Chicken Feet in Bean Paste Sauce

Each time we have a chicken we keep the feet and store them in the freezer until we have enough for this recipe. I have seen them for sale from the freezer in Chinese supermarkets. This dish is served as part of a buffet.

2lb/900g chicken feet (24 approx)	1¹⁄₂in/3.5mm piece fresh ginger
1 teaspoon oyster sauce	3 cloves garlic
1 teaspoon thin soy sauce	1 tablespoon bean paste
1 teaspoon thick soy sauce	2 tablespoons oil
1 teaspoon sesame oil	1¹⁄₂ tablespoons dried mushrooms, washed and soaked in
¹⁄₂ teaspoon five spice powder	2¹⁄₂ cups cold water for 30 minutes
freshly ground pepper	salt to taste
deep oil for frying	1 tablespoon cornstarch

SERVES 6

Wash the chicken feet well — trimming off the nails. Put the feet into a pan of boiling, salted water until they become stiff; drain. Mix the oyster and both soy sauces, sesame oil, five spice powder and pepper together. Pour this over the feet and mix well. Set aside for as long as possible, at least 1 hour. Heat the oil in a wok, fry the

feet until they are golden brown and crisp. If the fat splutters and splashes a lot you can cover the wok with a lid. Lift out and pop into cold water. Meanwhile peel and slice the ginger and garlic. Set aside one-third of each for frying and finely pound the rest with the bean paste. First fry the ginger and garlic in oil to bring out the flavor. Add the pounded ingredients and fry over a brisk heat. Stir in 1⁷⁄₈ cups of the juice drained from the mushrooms and taste for salt. Place the drained chicken feet in an ovenproof casserole. Pop in the mushrooms and pour over the sauce. Cover and cook in a moderate oven (approximately 350°F/180°C) for 30 minutes then reduce the heat to about 300°F/150°C, and cook for 3-4 hours or until the feet are tender. Mix the cornstarch to a paste with a little water, stir into the sauce to thicken just before serving.

Kao P'ai Ku
(Barbecued spareribs)

2lb/900g pork spareribs (sheets of ribs)	1 tablespoon thin soy sauce
2 teaspoons salt	3 tablespoons sherry
a few pinches five spice powder	2 tablespoons honey
freshly ground black pepper	1 tablespoon hoisin sauce
1 tablespoon thick soy sauce	2 cloves garlic, peeled and crushed
	3 tablespoons oil

SERVES 4

Wipe the spareribs and leave them in sections of several ribs as you bought them. Rub with salt, dust lightly with five spice powder and pepper; leave for 1 hour. Blend the soy sauces with sherry, honey, hoisin sauce and garlic. Finally stir in the oil. Pour this marinade over the ribs and spoon onto the surface. Leave for 2-4 hours, turning occasionally. Place on a wire rack above a roasting pan containing ¹⁄₄in/5mm of water to catch the drips of marinade from the ribs. Cook in a moderately hot oven (approximately 400°F/200°C) for 20 minutes. Baste again if desired, then reduce the heat to moderate (350°F/180°C) for a further 35-45 minutes or until the ribs are cooked. Cool a few minutes then divide into separate ribs and arrange attractively on a hot platter garnished with some scallion curls. You can serve these ribs with an accompaniment of salad and rice.

157

Korea

The Korean peninsular hangs like a jade pendant between China and the islands of Japan. Yet in spite of frequent invasions by China and Japan, the people of this tiny country, whose Mogul ancestors date back to prehistoric times, still retain their own language, culture and traditions. Confucianism is probably partly responsible for this as it is an inbuilt part of Korean life, reflected in relationships between seniors and juniors, men and women and respect for the elderly. The country itself is about the same size as Great Britain and, like Britain, has four definite seasons: hot, humid summers, cold, dry winters, blossom-filled springs and autumn harvesting time.

Autumn is also the time for making KIMCHI, *which is a spicy, peppery vegetable pickle, served as an accompaniment at all meals, even breakfast. This preparation of* kimchi *is a ritual that every family performs and there are countless variations on the basic theme, some hot or spicy, or both, some fermented. Until recently when living standards improved, it was possible to judge the wealth of the family by the* kimchi *they served. In wealthy homes it would contain all kinds of exotic and hard-to-come-by fruits and vegetables. In every home large, dark brown vats are inside or outside the house or apartment. The* kimchi *might be prepared from cabbage, radish, cucumbers, red* **peppers, onions, garlic, oysters, white fish, shrimp and chestnuts.** *The* kimchi *is left to ferment over a period of time, getting more pungent by the week. As a store for the latter part of the winter, when vegetables are difficult to find, the vat is sunk into the ground and covered with straw to prevent it freezing until it is required.*

A Korean home in the countryside will not have changed much over the decades. Usually it is on one storey, built of brick with a tile or metal roof. The heating system is called ondol — *an under-floor stone flue carries heat from the kitchen fire at the back of the house or ground level grates throughout the house. The agricultural land is well developed and well tended by the farmers. Large families are quite normal and there is little evidence of poverty. Traditional rural villages, the beautiful countryside, ancient palaces, shrines and temples, as well as country people in traditional costume, may be seen throughout. Women wear full pastel-colored skirts called the* chima chogori, *and the men a blouse and baggy trousers called* chogori pagi.

Festivals and family celebrations are very important; the first and 61st birthdays being the most celebrated. At the first the child is dressed in traditional costume and sits among piles of rice cakes, cookies and fruits, which are shared with all the relations. Sixty used to be considered the expected life span, so 61 is treated as bonus time and is still

Above *This Buddhist temple was first built in 751. It is situated in Kyongju, which was once the capital city of the Silla Dynasty. It was then restored in the 1970s, almost to its original grandeur.*

celebrated with a great family banquet, to be shared with family and loved ones. The New Year is a three-day holiday and traditionally the womenfolk prepare special dishes for the family ancestors. Wealthy families perform this devotion at a special shrine, while others might conduct it at home. The host entertains his friends with rice wine (suk), soup and meat. A rice dumpling soup (ttokkuk) is traditional fare from rich to poor, and glutinous rice (ttok), steamed and pounded to a dough then cut into bite-size pieces, is obligatory for all guests.

A traditional Korean meal is eaten at a low table, with the men eating first followed by the women, although this is less common than it used to be. Food is not eaten in courses, but served all at once, everyone taking their portion from the dishes in the middle of the table. It would be usual to have three, five or seven dishes for the main meal of the day, although in the homes of the wealthy and in the palaces, 9 or 12 would be normal. Breakfast used to be the main meal of the day, but this is now changing and is usually taken in the evening. The basic everyday meal, however, is quite simple, including a bowl of white rice, a meat or fish soup and kimchi. The rice is sometimes mixed with barley. Rice and soup are eaten with a porcelain or brass spoon, which must not be set down, except in the bowl, once you have started eating. Silver chopsticks were always used in the past as this metal quickly detects poison! Chopsticks must be set down to the right of the bowl after use — over the bowl denotes that the food has been offered to the dead.

Korean food is spicy and hot, particularly some of the kimchis. Taste, color and contrast in textures and flavors are very important and the slicing and cutting of meat and vegetables is a real art, which would take years to master. There are strong similarities in this aspect with Thai food and the sculpting of their fruit and vegetables. More time is actually spent in the cutting and slicing than the cooking, which results in almost raw vegetables and lightly cooked meats. It is a healthy diet and Koreans are always proud of their youthful looks, which they attribute to their style of eating. The five flavors that feature are sweet, sour, hot, tart and salty. Any dish worth eating will include garlic, ginger, scallions, sesame seeds and sesame oil.

Barley tea with a little ginseng added is normally served with the food. Ginseng is the 'cure for all ills'. It is believed to provide relief from insomnia, toothache, malaria and some people believe it prolongs life. In Korea white and red ginseng are sold. Red ginseng is the best quality and used for export. Korean ginseng claims to be the finest in the world.

Like most orientals, the Korean housewife's kitchen is extremely simple, yet practical. Cooking is usually done by boiling or frying, so she will have a sot — *the Korean version of the wok — a soup and rice kettle and cast iron pots. She may have a sinsullo pot, like a steamboat, and, if she is up to date, maybe even a pot for cooking* BULGOGI, *which looks like a sun hat with an upturned brim. The crown has slits in it to allow the heat through and then the juices collect in the brim. Food is eaten from stainless steel bowls nowadays, which are much easier to keep clean than brass and also less expensive.*

Left *The cuisine of Korea is a riot of colours, tastes and textures.* SINSULLO *is one of the most splendid, served in the traditional hotpot and laid out beautifully. It is seen in the centre of the picture.*

Bindaeduk
(A Korean pizza)

This dish is referred to as the Korean's answer to the pizza, although it is really a bean pancake. The filling can be varied to include *kimchi*, carrot and ginger, but pork and scallions are traditionally used. In Korea they are sold in drinking houses or cafes.

1⅓ cups split mung beans, washed	1 clove garlic, peeled and crushed
¼ cup glutinous rice	4 scallions, trimmed and chopped
1 tablespoon soy sauce	⅔ cup cooked lean pork, shredded
1 tablespoon roasted sesame seeds, crushed	salt and pepper to taste
½ teaspoon bicarbonate of soda	sesame oil for frying
1½ cups bean sprouts, blanched and dried	soy dressing for dipping (see Naeng Myon, page 163)

MAKES 16

Pick over then soak the split (or whole) mung beans and glutinous rice in the water for at least 8 hours. Rinse well, removing as many green skins as possible, drain then put into a food processor and grind to a batter the consistency of whipping cream. Add soy sauce, sesame seeds and bicarbonate of soda. When ready to cook, add the bean sprouts, garlic, scallions and pork. Season to taste. Heat the sesame oil in a pan. Spoon or ladle in just over ⅝ cup of the mixture and, using the back of a spoon, spread it into a thick pancake. Drizzle a little of the sesame oil over the surface, cover and cook over a medium heat until the under-side is cooked. Now invert a lightly oiled plate over the pancake. Remove from the heat and turn the frying pan over so that the pancake is on the plate. Slip the pancake, uncooked-side down, back into the pan, and continue cooking for a further 3-4 minutes. Keep warm while cooking the remaining batter and serve in quarters with the dipping sauce.

Left **Bindaeduk** *This pizza can be presented as though it really were a pizza, with the pieces arranged on top; or they may be mixed up and included inside the pancake.*

Naeng Myon
(Cold noodle soup)

5 cups chilled beef stock or 2 × 10oz/275g cans condensed consommé	a little chopped red chili
	1 tablespoon roasted sesame seeds
6 cups fresh or dried Chinese egg noodles	**Soy dressing**
	¼ cup soy sauce
To garnish	1 clove garlic, peeled and crushed
⅔ cup pressed beef or cold roast beef	2 tablespoons rice vinegar
¼ cucumber cut into even-sized slices	2 scallions, finely sliced from above
1 unripe pear, peeled and sliced and brushed with vinegar	sugar to taste
¼-½ white radish, peeled and grated	**Mustard dressing**
1 hard-cooked egg	1 tablespoon dry mustard
4 scallions, trimmed and chopped, reserve two for dressing	water or vinegar to mix to a soft paste

SERVES 8

Prepare the beef stock as much as a day ahead, if possible, so that it can cool and be skimmed thoroughly. Measure and reserve. Boil the noodles for 1 minute if fresh; soak for 10 minutes if dried, then cook for 3-5 minutes, drain and rinse with cold water. Leave to drain thoroughly. Cut the beef into even-sized pieces, about 2 × 3in/5 × 7½cm. Prepare the cucumber, pear, radish and reserve. Slice the egg. Chop the scallions and keep on one side together with both the chili and sesame seeds.

Divide the noodles between the deep soup bowls. Arrange the beef, cucumber and radish artistically on top of the noodles, but towards the outer edges of the dish. Set the egg slices in the center and scatter with chilli, the scallions and sesame seeds. Pour in the chilled beef stock, taking care not to disturb the garnish.

Prepare the soy dressing by blending together the soy sauce, garlic, rice vinegar, scallions and sugar to taste. Turn into a serving bowl. Prepare the mustard dressing and spoon it into a small bowl. Serve all at room temperature. Eat with chopsticks and soup spoons; each person takes as much or as little of the dressing as desired.

Gogi Kuk
(Beef soup with scallions)

Stock
¼lb/350g shin of beef
1-2 beef bones (if
    available), cut small
1in/2.5cm fresh ginger,
    scraped, bruised and
    cut in half
salt
10 cups water
1-2 fresh red chillies,
    seeded and
    pounded

1-2 cloves garlic, peeled
    and crushed
1 tablespoon sesame oil
1 tablespoon roasted
    sesame seed, ground
    to a paste (see page
    29)
3-4 tablespoons soy
    sauce
1 bunch scallions,
    trimmed and cut into
    2in/5cm lengths
salt and pepper to taste

SERVES 8-10

Cut the beef into three equal pieces. Place these in a pan with the beef bones, ginger, salt and water. Bring to the boil, skim well then lower the heat, cover and simmer for 1½-2 hours on a low heat or until the meat is tender. Strain the stock and skim away any fat. Discard the bones and ginger, but reserve the meat and shred finely. Mix well with the chili, garlic, sesame oil and paste and soy sauce. Return the stock to a pan and add all but a handful of the scallions then cook for 5 minutes. Meanwhile fry the meat mixture in another pan for just a minute then pour on the hot stock. Bring to the boil, season and cook for a further 5-10 minutes. Throw in the reserve scallions just before the end of cooking. These will add both color and flavor to the finished dish, and are worth taking the trouble over.

Kuchul Paan
(Nine heavenly varieties)

This is a very time-consuming dish to prepare, but it is very attractive and perfect either as a starter or as part of a buffet. Each person takes a pancake from the center and dots it with a little made-up mustard then adds a variety of fillings before rolling it up and dipping in the sauce. The examples given are just a selection of the fillings you may like to prepare, but any other chopped vegetables and meat will do just as well. The ones given are fairly traditional varieties to give you a flavor of the country.

⅓ large cucumber
1 teaspoon salt

1½ cups cooked
    shrimp
pinch salt

⅔ cup pork fillet,
    partially frozen to
    ease slicing
¼ teaspoon salt

⅔ cup fillet of beef,
    partially frozen as
    above
¼ teaspoon salt
2 tablespoons soy sauce
1 crushed clove garlic

1¾ cup button
    mushrooms
¼ teaspoon salt

1½ cups Chinese cabbage;
    finely shredded
¼ teaspoon salt

1 large carrot, finely cut
    into matchstick-like
    pieces
a little salt

2 eggs
3 tablespoons water
¼ teaspoon salt

½ white radish, grated
salt, if liked

Pancakes
2¼ cups plain flour
salt
2 eggs
2 cups beef stock,
    made from can of
    condensed consommé
    and water

sesame oil for frying
a little made-up mustard
pine nuts and spring
    onions to garnish

Dipping Sauce
⅝ cup soy sauce
3 tablespoons rice wine
    vinegar
2 chopped scallions
2 tablespoons roasted
    and crushed sesame
    seeds

MAKES 24 (approx)

First prepare all the varieties. Then make the pancakes by sifting flour and salt together, adding the lightly whisked eggs and sufficient beef stock to make a creamy batter. Next, prepare the fillings as follows. Cut the cucumber in half lengthwise and scoop out the seeds. Cut into 2in/5cm lengths and into fine strips. Sprinkle with salt and set aside for a while. Drain off any juice and squeeze lightly to dry a little. Drain on absorbent kitchen paper. Sprinkle the shrimp with salt. Finely slice the pork and cut it into shreds. Sprinkle with salt. Similarly cut the beef. Add salt, soy sauce and garlic and leave to marinate. Slice and salt the mushrooms, Chinese cabbage and carrots. Make two omelets from the eggs, water and salt. Roll up and cut into fine strips. Grate the white radish and sprinkle with salt and, finally, stir fry all the varieties separately and lightly, put them into a series of dishes around the central dish of pancakes. An hor's d'oeuvre tray is ideal for this.

Right **Kuchul paan** If you use one of this dishes only eight varieties can be arranged, but it does look authentic. Spring roll wrappers may be used in place of pancakes.

Kalbi Chim
(Beef spareribs)

3lb/1.4kg meaty ribs of beef, cut into chunky pieces (ask the butcher to do this for you)
1-2 tablespoons sugar
⅝ cup soy sauce
2 tablespoons sesame oil
2 cloves garlic, peeled and crushed
1 tablespoon sesame seeds, roasted and crushed
3-4 Chinese dried mushrooms, soaked in

2½ cups water for 30 minutes
2 scallions, trimmed and chopped
1 small Chinese turnip, peeled and cut into chunks
½ × 20oz/567g can of water chestnuts
seasoning
1 egg, separated and made into garnish (see page 172)

SERVES 4

Score the meaty pieces of the ribs and rub all over with sugar. Mix the soy sauce, sesame oil, garlic and sesame seeds together and rub into the pieces of beef. Marinate for 1 hour. Pour off the marinade and reserve. Drain and reserve the liquid from the mushrooms and slice the mushrooms. Fry the meat in a wok without oil to seal it on all sides, then pour over the marinade and reserved soaking water. Bring to the boil and cook over a gentle heat for 1 hour until the beef is almost tender. Remove the cover and add the mushrooms, scallions, turnip and water chestnuts. Cook for a further 30 minutes when much of the liquid will have evaporated. Taste for seasoning. Garnish on a hot platter with the egg strips or, if desired, cut them into diamond shapes, which is quite traditional.

Right **Kalbi chim** *These spareribs may be left plain or garnished with egg strips for color. Serve with rice.*

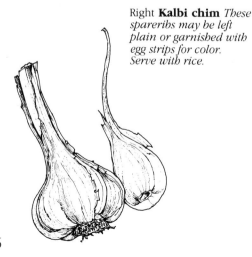

Sinsullo
(A Korean hotpot)

A century ago this exotic dish was eaten only by the Royal Household — a meal fit for a king!

Marinade
2 tablespoons soy sauce
2 cloves garlic, peeled and crushed
1 tablespoon sesame oil
1 tablespoon roasted sesame seeds, pounded
1 teaspoon sugar
freshly ground black pepper

2/3 cup fillet of beef, partially frozen and thinly sliced
1/2 cup ground pork
1/2 cup ground beef
2/3 cup calves liver, partially frozen and thinly sliced
4-6 Chinese mushrooms, soaked in water for 30 minutes

1/2 × 18oz/500g can bamboo shoots, drained and finely sliced
1 onion, peeled and sliced
2 carrots, peeled and sliced
4 scallions, trimmed and chopped into 2in/5cm lengths
sesame oil for frying
4-6 tablespoons flour
2 beaten eggs
4 cups beef stock, made from can condensed consommé and water

To garnish
1 1/2 tablespoons pine kernels
gingko nuts (optional)

SERVES 4-6

Marinate the beef slices in the marinade ingredients for 15 minutes. Lift out and set on one side. Add the marinade to the ground beef and pork. Roll the mixture into 12 even-size balls and set aside. Slice the liver. Drain the mushrooms and slice. Prepare the bamboo shoot, onion, carrot and scallions.

Now the cooking begins. Stir fry the beef slices in some sesame oil and then put aside. Wipe the pan in between frying. Repeat with the liver, which has been dipped in flour and then quickly into the beaten egg. Dip the meat balls in flour and beaten egg and again cook in a little sesame oil until cooked through; reserve. Drain the bamboo shoots. Lightly fry the onion first, lift out and then separately fry the carrots, scallions and sliced mushrooms.

Just before you take the Sinsullo to the table arrange the meats and vegetables together with the meat balls attractively in the moat of the hotpot, making sure that each layer is arranged in the same way so that each guest has a helping identical to his neighbour. Scatter the pine kernels and gringko nuts on top, if liked. Just before serving, flood in a little of the stock, cover and heat up rapidly. Add more hot stock before taking to the table. When the hotpot is in position at the table and the heat is satisfactory, carefully pour in boiling stock, taking care not to

disturb the foods. Guests help themselves with chopsticks and drink the soup at the end from bowls.

Any variety of chopped meat, vegetable and eggs may be used in this dish, provided they are laid out symmetrically.

Bulgogi
(Marinated and barbecued beef)

This is a very popular dish for entertaining outdoors, either in the garden or on a picnic. Traditionally, it would have been cooked on a Genghis Khan grill, which is shaped like the crown of a hat. I cooked the pieces of beef in the wok, lightly brushed with sesame oil. Like the Genghis Khan grill, the juices run into the well of the pan. Have another flame-proof dish ready to transfer the rapidly cooked pieces of beef while cooking the remainder.

2lb/900g fillet of beef or rump, cut thinly or ask the butcher to do it	2 tablespoons crushed, roasted sesame seeds
	4 scallions, trimmed and chopped
Marinade	freshly ground black pepper and salt to taste
⅝ cup soy sauce	a little oil for cooking
2 tablespoons sesame oil	
2 tablespoons sake	
1 clove garlic, peeled and crushed	slivers of garlic and raw chopped onion and lettuce to garnish if liked
1 tablespoon sugar	

SERVES 8

Place the meat into the freezer to firm it up so that the slices can be cut more thinly. Keep them all as even as possible. Mix all the ingredients for the marinade together and pour over the meat in a shallow glass or glazed dish. Leave at least 3 hours and preferably overnight. When required, broil over charcoal or in a heavy frying pan with a minimum of oil to just cook the beef. Serve at once.

Garnish as suggested; serve with rice and kimchi. course.

Left **Sinsullo** *Food served in a hotpot like this looks spectacular.*

Right **Bulgogi** *The juices from the meat collect in the moat of the grill.*

Korea is predominantly a rural country, with folk villages scattered throughout (centre top). The various islands provide these rural scenes, for example, this one on the island of Cheju (left). This is the largest of Korea's islands and is well worth a visit for its landscapes (top). With the miles of coastline that Korea has, fishing is inevitably an important part of agriculture. Boats of all shapes and sizes (top right) go out daily. These brilliant fields of rape are also quite a common sight (above). Religion also plays a large part in the Korean way of life. Popchusa Temple (far left) in North Ch'ungchong Province is a particularly well-known one.

171

Chap Chae
(Mixed vegetables with noodles)

8oz/225g rump or
    sirloin steak, sliced
    thinly

Marinade
1 tablespoon sugar
2 tablespoons soy sauce
1 tablespoon scallions,
    finely chopped
1 clove garlic, crushed
few crushed, roasted
    sesame seeds

$^3/_4$ cup transparent
    noodles, soaked in
    water for 20 minutes
4 Chinese mushrooms,
    soaked in water for
    30 minutes
1 onion, peeled and
    sliced

1 carrot, peeled and cut
    into fine
    matchstick-like pieces
2 zucchini or $^1/_2$
    cucumber, trimmed
    and cut into sticks
$^1/_2$ red pepper, seeds
    removed and cut into
    strips
4 button mushrooms,
    sliced
1 cup bean sprouts,
    washed and drained
3 scallions
sesame oil for cooking

To garnish
1-2 eggs, separated
    whites and yolks
1 tablespoon soy sauce
salt and pepper
sesame seeds, roasted

SERVES 4

Chill the steak so that it is easier to slice finely and cut it into 2in/5cm strips. Soak in marinade. Cook the soaked and drained noodles in boiling water for 5 minutes. Drain well and separate by pulling apart. Drain the mushrooms and slice. Prepare the onion, carrot, zucchini or cucumber, red pepper, button mushrooms, bean sprouts and the scallions. Reserve one of the scallions separately for garnish. Heat a little oil in the pan. Break the egg yolks and pour them into the pan. When they are set, remove them onto absorbent kitchen towels. Heat the pan again and pour in the egg whites. When these are set, drain, then cut up the yolk and the white into strips or diamond shapes to use as garnish.

Drain the marinade from the beef. Heat a little more sesame oil and stir fry the beef until it changes color. Add the carrot and onion next. Cook for 2 minutes then all the other vegetables, tossing all the time until they are just cooked. Add noodles and soy sauce and taste for seasoning. Cook for 1 more minute. Turn out onto a serving dish and garnish attractively with egg strips, chopped scallions and sesame seeds. This is a delicious dish and filling because of the number of ingredients.

Na Mul
(Cucumber salad)

1 large cucumber
2 teaspoons salt
3 scallions, finely
  chopped
1 tablespoon sesame oil
1 teaspoon chili powder

2 tablespoons soy sauce
sugar to taste
1 tablespoon roasted
  sesame seeds, lightly
  crushed

Halve the cucumber, trim the ends, cut it into 2in/5cm lengths, then into stick-like pieces, Sprinkle with salt and after 30 minutes squeeze to drain off any excess liquid. Fry the cucumber and two-thirds of the onion in hot sesame oil without browning. Add chili powder and cook for 1 minute. Stir in the soy sauce, sugar to taste and the sesame seeds. Turn onto a serving dish and leave for 2-3 hours before serving so that the flavors blend, then sprinkle over the top with the remaining scallions.

Left **Na mul** *As well as cucumber, bean sprouts or spinach may be used in this recipe, for example. Na mul is really a salad and is delicious served with most things.*

Below **Kimchi** *This national dish can be prepared with radish, cucumber, spring greens and Chinese cabbage. There are, in fact, hundreds of variations.*

Kimchi

1½lb/675g Chinese
  cabbage
1 large or 2 medium
  Chinese turnips
  (1½lb/675g) or 2
  hard pears
4 tablespoons salt
1 cup water

4 scallions, trimmed
  and finely chopped
4 cloves garlic, peeled
  and crushed
1in/2½cm piece fresh
  ginger, scraped, sliced
  and chopped finely
2-3 teaspoons chili
  powder

MAKES 2lb/900g

Shred the cabbage into pieces the length of your little finger. Peel and thinly slice the Chinese turnip or pears evenly. Sprinkle the vegetables with salt. Mix well, then press into a glazed or glass bowl and pour over water. Cover with a lid and leave overnight. On the following day drain off the salt water from the vegetables and reserve. Mix the vegetables with the scallions, garlic, ginger and chili powder; use rubber gloves if you have sensitive hands. Pack these into a large 2lb/900g jar or two smaller ones. Pour over the reserved salt water. Cover with plastic wrap and store in the warm sun or a warm cupboard for 2-3 days. Thereafter store in the refrigerator where it can be kept happily for several weeks.

Burma

Burma is shaped like a kite, sharing borders with India, extending to the Himalayas in the northwest and China and Laos to the east. The tail of the kite is the immensely long border linking Burma and Thailand, stretching down to a point just north of the equator. A great river, the Irrawady, flows from north to south through Mandalay, Ava and Pagan — all ancient capitals. Rangoon, its present capital, is situated near the lower tip of the kite on the Rangoon river well up from the sea. There are about 30 million people in the whole of this huge country — many working on the land. The monsoon winds bring torrential rain in May and rainfall can be expected until November, when the cool season starts. The odd shower in January, which the Burmese call mango showers, are auspicious; without these they reckon the rice harvest will not be so plentiful. From February to May the heat increases and the whole cycle begins again.

Burma has had a turbulent history and, even today, tourism is not encouraged in this Buddhist country as it is in neighbouring India and Thailand. It is a land of villages — three-quarters of the people live in rural areas. The small communities live in clusters of wooden houses and are surrounded by trees of all kinds — from mango to papaya, oranges, pomelos, limes, and beyond these lie the acres of paddy-fields. Rice is of course the main and most important crop: indeed, it is the staple diet of the people. In the days when Burma still had a king one of the rituals he would perform was to plough the first furrow before the planting of the rice. Other crops are cotton, tobacco, sugar-cane and sesame for the oil, which is so important in the Burmese kitchen. Teak is one of Burma's most famous exports.

The Burmese people are made up of four main groups — the Burmans, the Shans, the Mons and the Arakanese. Each group has its own language, but they are all Buddhist and the sharing of their faith is a uniting factor. At about the age of 12 each young boy will go to the monastery for his shinbyu, when he temporarily renounces the world for the saffron robe of a novice monk. He may in later years return to the monastery from time to time, if he feels the need for a period of retreat. Pagodas are everywhere. The most elaborate and well known is the Schwedagon in Rangoon, but there are many throughout the whole of the country, which have a monks' school and monastery close by. These are a constant reminder of the faith which links the different ethnic groups.

The Burmese people are renowned for their gentleness, charm and generosity and will readily invite you to their homes. In the country the house, set on stilts, will be constructed of bamboo or, for the more wealthy, wood, with a thatch or metal roof which covers a verandah all around the house. Cooking may well take place at a small fireplace in the ground or, in dry weather, outside. Each and every home will have its own altar to Buddha, at which there will be offerings of flowers, fruit and rice. It is therefore important to remove shoes before entering as a sign of respect. Furnishings in the home are sparse — there will be a low, round table, which is easily moved from place to place, for eating or food preparation; either low stools or mats for sitting on, perhaps the odd bamboo screen, which can be moved to divide the room.

Snacks are available throughout the day. It is quite customary for the hostess not to eat with her guests. She and her daughters will frequently eat prior to a large party so that they can fully concentrate on the needs of their guests. Two meals a day are the norm — both rice-based and plenty of it. Most people eat frugally, but when they can afford it they splash out on a more lavish spread, sharing it with neighbours and friends. In mid-April the Water Festival is a great excuse for a feast, followed by the Buddhist New Year. Weddings and the boys' shinkyus are popular at this time too, before the rains come and the planting of rice begins.

The Burmese are justly proud of their cuisine. The common borders shared with India and China have resulted in their adapting, they would say, the best from each. With many rivers and a lengthy coastline it is no wonder that fish features heavily on the menu (although fresh-water fish is said to be preferred and accounts for a high proportion of fish eaten). Dried shrimp are essential in the cuisine. In dried and powdered form they naturally do not require any refrigeration, which is an important factor in the monsoon climate. The shrimp are dried on mats in the sun and are then powdered. BALACHUANG is a sambal with a high proportion of powdered shrimp plus garlic and fried onions. This is immensley popular either to serve with curries or simply stirred into plain rice. There is also a strong-tasting shrimp paste akin to blachan called ngapi, which no self-respecting Burmese moves without.

Wet spices, as in Thai and Malaysian cooking, are traditional in Burma rather than the dry spices of India — they would be fried in peanut oil in preference to any other oil. Coconut milk is essential and would always be made from fresh coconut. Salads are popular, lethok literally means mixed by hand. Ingredients are carefully chosen to balance each other in texture, color and flavor with a dressing to complement all. Soups are generally clear, sometimes sour, but always with a few seasonable leaves thrown in at the last minute. The soup is eaten throughout the meal. MOHINGA (fish in a rich, creamy, coconut sauce) is perhaps the best known Burmese dish — hawkers and food stalls in the bazaars sell this from early morning throughout the day. PANTHE KAUKSWE is another popular dish, which uses chicken and,

The majority of Burmans are Buddhists and worship is often carried out within the many pagodas (left). Junior monks are often seen, each carrying their own alms bowls, collecting alms.

again, coconut and is served with a similar range of fascinating accompaniments as the Mohinga. Both are excellent party food.

Cooking facilities in the rural and urban home for most are very simple. To cook Burmese food I suggest that a Chinese wok with a lid will be invaluable, and either a granite pestle and mortar, food processor or electric blender, essential to grind and pound dried shrimp, as well as making up the wet spice mixtures. Serve a Burmese meal on a low table if available, from which the guests are able to reach all the dishes. Sit with the feet tucked up to your right or left. Each person will have a bowl and a plate, a spoon and fork. The rice will be served in a large dish and all the other sambals and accompaniments in smaller bowls. The bowls are never allowed to become empty. Dessert is rarely served. Fresh fruit is sometimes served, although this is often taken as a snack between meals, as are cakes and sweetmeats.

Hincho
(Vegetable and shrimp soup)

This is a poor man's soup, but it is eaten by everyone. The flavor can be changed daily by the addition of different green leaves or vegetables, depending on what is available.

6¼ cups water
⅓ cup powdered, dried
   shrimp or whole,
   dried shrimps,
   pounded in pestle
   and mortar
freshly ground pepper
2-3 cloves garlic, peeled
   and crushed
1 tablespoon fish sauce
   (see page 23)

dash soy sauce
   (optional)
salt to taste
¼-½ bottle gourd
   (boothi), peeled and
   seeds removed, or
   zucchini, diced
1½ cups green leaves
   such as spinach,
   sorrel, Chinese cabbage
   or watercress

SERVES 6

Pour the water into a pan and bring to the boil. Add the prepared, powdered shrimp, pepper, garlic, fish sauce, soy sauce if using and salt to taste. Simmer for a few minutes while preparing the gourd or zucchini. Add these and cook for several minutes until tender. Taste for seasoning. If you are using leaves only add them just before serving, so that they retain their colour and shape.

Right *The markets are as rife in Burma as they are all over the east. Here, a lady is selling peppers, which are weighed out, then bagged up.*

Far right **Chin hin** *This soup has a very* **distinctive flavor.** *The fish paste and sourness dominate, but they are not overpowering.*

Chin Hin
(Sour soup)

This is a sour soup, much loved by the Burmese who enjoy the balance of the sourness coupled with the strength of the fish paste (*ngapi*) or fish sauce. It is well worth trying.

10 pieces dried
   tamarind, soaked in
   4½ cups warm
   water for 30 minutes
2-3 tablespoons peanut
   oil
1 onion, peeled and
   very finely sliced
2 cloves garlic, peeled
   and crushed
¼ teaspoon turmeric
   powder

3 green tomatoes, peeled,
   seeded and
   chopped
½in/1cm ngapi
   (blachan), dry fried
   then mixed to a paste
   with tamarind juice,
   or fish sauce to taste
salt and freshly ground
   black pepper
a handful of shredded
   sorrel or spinach
   leaves

SERVES 4

Strain the tamarind into a jug and reserve. Heat the oil, fry the onions, garlic and turmeric together without browning. Add the tomatoes and strained stock. Bring to a boil, stir in the ngapi or fish sauce and seasoning. Simmer for several minutes. Add the leaves, taste for seasoning and cook until the sorrel or spinach leaves are tender.

Mohingha
(Curried fish soup with noodles)

Mohingha is perhaps one of the best known Burmese dishes. It is a delicious one-course meal available almost everywhere in Burma. Hawkers or Mohingha sellers pedal this complete meal with a long bamboo pole across the shoulder. At one end is a container with the charcoal fire and at the other all the bits and pieces to make up the meal on the spot. Few Burmese housewives would make this at home, relying on the excellence of the Mohingha sellers' 'take out'.

1½lb/650g huss, pilchard or mackerel	fresh coriander leaves
3 stems lemon grass	1lb/450g rice noodles, prepared according to packet directions, or cooked in boiling water and well drained, if fresh
1in/2.5cm ginger, scraped	
2 tablespoons fish sauce	
3 onions, peeled	
4 cloves garlic, peeled	
2-3 chilies, seeded	**Accompaniments**
1 teaspoon ground turmeric	3 eggs, hard-cooked and cut into wedges
peanut oil for frying	1-2 onions, peeled and finely sliced
3¼ cups coconut milk (see page 21)	lemon, cut into wedge shapes
4 tablespoons rice flour	1 bunch scallions, finely chopped
4 tablespoons garbanzo flour (see page 19)	fried chilies (see below)
pieces of banana trunk or heart, if available, or 1lb 3oz/540g canned bamboo shoot	crisp fritters (see below)

SERVES 8

Ask the store to clean the fish for you, but leave on the bone. Place in a pan with cold water to cover. Add two stems of lemon grass and half the ginger, just bruised. Bring up to the boil, add fish sauce and cook for 10 minutes. Lift out the fish and allow to cool while straining the remaining stock into a bowl. Discard the skin and bones from the fish and reserve the flesh, which will be in small pieces. Pound the lower stem of the reserved lemon grass together with the remaining piece of ginger, the onions, garlic, chilies and turmeric to a smooth paste in a food processor or with a pestle and mortar. Heat the oil and fry all these ingredients in it until they give off a rich aroma. Draw the pan off the heat and add the pieces of fish. Add coconut milk to the reserved fish stock. Add sufficient water to make up to 10 cups/2.4 liters. Blend the rice and garbanzo flours to a thin cream with some of the stock. Stir this into the remaining stock and allow it to come to a boil over a medium heat, stirring all the time. Add the slices of banana trunk or heart or bamboo shoot and cook for 10 minutes until just tender. Stir in the fish and spice mixture. Taste for seasoning, cover and leave until the rice noodles are cooked and the accompaniments are assembled. Do not allow the mohingha to cook for more than a few minutes or the fish will break up. Each person puts a helping of noodles into a deep bowl and pours or ladles over some of the prepared soup which has been scattered with coriander leaves at the last minute. Choose from the accompaniments as you wish.

Fried chilies

8-10 dried red chilies	1 teaspoon powdered shrimp
2 tablespoons peanut oil	

Dry roast the chilies over a gentle heat; the seeds can be removed to make them less hot. Pound the chilies, fry them in hot oil and stir in the powdered shrimp. Turn into a small bowl together with other accompaniments — make sure you use with discretion.

Crisp fries

⅓ cup canned garbanzos	few pinches sugar
¼ cup plain flour	¼ teaspoon bicarbonate of soda
4 tablespoons gram flour	
4 tablespoons rice flour	⅝ cup water
¼ teaspoon ground turmeric	oil to ¼in/5mm depth for frying
salt	

Drain the garbanzos. Blend the flours together with turmeric, salt, sugar and bicarbonate of soda. Mix to a smooth batter with water. Add the garbanzos. Fry in small spoonfuls in hot oil until they pale, then drain well. Return to the hot fat for a further minute to crisp up and turn golden brown. Guests break these over the Mohingha at the table.

Right **Panthe kaukswe**
This curry is exceptionally good if served with crisp fried rice noodles. Slices of lemon are also a good idea, with hard-cooked egg quarters, raw onions and raisins.

Sha Nga Boung
(Fish curry)

1¹/₂lb/675g fillet of
   haddock or cod
1 teaspoon turmeric
salt
1¹/₂ cups tomatoes,
   peeled, seeded and
   roughly chopped
3-4 fresh red chilies,
   seeded
1in/2.5cm fresh ginger,
   scraped

4 cups onions, peeled
a few dried garlic flakes
   or 2 fresh garlic,
   peeled
6-8 tablespoons peanut
   oil
1 tablespoon fish sauce
⁵/₈ cup water
4 scallions, chopped

SERVES 6

Skin the fish fillet and rub the surface with turmeric and salt. Cut into even-sized cubes (1in/2.5cm). Prepare the tomatoes and reserve. Place the chilies, ginger, one of the onions (slice the other and set aside) and garlic flakes or fresh garlic in a food processor. Do not allow this mixture to become too fine. Heat two-thirds of the oil and fry the pieces of fish in it for 2-3 minutes. Turn over once. Lift out onto a plate. Add the remaining oil to the pan and fry the spice paste, then, after 1 minute, add the sliced onion. When the onion looks transparent add the tomato and fish sauce. Pour in the water. Cover and cook gently for 15 minutes. Now add the fish and chopped scallions. Taste for seasoning. Shake the pan from time to time, if you stir you will break up the fish. Cook for 5 minutes then serve.

Panthe Kaukswe
(Chicken curry with noodles)

This dish has strong links with Chinese cooking in the days of the Mogul empire, and illustrates perfectly how the Burmese have cleverly combined something of both Chinese and Indian cooking, yet still retained a typically Burmese dish.

1 × 3lb/1.4kg chicken,
   cut into quarters
salt
1lb/450g onions, peeled
3 cloves garlic, peeled
   and crushed
4 fresh red chilies,
   seeded or 2
   teaspoons chili
   powder
1-2 teaspoons powdered
   turmeric
peanut oil for frying
3 cups coconut
   milk (see page 21)

3-4 tablespoons
   garbanzo flour
salt
1-2 tablespoons fish
   sauce
coriander leaves
6 cups egg noodles or
   rice noodles

Accompaniments
see Mohingha
crisp fried rice noodles,
   prepared as below.

SERVES 6-8

Break some of the rice noodles into 1in/2.5cm lengths and deep fry until crisp. Drain on absorbent kitchen towels. Place the chicken joints in a pan. Add 8³/₄ cups/2 liters of water and salt. Bring to the boil, then cover and simmer for 45-60 minutes or until the chicken is tender. Lift the chicken joints from the pan, cool and remove the meat and cut into small pieces. Discard the skin and bones. Strain the stock and reserve. Meanwhile pound the onions, garlic and chilies, or chili powder, to a paste in a food processor. Add turmeric. Fry in hot oil until it gives off a rich aroma. Stir in the coconut milk and 2 cups/1.2 liters of the reserved chicken stock. Simmer for 15 minutes.

Blend the garbanzo flour with a little of the cold stock or water to make a cream. Slowly stir one ladleful of liquid from the pan into the cream, then pour this back into the pan. Simmer over a low heat, stirring until the soup thickens a little. Add the chicken pieces, salt and fish sauce if liked. Turn into a serving tureen scattered with fresh coriander leaves.

Cook the noodles and, like the Mohingha, spoon noodles into the bowl first and top with the curried chicken. Serve the accompaniments separately.

Wetha See Pyan
(Pork curry)

2lb/900g lean pork, cut into 1in/2.5cm pieces	1in/2.5cm ngapi (blachan)
2 cups onions, peeled	1 teaspoon turmeric
8 cloves garlic, peeled and crushed	4 tablespoons peanut oil for frying
2in/5cm fresh ginger, scraped and chopped	salt to taste
2½ teaspoons chili powder	1¼ cups stock or water
4 stems lemon grass (see page 25)	coriander leaves to garnish

SERVES 6

Place the pork pieces on a dish. Slice half the onions and put the remainder into a food processor with the garlic, ginger, chilies, the lower 2½in/6cm of the lemon grass (bruise and reserve the top of the stem), ngapi and turmeric. Make these ingredients into a coarse paste. Fry the pork pieces in the hot oil to change color, then increase the heat and add the paste. Fry for 2 minutes, then add the remaining onion slices. When the pork is well coated with the spice mixture, pour on the stock or water. Add salt and the lemon grass tops. Cover and cook for 1½ hours or until the pork is tender. Cook uncovered for a further 15 minutes, if liked, to reduce the liquid. Remove the lemon grass. Add more chilli if a hotter curry is preferred. Sprinkle with fresh coriander and eat with rice.

Htamin le Thoke

This is the Burmese way of dealing with left-overs and is served cold. The noodles and rice are arranged on one large or several small platters with a myriad of accompaniments. It's an excellent summer party idea.

	Accompaniments
¼ cup long grain rice, boiled and allowed to cool a little	finely sliced raw onion
2 fresh red chilies, seeded	chopped scallions
1 small onion, peeled and sliced	fried onion flakes (see page 69)
2 tablespoons oil	crisp fried noodles (see page 117)
2 medium potatoes, boiled	roasted garbanzos, pounded
1 cup egg noodles	fresh coriander leaves
½ cup rice vermicelli	fish sauce (optional) (see page 23)
½ cup cellophane noodles (if not available, increase either of the above)	roasted, dried chilies, pounded
1 cup spinach or sorrel leaves	wedges of lemon or 1 tablespoon tamarind pulp, soaked in ⅞ cup warm water and strained (see page 16)
2¼ cups bean sprouts	

SERVES 6

Cook the rice. Pound the chilies with the onion, then fry in oil for 2-3 minutes. Stir into the cooked rice. Dice the potatoes and set aside. Cook the noodles separately in salted, boiling water and drain each with cold water thoroughly. Plunge the spinach into boiling water for 1 minute. Drain and repeat with the bean sprouts. The whole meal is eaten cold.

Now arrange the rice, noodles, potato, spinach and bean sprouts attractively on a large serving platter. Each person takes a little of what they fancy and tops it with some of the accompaniments, which are arranged in separate bowls. Squeeze lemon juice over the top or, to be more authentic, pour over a little tamarind juice.

Left *The Burmese use a number of different herbs and spices to liven up their curries. Ginger and laos or greater galangal are the favorites, but there are many more.*

Salad of Bean Sprouts and Bean Curd

3 cups bean
    sprouts
1 square bean curd,
    diced
oil for frying
1½ tablespoons
    powdered shrimp
2 dried red chilies, dry
    roasted, seeds

removed and
    pounded, or ½
    teaspoon chili
    powder
2 tablespoons oil
dash fish sauce
juice 1 lemon
fried onion flakes (see
    page 69)

SERVES 4-6

Soak the bean sprouts in cold water. Toss into boiling water for 1 minute, then drain and rinse with cold water. Fry the bean curd in fat until it is crisp; drain. Place the bean sprouts, powdered shrimp, chili powder, oil and fish sauce in a bowl and toss together. Squeeze over lemon juice. Taste for seasoning and, at the last minute, add crisp bean curds and top with fried onion.

Below **Salad of bean sprouts and bean curd** *This is a fairly tangy salad, but very good as an accompaniment to* *any main dish. It is delicious served with a topping of crisp fried onions and the addition of crisp bean curds.*

Balachaung

A spoonful or two of balachaung can be mixed into plain rice or served as accompaniment to curry, MOHINGHA or HTAMIN LE THOKE. In no way does the large amount of garlic dominate as you might expect. Adjust the amount of chili powder to your liking second time around.

1 whole corm garlic,
  peeled and finely
  sliced
4 cups onions, peeled
  and sliced finely
1¼ cups peanut oil
2¼ cups shrimp powder
  or dried prawns,
  pounded

2 teaspoons chili powder
1 teaspoon turmeric
1in/2.5cm cube of ngapi
  (blachan)
1 teaspoon tamarind,
  soaked in 2fl.oz/50ml
  water
salt

MAKES 1lb/450g

Dry the garlic and onion slices on pieces of absorbent kitchen towels, then fry each separately in the hot oil until crisp and golden. Lift out and drain well. Fry the shrimp powder or pounded shrimp in the same oil. Fry the chili powder and turmeric in this. Draw off the heat, blend the ngapi (blachan) with a little of the strained tamarind juice, then stir into the spice mixture in the pan. Draw off the heat. Cool, then stir in the onion and garlic.

Use as an accompaniment to any rice dish. Any leftovers can be stored in a screwtop jar for several weeks.

Below **Balachaung** A dried shrimp relish is probably the most apt description for this accompaniment. It is a favorite in Burma.

Right **Tha hnat** This is a refreshing salad to serve with hot curries. The cucumber will revive any assaulted taste-buds and add a special flavor.

Tha Hnat
(Pickled cucumber and sesame seed accompaniment)

1 large cucumber	1 onion, peeled, finely
juice ½ lemon	sliced and dried on
1 teaspoon salt	kitchen towels
4 tablespoons peanut oil	1 tablespoon roasted
1 tablespoon sesame oil	sesame seeds
3 cloves garlic, peeled	
and finely sliced	

Peel the cucumber, cut it in half and scoop out the seeds. Cut into even-sized chunks. Put 2½ cups water into a pan (stainless steel or enamel if possible). Add lemon juice and salt. Bring to the boil then lightly cook the cucumber pieces in this, but take care not to overcook. Drain and leave to cool. Heat the oils and fry the garlic, then lift out the pieces and fry the onion until crisp; lift out and drain. Reserve the oil and when cool pour over the cucumber. Toss well, then mix with the garlic, onion and sesame seeds. Serve with curries.

Moh-Let Saung
(Iced coconut milk with sago)

½ cup tapioca or	few tablespoons water
sago	3¼ cup coconut
½ cup jaggery or	milk (see page 21)
dark brown sugar	ice cubes

SERVES 4

Rinse the tapioca or sago, drain and put into a large pan with plenty of water. Bring to a boil and reduce to simmer. Stir often, cooking until the pearls of sago or tapioca become clear. Allow 10 minutes for sago and 20 minutes for tapioca. Drain and rinse with plenty of cold water until all the starch is removed. Dissolve the jaggery or dark brown sugar in water over a gentle heat, then cool. Spoon some of the sago or tapioca into a tall glass. Add syrup to taste, then the coconut milk and sufficient ice cubes to suit individual taste. It is important to serve this at once so that you are able to enjoy it at its very best.

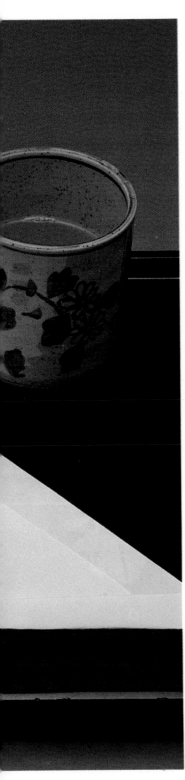

Japan

Japanese food is unique — it is an experience, an art form — each dish like a still life masterpiece. Why is the food of the islands of Japan so different? Other countries in South East Asia have borrowed ingredients and cooking styles from neighbours, each evolving its own special cuisine, but Japan has remained aloof from this pattern, retaining its traditional and ethnic style of cooking, especially in the country areas.

From 1640 all foreigners were prohibited entry into Japan as fears of colonization were a real threat; it was the time when the race for control of the Spice Islands was at its height and numbers of Spanish, Dutch and Portuguese had come to Japan already. This ban was to last for 200 years, which had a profound effect on the country as a whole. During this period they developed an exquisitely refined attitude to living, which is evident in their art, literature, architecture and gardening, as well as in the preparation and serving of food. Not until 1868 was the ban on foreigners lifted. Trade began slowly in those early years after the long period of isolation, but this has certainly been made up for since.

Japanese food is different, delicious and delights the eye and this applies to every dish that is placed before you. Presentation is just as important as taste and varies to suit the occasion; this might pertain to the season of the year, a religious or special festival, or perhaps in honor of a particular guest, a birthday or anniversary. The Japanese cook, whether housewife or professional chef, has a unique attitude to food that is sometimes difficult for the westerner to understand. To produce a delicious meal is not enough — creativity and imagination are essential attributes as well as skill in cutting vegetables and fruit into exquisite shapes. A profound subtlety is constantly demonstrated in the presentation of each and every dish. Even the plate on which the food is served is carefully chosen for the particular food, to complement colors, for example. The order in which the food is served is also important. You have a feeling that nothing is left to chance — it is all well planned. The Japanese like precision and order, and it shows.

Japanese homes are tiny compared with western homes. Rooms used as living rooms in the day become bedrooms at night with the clever use of a few bamboo screens; mattresses and quilts are rolled out each evening. The kitchen itself will probably be very small, too, and, as in many other countries of the orient, kitchen utensils are minimal; very basic, very simple and nothing superflous. A wok is standard equipment, plus a shallow cast iron pan with double hoop handles used for cooking SUKIYAKI. A more unusual, oblong pan is quite common and used for cooking omelets; however, an ordinary frying pan can be used instead. Barbecuing food is very popular and a hibachi charcoal grill doubles up as a heater during the winter months.

The early settlers who came to Japan probably crossed from Korea or Siberia. They developed a communion with nature that has left its mark on Japanese culture even today. Shrines to the gods of rice, Inari, *and the god of food,* Ukemochi-no-kami, *abound. Food has not always been plentiful and by most standards the food is basically simple, almost bordering on frugal. For breakfast a raw egg might be stirred into plain boiled rice, perhaps a soup with bean curd, a morsel of fish, vegetable and some pickle; green tea is served in pretty bowls. Lunch is simpler with the evening meal usually the most important of the day. This will consist of soup, rice, fish vegetables and* daikon — *a huge white radish that is either sliced or grated. The Japanese are passionately fond of this vegetable, which is known as moolie in Europe. Raw fish —*

Kinkakuji Temple, or the Gold Pavilion (right), *is situated in the ancient capital of Kyoto. Built c.1600, it was called the Gold Pavilion because its roof was originally overlaid with gold. From 794 to 1868 the emperors of Japan resided in this city. Another tourist attraction are the national parks throughout Japan. This one at Kitayamazake* (above) *is on the coast.*

every Japanese loves fish and consumes vast quantities of it — and an exquisitely arranged salad often features too; blossoms are frequently used as a garnish.

Eating out is quite standard, especially when entertaining. Many restaurants specialize in such foods as TEMPURA, SUKIYAKI, YAKITORI, SUSHI and SASHIMI. In a restaurant serving Sukiyaki, for instance, you will be ushered into a startlingly simply room — shoes are removed before entering. Everyone sits at a low table, a sukiyaki pan is set into a well in the center of the table over a burner, cunningly controlled to just the right temperature. On a separate platter is a veritable feast of foods for the Sukiyaki. These will vary according to the time of year. Fish of many different varieties and squid are frequently included instead of beef, which is vastly expensive (no wonder when you realize that the cattle are fed on beer and are hand massaged to produce the tenderest beef anywhere in the world). With everyone settled the hot sake and chatter begins to flow. The attendant waitress will place the raw foods into the hot-flavored DASHI. Portions of each ingredients are carefully placed into the pan in order, as you would expect. Even the sequence in which the foods are added is important. When still crisp, but cooked, guests help themselves and more of the raw ingredients are added. The soup in which these delicious morsels have been cooked is served at the end. Bowls and plates are expected to be left quite clean — no discreet left-overs to placate the gods here.

The art of table service is seen at its most impressive in the tea ceremony, inspired by the Buddhists of the fifteenth century. It is a ritual in the true sense of the word, which has developed into the purest and most formal style of Japanese cooking, kaiseki ryori (tea ceremony cooking). Time-honored rules are followed faithfully from the food, offering nourishment appropriate to the season, to the dishes — a black lacquer bowl for rice to an antique bowl for bamboo shoots and so on. This meal is a true composition, with serious and thoughtful regard to the fresh, seasonal, local food, served in tranquil and serene surroundings, and intended to refresh the spirit of all who partake.

New Year is the most widely celebrated festival. Food is prepared in advance and exquisitely packed into the tiered lacquer boxes, which are so attractive and becoming quite popular in the west. Ozoni is a special soup made in honor of the New Year, and a rice cake is made from this by dropping glutinous rice into it. UMANI is also a typical New Year dish. The celebrations last for almost a week.

Ingredients for Japanese cooking are less difficult to find than a few years ago. Wherever a Japanese community live there will always be an enterprizing person who sets up shop. Here are some of the ingredients, which are essential if you wish to achieve some degree of authenticity.

Japanese soup or stock is called DASHI, *served by rich and poor alike. It is made from* kombu *(kelp or dried seaweed), which is first wiped with kitchen towels, then soaked in the water to soften. This is removed on boiling as the flavor, if left, would spoil the balance of the* dashi. *The* katsoubushi *(dried bonito flakes) are then added. The flavor is much more meaty than the fishy taste you might have expected. When strained, the clear stock is ready for use.*

Japanese rice is medium grained, giving a fluffy result when cooked. Plain rice and soup are frequently served at the end of the meal. Noodles are very popular, particularly as a snack from a street stall or a café-type shop, specializing in noodles called soba. *Sake (rice wine) is served warm and is very intoxicating. It partners Japanese food very well, as does green tea, which is more frequently taken with meals. Sake in cooking can be replaced by medium dry vermouth or sherry, but do try to find sake if at all possible. Mirin is the sweet rice wine.*

A little goes a long way in the Japanese cuisine — 'small is beautiful' is an expression you feel must have been born in Japan. Raw fish and raw meats are cut paper thin, the skill of chefs and others who perform these miracles are a wonder to behold. As an alternative to cutting these items at home I suggest either find a Japanese shop where the foods are marketed in this way, especially the fish, or ask your favourite butcher to partially freeze the meat and then cut on a meat slicing machine, laying the slices one by one on plastic wrap to keep them separate.

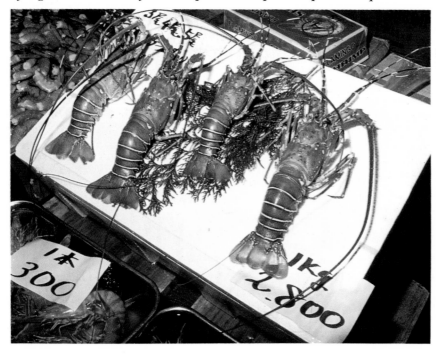

Tokyo (above) *is one of the world's most modern cities. Whatever the size of the city or village, however, all have their own festivals* (left). *They are also hard-working people, with tea as a major crop. Here, the green variety is picked by hand* (top). *Fishing* (far left) *also plays a large part in their agriculture — they are the leading producers in the world.*

Dashi
(Basic stock)

This basic stock is essential either to Japanese cooking as a soup in its own right with the addition of various ingredients and garnishes, or as an ingredient in cooking fish, meat and poultry dishes.

5 cups water	*1 tablespoon flaked*
4in/10cm piece dashi	*katsuobushi (dried*
kombu (dried kelp)	*bonito)*

MAKES 2 pt/1.2 liters

Pour the water into a large pan. Wipe over the dashi kombu lightly, being careful not to remove the powdery white film on the surface. Cut the kombu into strips with scissors. Place these in the pan of water and soak for 15-20 minutes. Now bring to a boil and remove the dashi kombu at once, otherwise it will make the stock too strong in flavor. Add the flaked katsuobushi and bring almost to a boil. Draw from the heat. When the bonito flakes have settled to the base of the pan, strain the stock through a sieve; otherwise ladle out the soup with care.

This first stock is the best quality and should always be used for soups. A second stock may be made using the same kelp and katsuobushi, but it is slightly inferior, although perfectly acceptable for use in dishes that have strong-flavored ingredients such as bean paste.

Right **Dashi** *This stock is used for a great variety of Japanese dishes, from soups to casseroles. It adds a unique flavor to the cuisine. The katsuobushi or bonito flakes can either be strained off, or a ladle can be used to draw off the liquid, leaving the flakes in the pan.*

Miso Shiru
(Bean paste soup)

Traditionally this soup would have been served at breakfast, together with rice, to sustain people for the morning. The amount of miso can be reduced if you find it rather strong in flavour.

3¼ cups prepared dashi	*¼ cup miso (see page 26)*
⅔-1 fresh bean curd	*a little chopped scallion*

SERVES 4

Heat the dashi in a pan. When boiling reduce the heat and add the bean curd, which has been diced. Cook for about 3-4 minutes Stir in the miso, which has been mixed to a thin cream with water. Cook for 1 minute without boiling, then pour into bowls with a few scallions.

Sushi *This is simply cooked rice, but may be accompanied with any selection of toppings, from raw fish to vegetables. It may also be rolled up in an omelet, seaweed, bean curd and so on.*
1 *Take a piece of the rice from the bowl into your fingers.*
2 *Mold it into a rounded oblong shape, which is used as a filling or base for other ingredients.*

Inarizushi
(Stuffed fried bean curd)

2 × 2oz/50g packets
    fried bean curd,
    (6 bean curds, 4
    × 2in/10 × 5cm)
¼pt/150ml dashi
2 tablespoons sugar
1-2 tablespoons soy
    sauce

Filling
Sushi rice (see page 193)

2 dried mushrooms,
    soaked in
    ½ cup water water
    for 30 minutes. Drain
    and reserve soaking
    juice
1 tablespoon soy sauce
1 tablespoon sugar
1 tablespoon roasted
    sesame seed
pickled ginger to garnish

MAKES 6

Pour the boiling water over the bean curds. Drain and dry on absorbent kitchen towels. Cut in half and open each one into a pocket shape. Mix the dashi, sugar and soy sauce together and cook with the bean curd over a low heat until the bean curd has soaked up the stock. When the prepared rice is cool, place in a bowl. Slice the mushrooms finely. Pour the soaking juices from the mushrooms into a pan. Add soy sauce and sugar. Cook the mushrooms until the liquid has evaporated. Cool quickly and add to the rice with the sesame seeds. Use this mixture to stuff the bean curds. Rub your hands with vinegar to make it easier to form the rice into a neat ball before popping it into the pocket-shaped bean curds. Tuck in the flaps and turn over. Set on a serving plate and garnish with pickled ginger and serve.

Sushi
(Cooked rice)

¼ cup Japanese rice
10fl.oz/300ml water
2 tablespoons rice wine
    vinegar

1 tablespoon sugar
¼ teaspoon salt

SERVES 6

Wash the rice and leave it to drain for 30-60 minutes then place it in a pan of water. Bring to a boil, cover and reduce the heat to very low. Cook for 15-20 minutes or until the rice is fluffy. Draw from the heat, leave covered for a further 15 minutes. Mix up the vinegar, sugar and salt. Sprinkle this over the surface of the rice and mix in. Cool quickly by fanning before using.

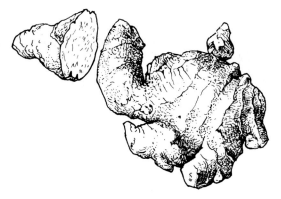

193

Tamago Yaki
(Egg roll made of several omelets)

The traditional pan in which this should be cooked is oblong and is available in Japanese shops. When cooking this omelet in a round frying pan cook in the same way, but if using the nori do not cut into such narrow strips.

4 eggs	*½-1 tablespoon sake*
4 tablespoons cold dashi	*½ teaspoon salt*
(see page 192)	*1 tablespoon sugar*
depending on egg size	*2 sheets nori (dried*
½ teaspoon thin soy	*laver) (optional)*
sauce	*a little oil for cooking*

SERVES 4-6

Beat the eggs. Heat the dashi, soy sauce, sake, salt and sugar and cool, then mix with the eggs. If you are using the nori, pass one side of each sheet over a gas flame to intensify the color and flavor, then divide into two or three strips. Lightly oil the pan. Pour in enough egg mixture to just cover the base of the pan, top with a strip of the nori and when the egg is set roll it up or fold. Lift to the end of the pan, lightly brush the pan with oil, if necessary, and again flood enough egg mixture into the pan to cover the base, lifting the rolled omelet at one end to allow the egg mixture underneath. Lift on nori, if using. Fold up in the same way when the mixture is set and repeat until all the mixture is used up and you have a large roll. If you have a bamboo mat (*suldare*) cover with a sheet of kitchen towelling. Place the omelet on it and roll up fairly firmly. Leave for several minutes then unfold. Cut across into slices to serve at breakfast, lunch or supper.

Above **Tomago yaki** *The Japanese use a rectangular omelet pan to ease the rolling up of the cooked omelet. However, a round pan* *can be used quite successfully. This is a delicious dish, suitable at any time of the day: breakfast, lunch or supper.*

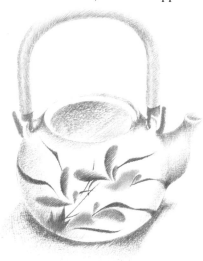

Nasu No Shigiyaki
(Eggplant with sesame seeds)

1¼lb eggplant
  (long and thin,
  preferably)
1 tablespoon salt
4 tablespoons corn oil
2 tablespoons sesame oil
2-3 tablespoons miso (see
  page 26)

2 tablespoons mirin (see
  page 26)
2 tablespoons sugar
5 tablespoons dashi
  (approx)
1-2 teaspoons roasted
  sesame seeds

MAKES 12

Wipe the eggplant and trim the ends. Cut into 1in/2.5cm thick slices and sprinkle with salt. Leave for 30 minutes. Rinse and dry well on absorbent kitchen towels. Fry in hot oils, turning all the time until they are brown. Stir the miso with the mirin, sugar and dashi. Cook without a cover to reduce in a small pan. Cool rapidly. Spread this mixture onto each eggplant slice then mark in a criss-cross pattern with a knife. Sprinkle each one with a few sesame seeds. Turn onto a serving dish and scatter with the remaining sesame seeds. Eat as a snack or part of lunch; it is a refreshing way of preparing aubergines.

195

Tempura
(Fish and vegetables in batter)

Right **Tempura** *The cut fish and vegetables are dipped in batter to produce a fan shape. For best effect the batter should be thin enough for the color of the vegetables to show through. Bright-colored vegetables are preferable.*

Tempura is perhaps one of the best known Japanese dishes, but care must be taken not to try and cook for a large number of people as the delicate, light, crispy texture of the batter only lasts about 2-3 minutes after frying. The batter is light and only just coats the vegetables, thereby allowing a glimpse of the vegetable colour to peep through after cooking, which greatly enhances its attractiveness.

8 large raw prawns
¼lb/225g monkfish fillets
1 eggplant, cut into shapes, sprinkled with salt and left 30 minutes
1 medium onion, peeled
8 mushrooms
8 okra
8-12 snow peas
4 flowers of cauliflower and/or lotus root slices
2 carrots, cut into matchsticks
8 green beans, left whole, ends removed
grated daikon to garnish

Sauce
⅞ cup dashi
4 tablespoons/50ml sweet sake (mirin)
4 tablespoons/50ml soy sauce
sugar to taste
vegetable or corn oil for frying

Batter, to be made at the last minute
1 egg
⅝ cup ice cold water (approx)
1 cup plain flour
salt (optional)

SERVES 8

Remove the heads and body shell from the prawns, but leave on the tails. Then remove the spinal cord if desired, by cutting lightly down the back and lifting the dark-colored cord out. Make three or four small incisions on the underside of each prawn to prevent curling when cooking. Cut the fish into small, even-sized strips about the size of your little finger. Rinse and dry the eggplant pieces, cut the onion into slices and leave the mushrooms whole, just wipe. Remove the tip from the stem of the okra and snow peas, but leave whole; rinse and dry. Cut the cauliflower into even-sized pieces and/or the lotus root. Cut the carrots attractively, and the beans into 1in/2.5cm pieces.

Prepare the garnish and set aside. Make the sauce by heating the dashi, sweet sake, soy sauce and sugar to taste. Cool and pour into small bowls, one for each person. When the oil is getting hot, quickly make up the batter by mixing the egg and water together. Pour into the sifted flour and salt. Do not overbeat. When the oil is at the correct temperature (350°F/180°C), firstly dip the fish in the batter then lower it into the hot oil. Do the same with the assembled ingredients until they are all cooked and crisp. Do not cook too many at once as the temperature will drop too much. The batter can be kept cold by standing in a large bowl of ice. Drain on absorbent kitchen paper. Serve on a hot platter, garnished with daikon.

Serve with hot sauce in small bowls in front of each person.

Slicing eggplant for Tempura
1 *Slice a 2-3in/5-7.5cm section from the eggplant.*

2 *Pare down the edges so that you are left with the outside pieces. These are to be cut further.*

3 *Place a piece, skin-side up and make cuts lengthways, but not right through. You should then be left with a fan shape.*

Slicing carrots for Tempura
1 *Slice lengthways down the carrot to make a long, rectangular shape.*

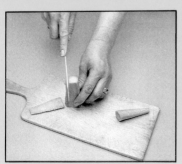

2 *Make equally spaced slits lengthways down the carrot, then turn to the adjacent side, repeating the slits.*

3 *Take a row of the resulting matchsticks, and dip them in batter to half cover; then plunge straight into hot oil.*

Shio-yaki
(Salt-broiled fish)

This method of cooking a whole fish is very simple and quite delicious. After marinating with salt, the fish is cooked over a high heat causing the oils and the salt to give a succulent, moist result.

2 small mackerel or red snapper (or any medium-sized fish), gutted but head and tail left on	**Garnish**
	finely grated daikon (white radish) or lemon slices
salt	*¼ cup soy sauce*

SERVES 2

Rinse and dry the fish on absorbent kitchen paper. Thread two skewers through the body of the fish as handles for grilling. Wrap the tail and fins, if liked, in small pieces of foil to prevent them burning when cooking. Sprinkle the surfaces of the fish, inside and out, with salt and leave for 30 minutes. Broil or barbecue for at least 5-10 minutes on each side, depending on the size of the fish. The flesh should look milky and flake easily. Do not overcook. Serve garnished with the daikon or slices of lemon and a bowl of soy sauce so that the fish can be dipped into it before eating.

Below **Shio-yaki** *Any type of small fish can be used for this recipe. It is served plain, apart from soy sauce for dipping the fish, and a quarter of lemon. Grated daikon is also popular.*

Skewering a fish
1 *Insert one skewer behind the head of the fish and bring out just before the tail fins. Sprinkle salt over the surface of the fish.*
2 *Thread a second skewer from the gills down to the fleshy part of the tail. This will ensure that they are secure for broiling.*

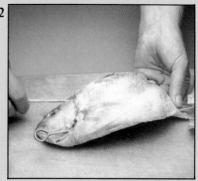

Yakitori
(Chicken pieces and chicken livers on skewers)

Marinade
6 tablespoons soy sauce
1/4 cup sake
1/2 cup mirin (or
   sweet sherry if
   unobtainable)

8 chicken livers
   (optional)
4 chicken thighs, boned
4 scallions, or 1/2
   green pepper,
   deseeded and cut into
   8 pieces

SERVES 4

Heat the soy sauce, sake and mirin together, stirring all the time until it comes to a boil. Cook without a cover for 2-3 minutes until it has reduced to two-thirds, then cool. Meanwhile clean the chicken livers, cutting away any threads with scissors. Remove the chicken thighs from the bone, then cut into even-sized pieces for broiling (1in/2.5cm). Cut the scallions into the same size lengths. Thread the halved chicken livers, if you are using them, onto skewers with the chicken pieces and scallions or green pepper. Pour the marinade into a jam jar and dip each skewer of food into this. Set under a hot broiler or over a barbecue. Dip in the marinade three or four times during the 10 minutes cooking period. **Serve at once to enjoy this succulent dish at its best.**

Above and left Yakitori
You could use a variety of vegetable pieces on these skewers, according to preference. It is the marinade that makes all the difference to the taste of this skewered meat.

199

Sukiyaki

Sukiyaki is actually cooked in front of the guests and, in order to create the correct atmosphere and setting, it is customary for guests to sit on a cushion on the floor with a low table placed in the middle. A modern table cooker and shallow metal pan or electric frying pan is placed in the center of the table, which must also be large enough to hold a platter of vegetables and one for meat, plus a bowl for the sauce. Each person has a plate, a bowl for beaten egg and a pair of chopsticks. It is also customary to have a bowl of clear soup and a small bowl for rice at each place setting. Warm sake is usually served and drunk in liberal quantities as the sauce is very salty and thirst making. The vegetables for the Sukiyaki can be changed according to the season, but combinations of color and texture and important.

1lb/450g rump or sirloin of beef, cut thinly (ask the butcher to do this for you)
1-2 (8oz/225g) packets shiritaki (Japanese vermicelli) (see page 29)
1 square bean curd, cut into quarters
4 small leeks, cleaned and cut into chunks
1 bunch scallions, sliced into lengths diagonally

watercress to garnish
a small piece of beef suet or oil

Sauce
⅝ cup light soy sauce
5 tablespoons sugar
5 tablespoons Dashi (see page 192) or 5 tablespoons sweet sake (mirin)

To serve
6 eggs

SERVES 6

Place the beef into the freezer for a little while to firm it up so that it can be sliced as thinly as two pieces of paper. Drain the shiritaki and cook in boiling water for 5-10 minutes. Drain well and cut into pieces. Cut the bean curd into quarters, slice the leeks and scallions diagonally. Wash the watercress and drain. Arrange all these ingredients like a 'still life' on a large platter or board. Place the suet in a large pan over a gentle heat and leave it to render for a while; otherwise you can use the oil and simply heat it.

Mix the soy sauce with sugar, dashi and sweet sake to make a sweet and sour sauce. This is very personal so add little by little to get the correct balance of flavors. When about to begin cooking each person breaks an egg into a small bowl and beats it up with chopsticks. When everyone is ready to eat, add half the meat to the pan, cook for a few minutes then add a little of the sauce mixture. Push the meat to the side of the pan and add half the other ingredients with some of the sauce. Keep turning over with chopsticks without breaking up any of the vegetables — they should only be lightly cooked. Now the guests can begin helping themselves to the Sukiyaki, dipping each mouthful in the beaten egg. The hot food will partially cook the egg, which in turn cools the food. Meanwhile add more meat and vegetables, other ingredients and sauce to the pan. Cook as before until used up.

Left **Sukiyaki** *The whole of this dish can, and indeed should, be cooked at the table by the guests. In the truly Japanese way, the vegetables must be cut and presented attractively. Serve with rice or noodles, if desired.*

Umani

(Simmered chicken and vegetables)

This is a very popular dish to serve at a New Year celebration when the root vegetables are available fresh from the country.

4 chicken thighs, boned and cut into pieces	*3 cups frozen satoemo, thawed (see page 28)*
8 dried mushrooms, soaked in water for 30 minutes and drained	*3 carrots, peeled and cut into chunks*
9oz/250g packet konnyaku (see page 24)	*1½ tablespoons oil*
	3oz/75g sugar
	⅓rd cup sugar
½ can (9.8oz/280g drained weight) gobomizuni, soaked in water	*½ cup mirin*
	3 cups prepared dashi
1 × 1lb 3oz/500g can bamboo shoot (optional)	*8 mange tout, blanched and rinsed in cold water, to garnish*

SERVES 6-8

Place the pieces of chicken on one side with the drained mushrooms. Remove the stalks from the mushrooms and mark the cap of each one in a criss-cross pattern if liked. Blanch the konnyaku in boiling water for 2-3 minutes. Lift it out of the pan and cut into chunky pieces about 1in/ 2.5cm. Cut the gobomizuni into similar size pieces, also the bamboo shoot if using. Leave the satoemo whole. Set on one side with the carrots. Heat the oil and sauté the chicken pieces until they are golden brown on all sides. Lift out. Add all the vegetables to the pan and konnyaku and toss well together. Lift them out into a large colander and pour boiling water over them. Leave to drain. Heat the sugar, soy sauce, mirin and dashi together. Add the drained vegetables, half cover the pan with a lid and cook for 1½-2 hours, or until the vegetables have absorbed most of the liquid.

Garnish in a serving bowl with mange tout (snow peas) and serve with rice.

Indochina

Each region of Cambodia (now Kampuchea) has its own favorite recipes. The Cambodians are proud of their diet, which they claim is very well balanced and healthy. Rice is the number one food — the best quality coming from Battambang, which is the rice bowl region of Cambodia. Most of the fish eaten are freshwater fish from the Mekong river and its tributaries, and its great lake, Tonle sap. This massive lake is teeming with fish and has great potential, should the fishing industry one day realize this wealth. Cambodian food shares many similarities to Thai and Laotian food; less with the Vietnamese cuisine, which is more closely related to the Chinese. This Buddhist nation shares many of the same personal characteristics as the Laotians, being gentle people of much the same temperament.

The New Year is celebrated around 13 April, when the chores of the harvest are over. Everyone goes to the temple for a blessing, taking lots of food to be shared with the monks. This celebration lasts for three days and three nights, with dancing in the village and young men perhaps on the look out for a future bride. A wedding in the family will also cover three days and three nights. Many guests will travel far and be given accommodation by relations and friends in the village. The food is often prepared by families of caterers who may live in the particular village or close by. Guests eat at round tables for 10 people. One delicacy, which is frequently served at such a celebration, is a young, green coconut. The top is taken off and filled with a snakehead fish or chicken, cooked in coconut cream with plenty of blachan and spices. The top is replaced and all is steamed; it is quite delicious.

The houses are usually brick-built in the towns and wood in the country, with characteristic red-tiled roofs. They are usually set on sturdy, round, wooden pillars, which provide a large resting area underneath the house, away from the hot sun. Much socializing goes on here, and so the kitchen is situated within easy reach. Cooking is done in a wok over a wood or charcoal fire. The kitchen is typically simple as in most of South East Asia, yet the food is very complex and time consuming to prepare.

Plants such as bougainvillaea, cannas, jasmine and marigolds flower freely. Every house will have its own herb garden. The Cambodians are passionate about leaves in their cooking so nearly always grow mint, lemon grass, turmeric (they use the leaves), some scallions and lengkuas, *to name but a few. On their way home they might pass a paddy-field where a green, grass-like herb can be picked to add to the soup, SAMLO MCHOU BANGKANG, we have used cumin seeds as the nearest substitute. Every garden generally has its own mango tree and a favor-*

ite snack with youngsters is a slice of green mango, lightly spread with a creamy mixture made from blachan, fish sauce, chili and sugar. In the markets the food is always very fresh and attractively presented in bamboo basets. The fish is mostly sold by the Vietnamese, the butchers are often Chinese and the vegetables sellers Cambodians.

Breakfast is an important meal and is almost always rice based, especially in the country areas, either served plain or as a rice noodle soup. This soup is made using a pork stock, perhaps with the addition of slices of dried squid and onion. The noodles, after cooking, are tossed in garlic and added to the soup before serving. There are many variations on this theme, finely ground pork is added, bean sprouts, fermented cabbage or scallion. For children rice porridge is popular, perhaps with dried fish or ground pork.

Lunch and dinner will again have rice as the main ingredient (cooked, as in Thailand, without salt), together with fish cooked with black beans and ginger or meat, usually pork or chicken, vegetables and always a clear soup to help the rice down, which is drunk throughout the meal. Chopsticks are rarely used — food is eaten with fingers or a spoon. Snacks to take to the fields are wrapped in banana or lotus leaves, which, as well as being efficient, also lend a little extra flavor to the food inside. Warm water or Chinese green tea is popular for drinking with food, or sometimes cold beer.

The five recipes given here, with a couple of alternative soup and fish dishes, constitute a very lavish meal by Cambodian standards — the preparation can be helped by preparing the fish stock for the soup, the sauce for the TUEK KROEUNG KHMER and the curry paste a day ahead. Serve the PHLEA SACH KO (beef and vegetable salad) first, followed by the soup along with the Tuek Kroeung Khmer and rice, then the curry and more rice. End the meal with jackfruit pudding.

Laos *is a landlocked country, but although there are no seawater fish, the Mekong river provides plenty of freshwater varieties. Laotians enjoy fresh meat and fruit and the markets pride themselves on their good-quality produce. However, more often than not, Laotians will have their own plot of land on which to grow herbs and vegetables. Sticky rice is the staple food and is generally eaten at every meal. The dishes have simple ingredients, which are then skillfully adapted to provide variety. Soup, a fish recipe, meat or chicken, and fresh or cooked vegetables, together with a hot sauce and sticky rice provide the basics. A bowl of fresh fruit and rice wine are also provided.*

Vietnam *has three distinct regions — in the north stir fry is a popular way of cooking and the food is less hot and spicy than that of the central region, where chilies and shrimp sauces are used extensively. In the*

Above *The people of Indochina make the most of their fresh vegetables. Food is usually presented in these traditional bamboo baskets, laid out in orderly rows or piles.*

hot, humid south fruit and vegetables grow in profusion and feature more fully in the cuisine. The two main meals of the day are breakfast and the evening meal, with a light snack in the middle of the day. These main meals would be based on rice with meat or fish and vegetables, along with a clear soup. Chicken, pork and duck are the most popular meats; beef is expensive and lamb or mutton rarely available. Although you might detect a French influence in foods in cities, the rural communities still cling to their traditional cuisine, which has a Chinese bias, but still with its own special Vietnamese character.

Rice is grown in the Mekong Delta in the south and in the Red River Delta in the north, as well as along every available river bank. Upland rice is also grown where irrigation is a problem. Glutinous rice is very popular for celebrations (the Laotians would prefer to eat it exclusively) along with nem, *which is another name for the* CHA GIO *— Vietnamese crab-filled rolls — traditionally made wrapped in rice paper, but here I have used the spring roll wrappers, available fresh or frozen from oriental food stores. The rolls, after frying, are wrapped in a lettuce leaf with mint sprigs, cucumber sticks and fresh coriander. The whole is then dipped in the famous* NUOC CHAM *sauce, which is as ubiquitous as soy sauce and tomato ketchup!*

The whole of the east side of Vietnam is exposed to sea — the South China Sea and Gulf of Thongking in the north. Fishing (below *and* left) is therefore a fairly large part of their farming. Cambodia also relies on fishing. The large lake, Tonle Sap, in the middle of the country and the sea provide a plentiful supply. Although Laos is landlocked by these two countries, as well as Thailand, Burma and China, its rivers, particularly the Mekong, also provide an abundance. All three countries produce fruit, vegetables and spices of a high quality (far left).

Samla Chapek
(Pork soup with ginger)

6¼ cups pork or
   chicken stock
2 tablespoons light soy
   sauce
1 clove garlic, peeled
   and crushed
1in/2.5cm ginger,
   scraped and sliced
1 medium-sized onion,
   peeled and sliced
1 tablespoon sugar
1 tablespoon fish sauce
   or to taste

1 tablespoon lime juice
   or vinegar
⅔ cup pork fillet,
   shredded finely
⅔ cup pigs liver, cut
   into small pieces
   (optional)
1-2 tablespoons seasoned
   cornstarch
2-3 tablespoons oil
seasoning
scallions or
   coriander leaves to
   garnish

SERVES 6

Above **Samla chapek**
*The ginger greatly
enhances the flavor of
this soup. The fish sauce
and vinegar are also
evident, but do not
overpower. It is quite a
meal in itself, with all the
meaty pieces. Tripe can
also be used in the recipe.*

Simmer the stock and soy sauce together while preparing the other ingredients. Pound the garlic, ginger and onion together in a pestle and mortar or blender and add them to the soup. Cook for 5 minutes, then add the sugar, fish sauce and lime juice or vinegar. Dip the pork and liver pieces in seasoned cornstarch. Fry in hot oil until the meats change colour, keeping the pieces of meat as separate as possible. Pour off any excess oil and add the meats to the soup. Simmer for 20-30 minutes or until the meat is tender. Taste for seasoning and serve garnished chopped scallions or coriander leaves.

Samlo Mchou Bangkang
(Prawn soup à la Cambodgienne)

The Thai's call this kind of soup Tom Yam, although they omit the tomatoes and pineapple and use chicken and prawn with plenty of chilies. Serve in small bowls or from a steamboat, which will keep the soup and second helpings hot.

*1½ cups cooked prawns
6¼ cups fish stock
5-8 dried tamarind slices
3 stems lemon grass, cut in half and bruised
½in/1cm lengkuas root, peeled and pounded
salt to taste
1 chicken stock cube
3 green tomatoes, peeled and quartered
2-3 slices fresh pineapple, not too ripe, chopped into neat cubes*

*6 green chilies, or less if preferred, seeded and chopped
2 tablespoons fish sauce
1-2 cloves garlic
2 tablespoons oil
1-2 tablespoons cumin seeds, dry fried and pounded
½ bunch scallions, trimmed into 1in/2cm lengths
1 handful coriander leaves and stems*

SERVES 8

Set the prawns and stock aside. Soak the tamarind slices in water while preparing the other ingredients. Leave them for at least 20 minutes then remove and add the tamarind juice to the stock. Prepare the lemon grass, lengkuas, tomatoes, pineapple and chilies.

Bring the stock to a boil with the bruised stems of lemon grass, lengkuas, salt and bouillon cube. Cook gently for 2-3 minutes then add the tomatoes, pineapple and chilies. Simmer for 10 minutes. Add the prawns and fish sauce. Cook for a further 5 minutes, but no longer, otherwise the prawns will be tough. Meanwhile fry the garlic in the oil, add the cumin and stir into the soup with the scallions, coriander leaves and chopped stems. Taste for seasoning and serve hot.

Tuek Kroeung Khmer
(Fish à la Cambodgienne)

*2 medium-large mackerel, filleted
salt and pepper
4 cloves garlic, peeled
½in/1cm piece lengkuas, peeled and sliced
1 teaspoon sugar
½in/1cm cube kapi or blachan, dry fried
6-8 tablespoons lemon juice
6 tablespoons boiled water
2 tablespoons fish sauce
extra fish stock or boiled water, if necessary, to get the right consistency
1 small onion, peeled and chopped*

*⅓ cup roasted peanuts, pounded (unsalted)
3-6 scallions, chopped
1 handful of coriander leaves, lightly chopped*

Raw vegetables to serve
*finger shapes of carrots, cucumber and green pepper
under-ripe tomatoes, quartered
florets of cauliflower
slices of green apple, tossed in lemon juice
green mango
green chilis*

SERVES 8

Season and broil the mackerel fillets on both sides until brown and just cooked. Cool, remove the skin and bones and flake finely. Meanwhile broil the garlic and lengkuas, then pound together and add to the fish mixture with sugar. Set aside. Dry fry the kapi or blachan. Remove from its foil parcel and blend to a paste with the lemon juice, water and fish sauce. Stir the two mixtures together. They should be the consistency of a thick batter, slightly sour and salty. Add fish stock or water if necessary. Stir in the finely sliced onion, peanuts, scallions and coriander. This can be done the day before and stored in a covered container in the refrigerator. Serve with a selection of raw vegetables, attractively arranged on a platter.

Kari Bang Khong Lasak
(Marinated and curried prawns with cucumber)

16 large prawns, head
and body shell
removed, but tail left
on
½ cucumber, sliced and
dried

Marinade
1 teaspoon cumin seeds
1 teaspoon fennel seeds
1 tablespoon coriander
seeds
2 cloves garlic, peeled
and crushed
½in/1cm ginger, scraped
and sliced
4 shallots, peeled and
sliced
½ teaspoon chili
powder

1 teaspoon turmeric
1 tablespoon sugar
⅝ cup fish stock or
water
2 tablespoons light soy
sauce
1 tablespoon fish sauce
juice 1 lemon or lime
salt

Batter for prawns
½ cup plain flour
6 tablespoons cornstarch
salt
⅝ cup water
(approx)
1 egg white, whisked
deep fat for frying
prawns

SERVES 4

Prepare the prawns and cucumber. Dry fry the spices for the marinade. Pound and add them to the garlic, ginger and shallots in a food processor, and blend to a paste. Add chilli powder, turmeric, sugar, fish stock, soy and fish sauces, lemon or lime juice and salt. Pour over the prawns and leave to marinate while preparing the batter. Sift the flours together, then add sufficient water to make a creamy batter, but do not add the egg until the last minute. Heat the oil. Dry the prawns on kitchen towels. Fold the egg white into the batter, dip prawns in this and pop them straight into the hot oil to fry until they are golden and cooked through. Meanwhile bring the marinade to a boil, then simmer for 5-8 minutes. Add some of the cucumber to the sauce if desired and reserve some for garnish. Pour over the prawns and serve hot.

Right **Kari bang khong lasak** *These prawns are coated in a fairly hot, spicy sauce and are best accompanied by rice. They are quite delicious, but you would be advised to supply a cucumber to refresh the taste-buds.*

Phlea Sach Ko

(Beef and vegetable salad à la Cambodgienne)

½lb/225g rump steak,
  cut into thin slices,
  or use best
  quality ground
  beef, if preferred
⅝ cup vinegar
pinch salt
½lb/225g tripe
1⅞ cup milk and
  water, to cover tripe
salt

Sauce
3 cloves garlic
3 shallots
½in/1cm lengkuas
good handful coriander,
  stems chopped and
  leaves set aside
reserved marinade from
  beef
1-2 tablespoons fish
  sauce
1 teaspoon sugar
seasoning
lemon juice (optional)
¾ cup roasted
  peanuts, skins
  removed and ground
  coarsely (see page
  42), or salted peanuts
fish stock or water

Vegetables for serving
½ daikon or moolie
  (long white radish),
  peeled and cut into
  strips
½ box bean sprouts,
  rinsed and drained
1-2 stems lemon grass,
  use lower 2½in/6cm,
  finely chopped
ground peanuts (see
  above)
½ red pepper, seeded
  and cut into strips
½ onion, peeled and
  sliced
¼ iceberg lettuce,
  shredded into
  1in/2.5cm strips
coriander leaves (see
  sauce)
1 handful mint leaves
1 bunch red radishes, cut
  into flower shapes

SERVES 8

Marinate the seasoned steak slices or ground beef in the vinegar for 30 minutes. The vinegar should cover the meat. When the meat looks 'cooked' squeeze any excess juices from it and reserve these with the marinade for the sauce. Cut the meat into fine strips. Meanwhile cook the tripe in salted milk and water to cover for 45 minutes, or until quite tender. Drain and cut into strips the same size as the beef.

Now prepare the sauce. Broil the garlic, shallots and lengkuas. Cool, skin and pound with the chopped coriander stems to a paste. Heat the reserved vinegar marinade from the meat in a small pan. Add this paste, cook for 1-2 minutes, then stir in the fish sauce, sugar, seasoning and lemon juice, if a tangy flavor is preferred. Thicken the sauce with ground peanuts. Stir in sufficient fish stock or water to reduce the sauce to just the consistency of thin cream, but no runnier.

To serve the salad, mix the beef, tripe, white radish, bean sprouts and lemon grass together. Taste for seasoning. Pile the mixture into the center of a large serving platter and scatter with some of the ground peanut. Arrange the red pepper on top attractively and the onion slices around the meats. Place the lettuce, coriander and mint leaves around the edge with the radishes. Serve the sauce separately so that each person takes some meat and salad and tops with spoonfuls of the sauce. It is easier for each person to satisfy their own desires and take as much or as little as they require.

Left *The peppercorn goes through quite a long and complicated process to remove the outer skin. Only after this are they put out in the sun to dry for three or four days. Pepper is used consistently throughout the east to spice up the cuisine.*

Samlo Kari Khmer

Braising steak, duck or wild game can be used instead of the chicken, but allow longer to brown the meat before adding to the curry, and a longer cooking period.

8 chicken legs, cut into drumstick and thigh portions	1 bouillon cube
6-8 tablespoons oil	salt
4 small onions, peeled and cut into quarters	sugar
	fish sauce
4 small potatoes, peeled and cut into quarters	curry leaves (optional)
3 cups desiccated coconut and 3¼ cups hot water to make coconut milk	1 handful coriander, stems chopped and leaves separated
	1-2 tablespoons ground almonds (optional)
full quantity green or red curry paste (see page 112)	1 eggplant, sliced, salted for 1½ hours and rinsed
	coriander leaves (see above) for garnish

SERVES 8

Brown the chicken all over and lift out onto a plate. Fry the onions and potatoes until brown. Set these on one side and pour off the oil from the pan. Spoon ⅝ cup of the coconut cream from the top of the coconut milk into a large pan or wok and add the prepared red or green curry paste. Lower the heat and cook, stirring all the time until the spices give off a rich aroma. Add a bouillon cube, salt, sugar and fish sauce to taste, along with curry leaves, if you are using them, and chopped coriander stems.

Add the meat to the pan, turning the pieces in the sauce until well coated. Add onions, potatoes and coconut milk. Bring to a boil, then reduce to simmer for 45-60 minutes. Shake the pan rather than stirring to prevent the meat from breaking up. When the chicken pieces are tender, thicken, if desired, with the ground almonds mixed to a paste and stirred into the mixture. Reheat for a few minutes. If you have chosen to cook a green curry, pieces of eggplant can be added 5.10 minutes before the end of cooking and before thickening with ground almonds.

Serve in a large bowl scattered with coriander leaves to garnish attractively.

Sangkcha Khnor
(Jackfruit pudding)

1½ cups packet desiccated coconut and 1¼ cups hot water to make just under 1¼ cups coconut milk	1 × 16oz/454g can jackfruit in syrup
	2-3 tablespoons sugar
	pinch salt
	5 eggs, whisked

SERVES 8

Prepare the coconut milk. Open the can of jackfruit and reserve the syrup. Cut into thin slices. Mix the reserved syrup with the prepared coconut milk and sugar. Stir until the sugar dissolves. Add a pinch of salt. Taste the mixture, which should be quite sweet, but not excessively so. Add the syrup mixture to the beaten eggs to form a creamy mixture. Strain into a buttered ovenproof dish, 10 × 8in/25 × 20cm. Cover with foil and set in a steamer over gently boiling water. When set, remove from the steamer and finish baking in the oven. Alternatively, place the dish in a roasting pan of water, to come half way up the sides of the dish, and bake in a moderate oven (approximately 325°F/160°C) for about 40 minutes.

Cha Gio and Nuoc Cham
(Crab-filled rolls)

We have substituted Chinese spring roll wrappers for the traditional rice paper that is used in Vietnam. Cha Gio are an immensely popular snack in Vietnam and the vegetable content of the filling can be varied as long as the flavours are complementary.

¼ cup cellophane noodles, soaked in water to cover for 10 minutes
10 wood ears, soaked in water to cover for 10 minutes
1 cup ground pork
1 cup crabmeat, fresh or canned
4 scallions, trimmed and finely chopped
1 teaspoon fish sauce
salt and pepper to taste

flour and water paste to seal
spring roll wrappers
oil for deep frying

To serve
lettuce leaves
mint and coriander leaves
matchstick-like pieces of cucumber
Nuoc Cham sauce (see below)

MAKES 15

Drain the noodles and cut into 1in/2.5cm lengths. Drain the wood ears and slice finely. Then add both of these ingredients to the pork and set aside.

Remove any cartilage from the crab and add the meat to the pork mixture with the scallions, fish sauce and seasoning to taste. Place a spring roll wrapper in front of you like a diamond. Spoon some of the mixture just below the center; fold over the point nearest to you and roll once. Bring the side points towards the center to enclose the filling, then brush the top edges with the paste and roll up to completely seal. Deep fry in hot oil for 8-10 minutes or until cooked through. If the oil is too hot the outside will be ready before the filling is cooked through. Drain well on absorbent kitchen paper and repeat until all the rolls are cooked.

Serve Vietnamese style by wrapping each one in a lettuce leaf with a few sprigs of mint and coriander and a stick of cucumber. Dip in the Nuoc Cham sauce (see below).

Nuoc cham

2 fresh red chilies, seeded and pounded
2 cloves garlic, peeled and crushed

1 tablespoon sugar
3 tablespoons fish sauce (nuoc mam)
juice ½ large lemon or lime

Blend the chilies, garlic, sugar and fish sauce together. Add lemon or lime juice to taste, and a little water if liked. Serve with a multitude of Vietnamese dishes.

Filling the cha gio rolls
1 *Having made up the filling, take one of the wrappers, place on a tray and brush over with a brush, dampened with flour and water paste.*
2 *If you are using these circular wrappers, you will need to fold over a piece of the edge nearest you. Then place a line of the filling on this edge.*
3 *Roll over this filling once, then fold over the two outside edges.*
4 *You may now continue to roll up the remainder of the wrapper. It should stick as a result of the brushed-on paste.*

Goi Tom
(A Vietnamese salad)

3 cups Chinese cabbage
2 carrots
1/2 cucumber
salt
2 red chilies, seeded and finely sliced
1 small onion, sliced into fine rings
4 pickled gherkins, sliced, plus 3 tablespoons of the liquid

1 clove garlic, crushed
1 teaspoon sugar
2 tablespoon cider or white vinegar
1/4 cup lightly pounded peanuts
1 1/3 cups cooked chicken, shredded
few stems fresh coriander

SERVES 4

Wash and shred the Chinese cabbage thinly. Peel and cut the carrots into matchstick-like strips. Trim the ends from the cucumber, cut in half lengthwise and scoop out the seeds. Cut in pieces the same size as the carrot, sprinkle with salt and leave for 15 minutes. Place the chilies, onion and gherkin slices altogether in a bowl. Blend the gherkin liquid with the garlic, sugar and vinegar. Rinse and dry the cabbage, carrot and cucumber, then add these to the liquid ingredients with the nuts and chicken, toss altogether and taste. Add more vinegar, if you wish, for a sharper taste. Garnish with coriander leaves.

Below **Cha gio and nuoc cham** *To serve these Vietnamese-style, they should actually be wrapped up in the lettuce leaf.*

215

Lap, Keng Som and Tchéo

Lap would almost certainly feature as part of a wedding banquet in Laos. Turkey has been introduced fairly recently so perhaps it is still considered rather special, although you will find that chicken is frequently used too.

Each person rolls up a ball of the sticky rice, then gathers up a little of the lap with it and eats. Bowls of soup are provided, as well as the Tchéo sauce and a bowl of raw vegetables.

1 × 5lb/2.25kg turkey (approx) or 1 × 4lb/1.75kg chicken	½-1 tablespoon chili powder, made from 4-8 roasted red chillies
Keng som soup	½in/1cm fresh laos, scraped and sliced
skin, bones and giblets from above	1 stem lemon grass, use lower 2in/5cm
7½ cups water	½-1 onion
2 tablespoon tamarind pulp, soaked in 1¼ cups warm water for 15 minutes	fish sauce, if liked salt and a little sugar to taste
1 stem lemon grass, bruised	coriander leaves and spring onion to garnish
3 green tomatoes, washed and cut into wedges	**Tchéo chili pepper sauce**
1-2 tablespoons fish sauce	5 green chilies, seeded and pounded
salt and sugar, if liked fresh coriander leaves and scallion tops to garnish	2 cloves garlic, peeled and crushed
	2 tablespoons fish sauce
Lap	1 handful fine coriander leaves
½ cup glutinous rice flesh from the above turkey or chicken	platter of raw vegetables: carrot, cucumber, cauliflower, cut into small pieces
juice 1 lemon	
2 tablespoons padek or bagoong (anchovy) (see page 16)	

SERVES 6-8

Set the flesh from the turkey or chicken on one side while the soup is prepared. Put the skin, bones and rinsed giblets into a large pan. Bring to a boil, skim, then add the juice from the tamarind, lemon grass and tomatoes. Bring to the boil again, then reduce to simmer and cook for 30 minutes. Lift out the chicken liver and gizzard and finely slice to add to the soup later. Continue cooking for a further 30 minutes. Add the fish sauce, sliced liver and gizzard from the chicken or turkey and seasoning then, when the lap is ready, skim and strain into a hot tureen. Garnish with coriander leaves and spring onion tops.

TO PREPARE THE LAP Dry fry the rice in a frying pan or wok, turning all the time until the rice is roasted and golden. Pound or put in a blender or food processor until fine. Finely chop or grind the turkey or chicken flesh. Half fry this in the wok, breaking up with a fish slice so that the meat begins to change color. Add the pounded rice to the meat little by little along with the lemon juice and the padek or bagoong and some of the chili. Pound the laos root and lemon grass together, stir into the mixture with very finely chopped onion and more chili, if liked. Add fish sauce, salt and sugar to taste. Mix well with your hands, adding a little of the soup if necessary. The mixture should be moist not wet.

TCHÉO Pound the chilies, garlic and coriander leaves together, then add as much fish sauce as is necessary to suit individual taste.

Thora Sin Moo
(Stir fry pork)

1lb/450g fillet of pork	2 cups green beans, cut into 1in/2.5cm lengths
1 piece of pork fat or oil	1½ teaspoons fish sauce
1 onion, peeled and chopped	salt and sugar to taste
1 clove garlic, peeled and crushed	coriander leaves to garnish
2 green chilies, seeded and pounded	plain boiled rice to serve

SERVES 4-6

Trim the pork and cut into small pieces. Render the fat from the pork. When all the fat is in the pan, discard it or heat the oil, if preferred. Fry the onion, garlic and chili until it gives off a rich aroma; do not allow to brown. Push to the side of the pan and stir in the pork fillet pieces. Turn all the time until the meat changes color. Cook for 2-3 minutes. Now add the beans and toss all the ingredients well. Add the fish sauce, sugar and salt to taste. Garnish with fresh coriander leaves and serve with plain rice and a raw vegetable platter and perhaps the Tchéo sauce.

Glutinous Rice — Steamed

In Laos a proper rice-steaming basket would be employed for the cooking and serving. This is a woven basket, which sits in a flameproof pot set over charcoal.

8oz/225g glutinous rice, soaked in water to | *cover for up to 6 hours*

SERVES 4

Drain the rice then place in a steamer lined with muslin. Set over bubbling water and cover. Replenish with boiling water as necessary. Cook until the rice grains are soft. The longer the soaking period the shorter the cooking time. Serve hot.

Yaew Mak Len
(Tomato dip)

5 cloves garlic
2 red onions or 3oz/75g shallots
1 coriander root
2 big chilies, dried

8 small tomatoes, skinned and deseeded
fish sauce
1 tablespoon chopped coriander to garnish

Dry fry the garlic, onions or shallots, coriander root and chilies briefly. Fry the tomatoes until lightly cooked. Pound the garlic, onions or shallots, coriander root, chilies and tomatoes to a thick paste in the food processor. Add fish sauce to taste and garnish with the chopped coriander leaves. Serve with an assortment of raw vegetables.

Left **Yaew mak len** *This tomato dip is an excellent accompaniment to all kinds of steamed vegetables. Arrange them on a platter with the dip in the center.*

The markets of Laos are no less impressive than the rest of the orient. A range of root vegetables and fruits (left and above) are available. Cooking in the market is not an uncommon sight (right). The steam- and aroma-filled streets are synonymous with the east. The countryside of Laos is also quite spectacular, particularly the mist-shrouded uplands (top).

Index

Page numbers in italics refer to the illustrations

221

223